A JOURNEY TO HOPE
WITH A DETERMINED GOD

*365 Devotionals of hope,
encouragement and love from God's Word*

KELLY ADKINS

Scripture quotations taken from the New American Standard Bible® (NASB),

Copyright © 1960, 1962, 1963, 1968, 1971, 1972, 1973, 1975, 1977, 1995 by The Lockman Foundation

Used by permission. www.Lockman.org

ISBN 978-1-7359487-7-5

Front Cover Art:

Profound thanks and gratitude go to my super-talented, wonderful friend and co-worker Daiane Menezes de Oliveira dos Santos for this powerful, emotional, original work of art. She drew this for me to illustrate the soul-shaking hope that is contained in Hebrews 12:2, which says: "fixing our eyes on Jesus, the author and perfecter of faith, who for the joy set before Him endured the cross, despising the shame, and has sat down at the right hand of the throne of God."

As you gaze at the image, it is impossible to NOT fix your eyes on Jesus, who guarantees that we don't have to depend on our own strength in order to have faith. It is Jesus who creates our faith, and it is Jesus who perfects our faith. This truth is borne out by "the joy set before Him." His joy isn't knowing that He will, in the end, have victory over His cross. His joy is knowing that our own cross will forever be empty because He has already paid the price for our sin, and has risen victorious over death and the grave.

Table of Contents

Dedication

This book is dedicated to five of the best people this world has ever known.

Bert and Elsie Adkins — my maternal grandparents who raised both my sister and me from before my second birthday until I was grown and left home. And after that, I came back when I had messed up my life and lived with them some more. There is simply no words that can describe the love and support they showed me for my whole life. Through thick and thin, good and bad, laughter and tears, until they went to be with the Lord they remained the most unshakeable pillars of love, encouragement and inspiration in my life. It never mattered to them when I didn't deserve it. All that mattered to them was that they loved me ... and they never stopped. To this day, I would give all I own just to be able to spend one more day with them.

Lorene Jones — my sister. My one and only sister. The memories of growing up with her as my sister remain to this day among the supreme joys of my life. And they continue, even today. A number of years ago, when I was passing through what was by far the worst time of my life ... when sadness poured out of my eyes as tears every day, literally, for two solid years, God reminded me of just how special she is. Just about everyone else in my life had turned their backs and didn't want to know — but — she and my brother-in-law, Mike (who has gone on to be with the Lord) and their son, Cody, stayed in my corner, supported me and cheered me on, loved me and always gave me hope that tomorrow would be a better day. During that same time, when I had no place to stay she took me in and showered me with love and kindness every day. An enormous amount of the hope, love and encouragement you will read in this book flows from my heart after having experienced all three first hand, from one of the very best. My sister.

Dolores Bertrand — my mother. My wonderful mother. Because my grandparents raised me several hours from where my mother lived, I grew up feeling like my mother was more like a best friend I got to be with several times a year. As a kid growing up, I loved it because it made my mother seem like, well, my mother of course, but something extra special as well. I only learned of my mother's truly special love after I had become a grown man and didn't have my grandparents any more because they had already gone home to be with the Lord. I learned of it in an even more special way when I came to her broken-hearted and didn't have a place to stay — as a 50-year-old man. I know, and am truly happy, that many people have special moms, but I will put mine up there right beside the best of them. A lot of the beauty of hope, love and encouragement you will read here comes from my mother's heart, too.

<u>Claudia</u> — my wife. Where would I be today without her? I don't even like to think about it. My best friend in life. My partner in life. My greatest champion in all I attempt, and the wind beneath my wings every day. Without her, this book would have never even happened. My prayer is that you will be as blessed reading it as I was writing it.

Foreword

A Journey to Hope with a Determined God, is an inspiring series of devotionals that are biblically based and contextualized to address questions we ask and situations we face during the various seasons of the year. These intentionally brief devotionals focus very specifically on instructive biblical truths and leave the readers with the desire to meditate and learn more about their spiritual journey.

It is evident that these devotionals come straight from the heart of a person who dearly loves the Lord and has related in a very personal and caring way to people during his extensive years of missionary service.

I wholeheartedly recommend this book to individuals as well as groups of people who are seeking a walk with the Lord filled with hope and assurance of a victorious life and a glorious anticipation of the eternal celebration at the end of their earthly journey.

Daniel R. Sanchez, D.Min., Ph.D.
Distinguished Professor of Missions
Ambassador, World Missions Center
Southwestern Baptist Theological Seminary

Special Thanks to the Following Deserving People:

My many life-long friends with whom I grew up in Madisonville, Texas.
These are friends whose wisdom, lives and laughter (mixed with a little craziness every now and then) have made beautiful, indelible marks on my heart, and whose lifetime of influence on my life is reflected throughout these devotionals. Just one example of how special they are: A number of years ago, when I had not been able to go back home or see my family for a very long time because I simply didn't have the money, a large number of these friends joined together and bought tickets for my wife and me to go home – even though I hadn't seen most of those friends for over 40 years.

Dr. Bob Utley.
In these devotionals there is one source I used on a regular basis when I wanted to verify the scholarship from other sources, and to which I would like to call special attention: The critical commentary work of an incredibly accomplished scholar and beautiful Christian servant of the Lord, Dr. Bob Utley. His brilliant work in its entirety can be accessed and used free of charge at his website: www.freebiblecommentary.org.

Dr. Danny Pickens.
My wonderful, Director of Missions friend from Texas whose help on my own mission field I have never forgotten – also just happens to be a world-class photographer. You will see some of his beautiful work in this book. If you would like to see more, go to his incredible website: www.pickensphotos.com.

Dr. Daniel Sanchez
Profound thanks to my special friend and professor from my seminary days for writing such an elegant foreword for my book.

Preface

I believe there is a serious need for hope and encouragement in our world. I also believe there is a God in heaven serious about giving that hope. 48,344 deaths by suicide in the U.S. and 1.4 million attempts (2019) is proof of the first sentence. The death of Jesus on the cross is proof of the second. Through a year-long, daily journey that will make stops in every one of its 66 books, I have tried to create a connection between the one who needs that hope, and the One who unfailingly provides that hope through the greatest "self-help" book ever written — we call it the Holy Bible. It is truly God's love-letter to man.

This book of devotionals began, actually, on the western edge of the Atlantic Rainforest in the southern state of Paraná, Brazil, where we owned a chácara (small farm) that was secluded enough to feel like the middle of nowhere. Even still, through a very, very slow antenna internet connection, I was able to stay in touch with friends and family back home by email and facebook. This slow, and thin social "lifeline" was where this book was born. Conversations on facebook led me to the realization that there were many people "out there" who were hurting and searching for hope and encouragement — even Christians.

The fact that many of these people were lifelong friends I had grown up with, would not stop pulling on the strings of my heart. I made the commitment to them to post for one year, a daily devotional of hope and encouragement from God's word that we could all share together. During our year-long journey, some friends began encouraging me to put all the devotionals into a book. Up to that point, I hadn't even thought of that possibility, because I was just trying to help my friends with some spiritual encouragement. Eight years later, what you now hold in your hands is the result of their encouragement and our year-long journey together, discovering the beautiful and endless hope contained in God's love for us.

The "source material" for all the devotionals (other than the Bible itself) comes from a rich and wide array of sources. Some of it comes from notes written down as long as 36 years ago when I was a student at Southwestern Baptist Theological Seminary, where I had the privilege of learning from some of the finest Christian professors the world has ever seen. Notes written along the edges of pages in quite a number of my Bibles are there, too. Phrases from sermons I have heard as well as those in everyday conversations, into which God dropped a nugget of truth that burned itself unforgettably into my memory — they are there as well. I consulted critical sources like Robertson's Word Pictures and Kiel and Delitzsch when I wanted to confirm or unfold in a fuller way, the richness of the original languages and expressions from the biblical era.

Throughout the entire book, I have studiously avoided even the appearance of infringing on any copyright, or copying anyone else's work — published or unpublished. If any comment in any of these devotionals seems similar to other content, I can assure you it is a complete accident unless I have called attention, and given credit, to a specific quote. At the absolute top of the source material list, all credit goes to the love of God which is written down plainly in the scriptures, and to the pen of the Holy Spirit, which He gave me the privilege of holding while He wrote. Any inspiration you feel as you read this book is all His work, any mistakes you see are all mine. I pray that you can feel His presence as you read, the same way I felt it as I wrote.

Introduction

As you read these devotionals, we will wrestle with real life together. When hurt is real, you won't find me painting a flowery picture that minimizes that hurt. But — neither will we shy away from the fact that God offers us real hope and real encouragement right in the middle of it all, and you will discover in these pages that the Bible is drenched with hope and love and encouragement if you will just reach for it. You can reach for it from Genesis to Revelation. There is at least one devotional here from every book in the Bible. Hope and encouragement and love is there, and it is real, even in the middle of a broken heart and broken dreams. It is there, and it is real, even in the middle of desperation and fear. It is there, and it is real, even when you believe that all hope is gone. I can assure you of this truth because I have lived through every single one of those things in my own life.

In the preface I characterized the Bible as God's love letter to man, and it is. What I have learned about that love-letter in my journey of many years (from being a brand new Christian, to seminary student, to pastor, to crusade coordinator, to missionary in Brazil) is hopefully reflected in the lessons of hope and encouragement contained in these devotionals. It is a journey in which I have experienced both exhilarating highs and crushing lows, and I make no attempt to hide them — because that is real life. My hope and prayer is that you will discover the same thing I did as you read these devotionals: If you open your heart and read honestly, you will not be able to hide from the hope and encouragement of God. His love is endless, beautiful and relentless all at the same time. Many times we give up on ourselves, but God never does.

If you are determined to give up, it might prove to be a challenge, reading this book. You will discover that it won't let you give up, because the hope and encouragement and love of God that pours out from these devotionals is infectious and irresistible. On the other hand, if you dare to be filled with joy and hope — read on.

HOW BEST TO READ THESE DEVOTIONALS: A LITTLE NOTE BEFORE YOU BEGIN

You will quickly notice a couple of things as you begin reading these devotionals:

1. <u>Some are shorter (some take only 5 to 10 seconds to read), some are longer, and some are in between.</u>
   This is completely on purpose. First of all, everything needs a little variety, even devotionals. But the main reason they are this way is because commentary would only detract from the power and the message of the raw word of God. Many times God's word can become a sword ... or a salve — in a single, short sentence.

2. <u>Some of the scripture references are very short just like some of the devotionals.</u>
   This is completely on purpose as well. In fact, some of the scripture references mention only a portion of the whole passage used in the devotional. The goal is to foment in your mind and heart a curiosity to know "the rest of the story" — to read on a bit; to want to know more.

For the occasions when either the scripture passage or the devotional is short, I would like to offer you some beautiful, wise, and very helpful counsel that was taught to me in class one day by one of the finest Greek professors who ever lived, Dr. Curtis Vaughan. This man, who could read the Greek New Testament as easily as you and I could read "Fun With Dick and Jane" told us one day that the very best advice he could give us in studying God's word was to force ourselves to slow down as we read it. His advice: Take a small amount of scripture and read it slowly. Then read it again, even slower. Then one more time, even slower. Repeat that process at least 10 times, until your mind is forced to slow down and really absorb what God's word is trying to say to you — you will find that the voice of God is better than any commentary you could ever read.

That was one of the most valuable lessons I learned during all my years at the seminary. It revolutionized how I study the Bible — and it works for the scriptures in these devotionals, too. Many times you will find yourself not only discovering more, but thirsting for more. If that happens, one of my main goals in these devotionals will have been achieved.

*and now
we begin
our journey ...*

"For I know the plans that I have for you, 'declares the Lord,' plans for welfare and not for calamity to give you a future and a hope."
— *Jeremiah 29:11*

God's New Year's Greeting

Many of us look to the beginning of a new year as a chance to "re-boot" our lives — to erase the blackboard and start with a clean slate. A new set of spark plugs for our engine called "hope." Look no further.

Close to 2,600 new years ago these words from God were written by Jeremiah, to whom Biblical historians refer as the "weeping" prophet. But this verse is about as far away from weeping as you can get, and on this first day of a brand new year it reaches across all those years that went before, all the way to us today ... and its words fill our hearts with the best kind of hope and encouragement possible for the beginning of a new year: the kind that comes straight from God's own personal plans for you and me.

Make this verse your very own promise from God for this new year like this:

(**Your first name**), I know the plans that I am weaving together for you as this new year begins," declares the Lord, "plans for welfare (peace), and not for harm, in order to give you, (**your first name**), a future and a hope."

"That which is born of the flesh is flesh, and that which is born of the Spirit is spirit. Do not be amazed that I said to you, 'You must be born again.'"
— *John 3:6,7*

Starting Over

I'm betting that I am not the only one who has ever had this wish about their life. If I could just start over with what I know now ... If I could just start over, I could eliminate so many mistakes I have made with my life ... If I could just start over, I could undo the hurt I have caused so many people ... Where we are right here in the Bible, talks about this very subject — starting over. It is the account of a meeting between a noteworthy figure in the community, and the breath-taking beauty of the lesson that Jesus taught him.

The noteworthy figure — Nicodemus. A leader of the Pharisees, and referred to by Jesus Himself as no less than "THE teacher" of Israel. Most of us will never have the social, or religious pedigree of Nicodemus, but, most of us CAN identify with Nicodemus in the way he approached his encounter with Jesus. He went in the middle of the night — for fear of being publicly exposed as someone who was interested in Jesus. It is easy to pretend to be a bold follower of Jesus inside the safety of the church. Outside is another matter altogether, is it not? The encouragement we get from Nicodemus, however, is seen in his step-by-step improvement: When the Pharisees met to discuss eliminating Jesus, he instead spoke of justice, then, after the crucifixion he joined with Joseph of Arimathea in asking for Jesus's body. Through the life of Nicodemus, we learn that what God looks for is steady growth, not instant perfection.

Then, there is the beautiful spiritual lesson Jesus taught him. You must be born again. Not simply a "make-over." A complete "start over." Throughout its history, the Bible records some pretty remarkable births. People who God used to change history itself. To name a few: Noah, Moses, David, John the Baptist, Joseph and Mary ... which brings us, of course, to the most incredible birth of all — Jesus. There is another remarkable birth, however, and Jesus speaks of it here — yours. If you have believed in Jesus as your Savior, you are the recipient of a VERY special birth. A spiritual one. An eternal one. It is not a "make-over." It is a brand new birth. You are a brand new person. You are not a melted down and re-molded version of the old you. In God's eyes, you are completely new — and His eyes are the only ones that matter.

And Jesus turned and saw them following, and said to them, "What do you seek?" They said to Him, "Rabbi (which translated means Teacher), where are You staying?" He said to them, "Come, and you will see."
— *John 1:38,39*

An Old Invitation

Most of us have what we call "scrapbooks." Strange name, considering what is usually kept in them isn't scrap at all, but precious memories and mementos, of special people or special events in our lives. Many times we will see old invitations that are no longer valid in these "scrapbooks." Invitations to a birthday party or a dance from when we were just teenagers, baby showers, invitations to weddings that all happened years ago. There is an old invitation right here where Jesus called His first two disciples, too.

The exchange between Jesus and these two men, before the invitation is really special. It is significant that Jesus didn't ask them "<u>Who</u> do you seek?" He asked them, "<u>What</u> do you seek?" He knew they had questions. Their response was special too: "Where are You staying?" which was a way in that day of saying, "Is there a place we can go where we can spend some extended time with You?" Jesus responded with an invitation ... "come" ... and a promise — "you will see."

That old invitation Jesus gave over 2,000 years ago is different from our old invitations. That invitation He gave is just as good today as it was when He gave it to His first two disciples. It is still valid. You may have questions for Jesus today just like they did. Some of them may be really tough questions. That's ok with Jesus. If you want answers bad enough to spend some extended time with Him the way these men did, His answer to you is that very same invitation ... "come" — and that very same promise — "you will see."

If you were to ask Jesus today, "Where are you staying?" He would respond to you, "Well, one place is right in your hands every time you pick up your Bible. You can always find Me there." If you have already asked Jesus to be your Savior, the answer is even better. It is written down forever in Matthew 28:20 — "I am with you always, even to the end of the ages." He is as close as a whispered prayer, and, in the middle of all the trials of your life and all your questions, if you will seek Him out — Jesus's invitation is still, "Come ... and you will see."

He does not forget the cry of the afflicted.
— *Psalms 9:12b*

He Remembers

It's not much fun to be forgotten. Especially on special days, or during hard times. That second category is probably the most difficult of all because it is really hard to hurt alone, isn't it? One of the most beautiful and comforting things about God is that He never does that to us. He always remembers.

So very short, but so very full of hope and encouragement is this little one half of a verse from the Psalms. Sometimes when we are hurt, or confused, or lonely, it is easy to feel as if no one cares and that God has abandoned us. He hasn't. And He never will.

When we bend the knees of our hearts and our pride in prayer, God always hears, and never forgets. Sometimes God's timing and God's answer is much different than what we might want or think, but rest assured, the cry of the afflicted has a special place in the heart and mind of God. If it were not true, it wouldn't be in God's word. And God is always as near as a whispered prayer ...

for all have sinned and fall short of the glory of God,
— *Romans 3:23*

The Ugly Duckling

Almost everyone has heard the famous story written way back in 1843 by Hans Christian Andersen, where there was a "duckling" hatched who was so ugly and different that all his own brothers and sisters and the other barnyard animals made fun of him — then at the end of the story he actually became more beautiful than all the rest because he was actually a swan and not a duck.

I think this would be a wonderful story to tell in church — to the generation of today. Too many times, even in church, there is a tendency to "judge a book by its cover," instead of loving unconditionally, the way Jesus tells us to love, and it leaves people, especially new Christians, feeling often times like the little ugly duckling. Ask me how I know.

If you know how it feels to be treated like the ugly duckling, this little verse in Romans is beautiful encouragement. It lets all of us know, who are so aware of how far from perfect we are, that everyone else is a long way from perfect, too — "ALL have sinned and fall short of the glory of God." Yes, even those who treat us like the ugly duckling. The Bible tells us that all our "righteousness" is like a filthy rag in the sight of God, but don't despair my friend! Just like the "ugly duckling," you also, are in the process of changing into something beautiful. God is not finished with you yet ... and who knows how beautiful the final "you" will turn out to be.

Rejoice greatly, O daughter of Zion! Shout in triumph, O daughter of
Jerusalem! Behold, your king is coming to you; He is just and endowed
with salvation, humble, and mounted on a donkey, even on a colt, the foal
of a donkey. I will cut off the chariot from Ephraim and the horse from
Jerusalem; and the bow of war will be cut off. And He will speak peace to the
nations; and His dominion will be from sea to sea, and from the River to the
ends of the earth.
— *Zechariah 9:9,10*

Extra ... Extra ... Read All About It!!

The familiar shout of paper boys from days gone by announcing exciting,
or breaking news could be well-applied to this passage in the prophecy of
Zechariah. It has joy and excitement and hope and encouragement that
spans history from Zechariah's day to ours and on into eternity.

God sent word right here through His prophet, of the triumphal entry
of Jesus into Jerusalem (Matthew 21:1-9) 500 YEARS before it would
happen. You think that is a long time? Well, God has known you — and
loved you — for even longer than that (Ephesians 1:4) — since before He
created the Earth and everything in it.

And not only that. Zechariah lets you know even more. One day the
Lord is coming for you. One day He will remove all your enemies, and
the only reigning power will be His. Why? Because He really is the
Alpha and the Omega, the Beginning and the End, the Kings of Kings
and the Lord of Lords. Our God IS God!!!

Rejoice greatly? Oh my, yes!!! Shout in triumph? Absolutely!!!

Blessed is a man who perseveres under trial; for once he has been
approved, he will receive the crown of life which the Lord has
promised to those who love Him.
— *James 1:12*

What Happens Next

A common misconception about the Christian walk of faith in Jesus,
especially by those on the outside of that faith looking in, is that we
believe it causes life to become perfect, and being a Christian magically
fixes everything, and God is sort of like a spiritual Santa Claus. That is
simply not true, and the Bible never teaches it — anywhere.

What it does teach is what James shares in this verse: Christians have
the same trials in life as everyone else. Disappointment can crush our
hearts, tragedy can kill our joy, failure can steal our hope, rejection can
make us feel worthless. What makes a Christian different is not the
absence of trials. What makes a Christian different is a living, breathing,
active faith in God that refuses to give up in spite of those trials. That's
what "persevere" means.

Like the nitric acid test which proves that gold is genuine, perseverance in
trials proves how genuine our faith is. Genuine faith gives us the strength
to endure what happens now — because we already know what happens
next. The crown of life. The Lord has given us His promise.

They were amazed and astonished, saying,
"Why, are not all these who are speaking Galileans? And how is
it that we each hear them in our own language to which we were
born?
— *Acts 2:7,8*

Calling All Galileans...

I bet just about everyone is saying, "Well, I'm not a Galilean.", right?
Well ... there may be all sorts of ways to be a "Galilean" that you haven't
thought about. The words here were spoken in a sense of disdain and
disbelief. If I may offer an interpretation using the language of today:
"and everyone was stunned speechless and couldn't believe their ears,
saying to each other, "Good grief!! Aren't all these speaking just a group
of crude Galileans?"

Galileans were known for their crude Aramaic and crude Greek vernacular,
being very weak in correct language skills, and yet — here those Galileans
were, all miraculously speaking in other languages, with their audience
understanding everything they were saying, each in their own language.
All at the same time. It is truly amazing, isn't it, what can happen when
the power of the Holy Spirit takes control?

There may be someone reading this today who may know what it is like
to feel that you are outside the "upper crust" of society — sort of like
a Galilean. You may not have a degree in the English language, and you
feel that you don't express yourself very well. You may even slaughter our
language just a bit, like I do. You may not have a degree in theology, you
may not have a voice that lets you sing a solo in the church choir, you may
not be a deacon or other leader in the church, you may be someone who
very few listen to. If you think you are of little position or importance,
join the Galilean Club. But — the same is true today as when this group
of Galilean disciples spoke instantly in other languages — it is amazing
what can happen when the power of the Holy Spirit takes control.

You don't have to be well-spoken, well-educated, well-off, well-thought-of,
well-positioned, well-liked, or well-anything else. All you have to do is let
the Holy Spirit work through you. It is amazing what He can do — and
He can be amazing through you too!

"For My hand made all these things, thus all these things came into being," declares the Lord. "But to this one I will look, To him who is humble and contrite of spirit, and who trembles at My word."
— *Isaiah 66:2*

Beauty is in the Eye of the Beholder

Long years ago, it was my grandfather who taught me the inspiring encouragement of this truth. It counteracted the poison of cruel words someone had directed at me when I was very young. I never forgot the lesson and the loving way my grandfather taught it to me. God does exactly the same thing here for all His children.

God frames the beauty and majesty of all heaven and earth with His words, "all those things My hand has made ..." (see verse 1). And yet, with all of that in His field of vision — what He chooses to look at, what He chooses to consider as more beautiful still, is one of His children who has a humble spirit and who gives reverent honor to His word.

You don't need to be famous, you don't need to be successful, you don't need to be important on the world stage, your appearance doesn't need to turn heads when you walk by. If beauty is in the eye of the beholder, and your Beholder is your Heavenly Father, it is easier to be beautiful than you might think. In a beauty contest with heaven and earth, what captures the eye of Almighty God is His child who has a humble heart and honors His word. Is that child you, dear friend?

He said to Simon, "Put out into the deep water and let down your
nets for a catch."
— *Luke 5:4*

Fishing With Jesus

We who love to fish, also love to tell stories of "how the big one got away," or other similar yarns that are many times very hard to believe. What Jesus said right here is the beginning of one of the greatest fishing stories in the entire history of fishing stories. It is easy to read the whole story, Luke relates all of it in only 8 verses.

Here are all the ingredients that make this such an incredible event (if you read through verse 11):

1. Jesus asked them to put back out in the day time. **WRONG TIME**. In Jesus's day the time to fish was at night. In fact, they had just finished fishing all night and had caught absolutely nothing.
2. Jesus asked them to put out in the deep part of the lake (Sea of Galilee). **WRONG LOCATION**. In Jesus's day the place to fish was close to the shore, as the structure of their boats demonstrated — shallow drafts, flat bottoms.
3. Jesus asked them to put their nets down for a catch in the deep water. **WRONG STRATEGY**. In Jesus's day the place fish were caught was in the shallow water.
4. Peter obeyed Jesus, but not with much faith or enthusiasm. They were all already exhausted from fishing all night and catching nothing, and Jesus had just asked professional fishermen who knew how to fish, to do three wrong things that had to have seemed incredibly stupid to them. Still, to Peter's credit, he obeyed and said, "At Your word I will let down the nets." And it's a good thing he did, because …
5. They caught so many fish that their nets began to tear and their boats began to sink.
6. The reaction of Mr. Expert Fisherman, Peter — he fell at the knees of Jesus right in the middle of all those fish and said, "Depart from me, Lord, because I am a sinful man!" Amazement had seized him and all those who were with him at the size of the catch of fish they had just brought to the shore.

What's the point? In your own life, in your own business, or in whatever experience in which you consider yourself an expert — if you feel Jesus telling you someday to "Put out into the deep water and let down your nets for a catch." Do it! And trust Him like Peter did, even if you would do things differently –

And get ready ... because Jesus is in control of absolutely everything. Even where the fish swim.

For God has not given us a Spirit of timidity, but of power and love
and discipline.
— *2 Timothy 1:7*

God's Knockout Combination

If anyone tells me they have never been fearful of something in their lives,
I am going to think one of two things: One, I am talking to Chuck Norris,
or two, I am talking to someone who is either deluded or dishonest. The
good news is, in the boxing ring we call "life," God has given us the Holy
Spirit, who really is afraid of nothing, and who has a devastating, heavenly
three-punch combination to fight fear.

"Power" — the Greek word here is 'dunamis' and it is where we get our
word 'dynamite.'
"Love" — the Greek word here is 'agape,' the strongest word for love in
the entire Bible.
"Discipline" — the Greek word here is 'sophronismos,' a mental self-
control as strong as steel.

First, if you are experiencing fear you can rest assured that this fear isn't
coming from God. Second, what you have that IS from God is more
than enough to overcome that fear. The right cross of POWER to the
head of fear, then the uppercut of LOVE to the jaw of fear, followed by
the gut-hemorrhaging body blow of DISCIPLINE direct to the ribs of
fear to finish it off. Your fear — on the canvas — out for the count.

(P.S. If you think love can't be tough, take a really, really good look at
Jesus.)

O Lord, our Lord, how majestic is Your name in all the earth!
— *Psalms 8:9*

What's In A Name?

By some accounts (including the names for Jesus as well) there are over 900 names for God in the Bible. Obviously we can't look at all of them here. My bet is, however, that we can look at enough of them to make you want to shout with King David in this Psalm, "O Lord, our Lord, how excellent is Your name in all the earth!"

1. **Adonai — The Lord is master**. No matter our situation in life, no matter how unsolvable we think a problem is, no matter how confusing or intense a hurt may be — we can rest in the knowledge that our God is master of it all, and over it all.

2. **Jehovah Jireh — The Lord will Provide.** No one could have felt the beauty of this any more than Abraham when God commanded him to sacrifice his only son. When he and Isaac arrived at the altar and Isaac asked his father where was the ram for the sacrifice, this was Abraham's response: "Jehovah Jireh." Today, no matter how desperate your situation may seem, the Lord is still Jehovah Jireh.

3. **El Shaddai — The Almighty God.** There is no power — in heaven, on the earth, or under the earth that is greater than the power of our God. Mightier than all the angels. Mightier than the devil — and therefore, mightier than any temptation or evil plan the devil might be throwing your way.

4. **Jehovah Shalom — The Lord is Peace.** Got stress? Got anxiety? Got fear? The person who will place God on the throne of their life has a cure for every bit of that.

5. **Jehovah Rohi — The Lord is my Shepherd.** The beauty of this name means that Psalm 23 was written for you. Green pastures, still waters, protection, company in the valley of the shadow of death — and more. All yours.

6. **Yahweh — I Am.** Much too profound for a few simple words, but this is the name that God Himself used to set Himself apart from any other god. It speaks to the eternal existence and the eternal presence of the Lord God in the life of His children. Whatever your need, God says, "I am the answer." And He will never — that's never — leave you or forsake you.

7. **<u>And my personal favorite: Savior.</u>** Perhaps most beautifully announced by the angel on the night God came to us in a manger in Bethlehem — "Behold, I bring you good news of great joy which will be for all the people; for today in the city of David there has been born for you a Savior, who is Christ the Lord." Hell has no temptation that can take it away, life has no problem, sadness or sorrow that can take it away, I have no personal weakness than can take it away. And one day, in spite of everything, I will see Jesus face to face because He is my Savior.

(you) who are protected by the power of God through faith for
a salvation ready to be revealed in the last time.
— *1ˢᵗ Peter 1:5*

Under Lock and Key

Small verse. Huge encouragement. I can't speak for anyone else, but
I can speak for me. And what I speak is this: I am glad — very, very
glad — that the security of my salvation, the certainty of my home in
heaven does not depend on my own strength to protect and guarantee it.

Praise and glory be to the Lord that when I appear before Him some day,
I don't have to produce a list of reasons why I deserve His forgiveness,
because there ARE none. I don't have to produce test results that show
"sinless life" because in my case, it doesn't exist. I don't have to produce
a certificate that says "worthy," because I am not.

On the day you enter heaven, it will not be because you protected your
salvation by anything at all that you did or deserved. You don't preserve
it with your own power. You will enter heaven because your salvation is
under lock and key. The lock of Almighty God's power, opened with the
key of your faith in Jesus Christ. It is not in doubt. Not even a little bit.
In fact, it is already finished and ready to be revealed.

Seeing them straining at the oars, for the wind was against them, at
about the fourth watch of the night He came to them, walking on
the sea; and He intended to pass by them.
— *Mark 6:48*

Row, Row, Row Your Boat

Have you ever taken a turn at the oars of a boat? Ever tried it against the
wind? If you have, you know that it doesn't take much of a contrary wind
to make rowing a boat a really tiring and frustrating task.

Here, Jesus's disciples got a lesson in just HOW tiring it can be. About
3:00 a.m. in the morning, 8 to 9 hours rowing in the face of a ferocious
wind, less than half-way into their journey across the lake — their muscles
had to be screaming from exhaustion. Then Jesus came to them. Not IN
the water — ON the water. Walking on top of it. And when the Master
of the sea and the wind got into their boat (verse 51), the wind stopped.
Instantly.

So many times in our own lives, we are just like the disciples, aren't
we? Frantically, frothing at the mouth we row, row, row our boats alone,
against the storms and howling winds of life until we are ready to drop
from bone-deep stress and exhaustion. There is a better way. Let the
Master of the sea and the wind get into your boat.

> But King David said to Ornan, "No, but I will surely buy it for the
> full price; for I will not take what is yours for the Lord, or offer
> a burnt offering which costs me nothing." —
> *Chronicles 21:24*

Burnt Offerings

I had the privilege of growing up in one of the finest horse and cattle counties in the entire country: Madison County, Texas. There are a lot of folks there who are razor sharp when it comes to recognizing the value of a fine horse, or cow, or bull. If I was to go to any of them and offer, for example, 25 cents for a registered Shorthorn bull, or 50 cents for a registered quarter horse, they would probably do two things: First they would look at me with a "Have you lost your mind?" expression, and then they would probably fall over laughing.

Have you ever wondered what God must think when we offer as much to Him? Burnt offerings that look more like "fried to a crisp offerings," instead of a sacrifice worthy of the Lord. Less than 10% of the people who go to church are tithers (give a Biblical tenth of their income), and many give nothing at all — not even 50 cents — for the God whose love for us never sleeps or fails.

King David gives us here a statement for our lives today that is nothing short of magnificent: "I will not offer burnt offerings to the Lord with that which costs me nothing." These were the words of a man whose integrity recognized the level of giving and service of which our Lord is worthy.

John 3:16 says, "For God so loved the world that He gave His only begotten Son, that whosoever believes in Him will never perish, but will have everlasting life." As we look at what God sacrificed because of His love for us, may that be our encouragement as we bring our own "burnt offerings" to a God who deserves our very best — every minute of every day.

It is a trustworthy statement, deserving full acceptance, that Christ
Jesus came into the world to save sinners, among whom I am
foremost of all. Yet for this reason I found mercy, so that in me as
the foremost, Jesus Christ might demonstrate His perfect patience as
an example for those who would believe in Him for eternal life.
— *Timothy 1:15,16*

Mercy's Poster Child

Before his encounter with the risen Lord Jesus Christ on the road to
Damascus, the man who penned these words was renowned for his
sustained, vicious, and ardent opposition to Christianity. He seethed on
the inside, waiting for each opportunity to persecute Christians and the
church. He held the coats of the men who stoned to death the first
Christian martyr, Stephen. He brought men, AND women in chains to
face prison and the fury of those who opposed Christianity. In his own
words he was a blasphemer, a persecutor, a violent aggressor, the foremost
sinner of them all. Yet, when he met personally, the risen Lord Jesus
Christ on the road to Damascus he was transformed, and persecution's
poster child because mercy's poster child.

There may be someone reading this today who, because of the depth of
their sins, feels they are beyond the reach of God's mercy. You're not.
That you are beyond God's forgiveness. You're not. That you are beyond
being useful to God because of what you have done. You're not. The
apostle Paul's trustworthy ("you can take it to the bank") statement here is
for you, too. Erasing your sin is why Jesus came into the world, and just
as He did with Paul, He can use you too — to demonstrate His perfect
patience and perfect love in your own life if you will just give Him the
chance. You can be mercy's poster child too!

"I am the good shepherd; the good shepherd lays down His life for
the sheep."
— *John 10:11*

Working With Heaven's Livestock

I and a whole lot of my friends grew up in the country. Proud of it, too.
We may not know much about "city life," or which fork to start eating
with first in a fancy restaurant, but, at the same time, if I asked my city
friends to hand-make an 8-plait bosal for my horse, I would be willing to
bet that just about 100 % of them would give me a blank stare and ask …
"Make a what?"

If you grow up in the country, one of the things you normally get a lot of
experience doing is working with livestock. It can be a scary job — like
if you surprise a mama cow with a new baby. Just ask my sister, Lorene
about that. Many times it is a dirty job, especially if you are working in
a confined space in the rain. And … almost always, it is a frustrating job.
Any cowboy can give you an almost endless list of reasons why.

Working with livestock is not easy. It takes dedication, patience, sacrifice …
and many, many hours of very hard work. I have known ranchers who
did that year after year after year. In the cold, in the heat, in the rain.
But — I never met a single one who would say they would be willing to
die for one of their cows, or a horse — or a sheep — no matter HOW
valuable it was.

But that's what Jesus did, isn't it? He said He would do it right here —
and He did. The Bible tells us that we are His "sheep," and all of us …
every single one of us, have gone astray. And even with His entire "herd"
scattered to the four winds and prone to wander off repeatedly, Jesus still
said, "The Good Shepherd gives His life for the sheep." And on a cross
stained with His own blood, on a hill called Calvary, He kept His word.

Why? Because in God's heart you are worth more than all the animals
on earth put together. Because He loves you more than you can ever
imagine. Because at the end of your "day" here on this earth and with
eternal life in heaven in the balance … He wanted to make sure that He
brought you home safely.

You will make known to me the path of life; in Your presence is fullness of joy; in Your right hand there are pleasures forever.
— *Psalms 16:11*

A Walk With The Lord

And what an incredibly beautiful walk it is indeed!! Did you notice there is not a single "might be" or "maybe" anywhere in it? Look where this walk takes us!!

*** "path of life" — God Himself reveals it. It is a beautiful expression in the Hebrew language meaning a journey, as the word "path" suggests. A journey that contains life from God, with God, and in God — the living God.

*** "fullness of joy" –A few drips of joy? No. Fullness. Where? In His presence. Side by side with God. How do you get there? By spending time in His word, time on your knees, and time in His path.

*** "pleasures forevermore" — What a walk we are having! Walking hand in hand with the Lord is pretty cool, isn't it? Pleasures from the hand of the world are many times sin-tainted, ALWAYS fleeting ... and many times the world's hand is empty. Pleasures from the hand of God are spotless and secure. And God's hand is never empty.

> Blessed be the God and Father of our Lord Jesus Christ, who
> according to His great mercy has caused us to be born again to
> a living hope through the resurrection of Jesus Christ from the dead,
> to obtain an inheritance which is imperishable and undefiled and
> will not fade away, reserved in heaven for you ...
> — *1 Peter 1:3,4*

The Face of Salvation

Remember that salvation protected by God Himself, that we looked at a few days ago in verse 5? Well, here is that salvation in a word picture from the previous two verses. We may not be able to draw the face of salvation, but using the descriptions in these verses we can touch the face of salvation with our hearts:

1. A salvation that flows not from our own efforts, but from the perfect mercy of God.
2. A salvation that promises a living hope after death, as proved by the resurrection of Jesus Christ Himself. How different than putting hope in an obscenely obese, fat man who is dead, sitting on folded legs, or praying to a carved wooden idol. Or any other of a long line of dead, false gods. Our God and Savior IS God ... and is alive forevermore.
3. A salvation that inherits together with Jesus, all that is in eternity.
4. A salvation that already exists, remains perfect, and is reserved — eternally.
5. A salvation whose full beauty will unfold in heaven itself. And it is all yours. Forever.

'For I will pour out water on the thirsty land and streams on the dry
ground; I will pour out My Spirit on your offspring and My blessing
on your descendants; and they will spring up among the grass like
poplars by streams of water.'
— *Isaiah 44:3,4*

The Oasis

Sometimes life is not a bed of roses, is it? Sometimes it can be dark and
cold, or confusing, or heartbreaking, or a desert of dried up dreams. Have
you ever lived through some of that? Have you ever wondered where
God is sometimes when life becomes a desert?

I love the way Isaiah approaches that very thing right here in these two
verses. He doesn't try to paint a believer's life like it is a path strewn
with rose petals — because it's not. Sometimes the needs of our heart go
thirsty, and the future can seem like endless dry ground stretching out in
front of us. But — the wonderful news from God's word is that it won't
always be that way.

The promise of God for His children is that He will renew the heart that
is aching and thirsty. He will send floods of refreshment to your life.
Sometimes it is still in the future, but it is there. It will come. Don't give

up. Our part is to have faith in the truth of God's promise. God's part is the oasis. Imagine if a weary traveler gave up just on the other side of that mountain of sand in this picture. He would never know that there was a beautiful oasis waiting just on the other side.

And there's more. You may not ever be able to pass along to your children a mansion, or bank accounts full of gold, but you can give them something much better — the Creator of the oasis.

... make it your ambition to lead a quiet life and attend to your own business and work with your hands, just as we commanded you, so that you will behave properly toward outsiders and not be in any need.
— *1ˢᵗ Thessalonians 4:11,12*

Mind Your Own Business

It might surprise a lot of people to know that this well-known admonition, "mind your own business," is actually Biblical advice. My mother is a reflection of this advice and I have enormous admiration for her. The great majority of her life, she has lived as a single woman. As a single-parent mom, she raised my two half-brothers all by herself. For many years she held down two jobs at the same time — and sometimes three. An accomplished and talented bookkeeper, at one point she kept five sets of books all at the same time (and that was back before computers and Excel spreadsheets). Today at 85+ years of age, she remains single, independent, self-sufficient, beholding to no one — and respected by everyone.

These two verses from the apostle Paul's earliest writing could be titled, "The Power of Positive Living." He lays out the process in a way that all of us can easily understand. He exhorts the Thessalonians — and us — with the integrity of minding our own business instead of inserting ourselves (wanted or not) into the affairs of others, and the dignity of hard work. He also describes the way we are to go about it: ambitiously — an eager and earnest desire to apply ourselves to the task. Taken together, they constitute a simple formula that can bring hope, encouragement — and success — to your life.

My mother is a living example that it works. And it can work for you, too.

You shall love the Lord your God with all your heart and with all
your soul and with all your might.
— *Deuteronomy 6:5*

Do This First

Our life is full of lists, isn't it? Shopping lists, priorities at work lists, kids
activities at school lists, honey-do lists, birthdays to remember ... lists,
lists, lists. Sitting on top of all of them should be this verse right here in
Deuteronomy. This was the advice of Moses to the children of Israel on
how to keep the very first commandment: "You shall have no other gods
before Me." It is still the best way to keep the first commandment today,
when we are besieged from all sides to put a long list of things ahead of
God. Anything placed ahead of God becomes a god (with a little "g") in
our lives, and our list of excuses to put them there is almost endless. This
one verse cures that.

Over the years I have had any number of people not truly interested in
a relationship with God tell me, "There's no way I can keep all those
commandments." I always, always, always respond: "You don't have to.
Just keep the first one and all the rest will take care of themselves." This
one verse tells you how to do it.

But Jesus, aware of their reasonings, answered and said to them,
"Why are you reasoning in your hearts? Which is easier, to say,
'Your sins have been forgiven you,' or to say, 'Get up and walk'? But,
so that you may know that the Son of Man has authority on earth
to forgive sins,"-He said to the paralytic-"I say to you, get up, and
pick up your stretcher and go home."
— *Luke 5:22-24*

I'm Going To Make An Example Out Of You

Anyone besides me ever heard those dreaded words? Normally, they would strike fear into us, especially when we were younger because it meant the following: we had done something wrong, and someone like one of our teachers or our parents would administer some really painful "correction" to prevent anyone else from wanting to do the same thing.

A wonderfully opposite application of this declaration, however, can exist when it involves Jesus and those who believe in Him. It is very positive and encouraging. In this setting in the fifth chapter of Luke, the scribes and Pharisees were all indignant about Jesus pronouncing forgiveness of the sins of a paralyzed man. Jesus read their minds without them even opening their mouths and what happened next is recorded in these three verses.

What is so encouraging for you and me is that Jesus doesn't need a theologian, or a pastor, or an evangelist, or a popular leader in the church to create an example. He can make an example out of you as surely as He made one out of this paralyzed man. An example of His power, an example of His forgiveness, an example of His love.

All you have to do is make yourself available, just like the paralyzed man in this text.

"… You have kept the good wine until now!"
— *John 2:10d*

Home Brew

We're going to have some fun with this today, and hopefully it will bring a blessing alongside at the same time. I know I say this a lot, about a lot of different verses, but … this verse is part of one of my favorite stories in the whole Bible.

Here's the fun part:

Jesus's very first miracle recorded in the Bible was turning water into wine. The One who made the stars, just made some home brew. Down through the years I have had a lot of fun with some dear Christian friends who try to say that this (and other wine mentioned in the Bible) was non-alcoholic — in other words, grape juice. It wasn't grape juice — and there is no textual evidence, linguistic evidence, or cultural evidence that can make it grape juice. It was wine. Real wine. And Jesus made it. Home brew. And it made Him the "life of the party." In Jesus's day, normally a party went like this: good wine at the beginning to impress the guests, then when everyone was "well-pickled" they brought out the cheap stuff because no one would be able to tell the difference. What Jesus did was exactly the opposite — the best was saved for last — which is what this little verse records in the second chapter of the gospel of John.

Here's the blessing part:

Think of this party in the Bible as your own life. Your "party" has been going on for quite some time … years and years, in fact. Jesus has no trouble at all working with that, even at the sunset of the party. Your part is giving Him your heart to work with. If He has that, He can be the life of your party too. Jesus's home brew of love in your life. He can still turn water into wine.

... there was given me a thorn in the flesh...
— *2nd Corinthians 12:7c*

A Thorn in the Flesh

Ever get one of those? A thorn in the flesh? Did you enjoy it? Stupid question, right? I know what you must be thinking — if this is a book of devotions about hope and encouragement, why on earth is there a verse about a thorn in it? We will get there, I promise. I purposely left off the surrounding scripture (which you should look up) because that is what we do almost all the time in real life. We concentrate on the thorn, the irritant, the flaw — and spend very little time considering why we have it, and what God can do with us in spite of it. The scripture before and after verse 7 talks about those very things.

First of all, stop worrying about your flaws. Verse 8 shows you that you might NEVER get rid of them. Second of all, consider — as verse 9 shows you, positive thing #1 — God's grace in your life is greater than your weakness, and positive thing #2 — your weakness, your flaw, allows God's power to be magnified in your life.

Thirdly — I don't know anyone who loves jewelry and does not love the serene, elegant beauty of natural pearls, do you? The only gem that isn't mined from the earth. It is created inside a living thing, an oyster. Well, every single pearl ever formed in an oyster started with an invasive grain of sand, an irritant — a thorn in its flesh. For a saltwater pearl to form, the oyster needs between 5 to 20 years, slowly building the pearl around its "thorn in the flesh," but just look at the beauty when it is done, even with the flaw still inside the pearl. All different kinds of colors, sizes and shapes, but all beautiful just the same.

Now — if a grain of sand can become a beautiful pearl inside a living oyster — imagine what you can become in the hands of the living God.

"Answer me, O Lord, answer me, that this people may know that You, O Lord, are God, and that You have turned their heart back again." Then the fire of the Lord fell and consumed the burnt offering and the wood and the stones and the dust, and licked up the water that was in the trench.
— *1ˢᵗ Kings 18:37,38*

In Tune

Anyone from the world of music knows instantly what "in tune" means. It means that an instrument ... be it a flute, clarinet, trumpet, violin or piano, is properly adjusted so the sounds it makes are harmonious with all the other instruments. The opposite condition is "out of tune." If the instruments of an orchestra are "out of tune" the greatest works of even Beethoven or Mozart would just sound like so much backyard noise.

Have you ever wondered what being "in tune" with God might be like? Well, here is one of the best examples in all the Bible. The setting: a confrontation between the prophets of Baal (a false god) and Elijah, the famous prophet of the Lord God Almighty. The test: two altars of sacrifice were constructed. The prophets of Baal would "pray" to their God, and Elijah would pray to his God. It was agreed that the one who answered with fire would be considered the true God. The prophets of Baal prayed and chanted and danced around their altar — then even beat themselves on their backs with whips trying to summon their "god." All day. No answer. Then it was Elijah's turn. His prayer (which actually starts one verse earlier) takes about 20 SECONDS to speak — and the results are there before your eyes. That is what it is like to be really "in tune" with God.

Now — can we all be mighty prophets of God? Will we all equal the feats of Elijah? Of course not. But — we CAN all be "in tune" with God. Spend time with Him the same way Elijah did and watch what happens.

> For He rescued us from the domain of darkness, and transferred us
> to the kingdom of His beloved Son, in whom we have redemption,
> the forgiveness of sins.
> — *Colossians 1:13,14*

Verb Tense Excitement

I know that for many people the "title" of this devotional sounds almost like an oxymoron: verb tense — excitement. Maybe it brings excitement for our English teachers, but for most of us? Well …

Verb tenses in the Bible, however, can reveal for us how God sees things from His perspective, and they can actually be VERY exciting in certain places in the Bible. Right here is one of those places. Note the past tenses Paul used here: "rescued us," and "delivered us." From God's perspective (get ready) the battle is ***already won*** and our home in heaven ***is already secure***. We don't have to wait and wonder. AND — redemption is not something we have to wait for either, or hope we have, or continually earn each day. We ***already have it***. As in right now. Secured forever by the blood of the Lord Jesus Christ.

Be gracious to me, O God, be gracious to me, for my soul takes refuge in You; and in the shadow of Your wings I will take refuge until destruction passes by.
— *Psalms 57:1*

Safe And Sound

What is it they say? Sometimes a picture is worth a thousand words.

Psalms 57:1

In Him was life, and the Life was the Light of men. The Light
shines in the darkness, and the darkness did not comprehend it.
— John 1:4,5

Where's The Flashlight?

My bet is, that I am not the only one who has needed to ask that
question in the pitch black. Am I right? We almost never ask it when
the electricity is working, do we? Usually we ask it when the electricity
goes off unexpectedly at night, and even if we actually KNOW where
the flashlight is, it isn't all that easy to get to in the dark, is it? Even
in a house we are familiar with, we have to walk slowly, and we stumble
around in the dark.

This can happen in life too, can't it? One minute everything is as clear
as day, everything is going great — and suddenly the lights go out and
we are left in the dark, wishing we knew where the flashlight was. That
relationship that you knew for sure would last forever, came to a crashing,
heartbreaking end. And the darkness of sadness overcomes you. That
job that you thought would carry you into your sunset years with benefits
and solid retirement — disappeared like morning mist on the lake with
unexpected "downsizing." And the darkness of desperation overcomes
you. There are many ways the light can go out, aren't there?

The good news is that, if you have Jesus as your Savior, you never have to
worry when the lights go out. And you never have to wonder where the
Flashlight is — because the Flashlight is Jesus and He is with you all the
time. These two wonderful verses from the gospel of John are primarily
about the victory of Jesus over the darkness of sin and evil in our lives. In
fact, the more literal translation of "did not comprehend it" is actually "did
not overcome it." Evil loses. In fact, evil has already lost. Now … it isn't
always evil and sin that cause the lights to go out in our lives, but when it
happens, evil for sure tries to keep us there, defeated in our darkness. In
Jesus, you have a Holy Flashlight — use it. He never needs batteries, He
never needs recharging, He is always ready, He is always shining — and
He will defeat your darkness. Every single time.

For if you remain silent at this time, relief and deliverance will arise
for the Jews from another place and you and your father's house will
perish. And who knows whether you have not attained royalty for
such a time as this?"
— *Esther 4:14c*

Your Time To Shine

Esther rose from being a Jewish harem girl to being the queen of the
king of Persia. Her story is thrilling to read, but if you want to know it
you will need to read the whole book. I will say only the following, to
tease you: In one of the most remarkable displays of courage and faith in
the entire Bible, Esther used her position as queen to save, quite literally,
the entire nation of Israel. It was her time to shine in God's plan.

What is so exciting about this little phrase is that it can be just as true
today — in your life — speaking to you right out of the pages of God's
word. To distill the eternal truth of this phrase for your life, translate it
this way: "... and who knows whether you are where you are today for
such a time as this." — A time to share a word of encouragement, a time
to be a Christian example, a time to help heal a broken heart because
you've been there and know how it feels — or a time to share the hope
of the gospel for someone who will cross your path because you are where
you are — even if it is a difficult time in your life. Esther literally put her
life on the line as queen to save the nation of Israel.

Example: Let's say your job is sweeping and cleaning a bus stop, graveyard
shift. One night a person sits down to wait for the bus. You can see that
for some reason this person's heart is shattered. You know how that feels.
They sit there with a sadness that almost wrings tears out of the night
air. You share the hope of the gospel and the person asks Jesus Christ
to come into their heart. "For such a time as this" ... one lonely night at
the bus stop, God used you to not only change history — but to change
eternity for a living human being.

Maybe it is your time to shine wherever you are today — for such a time
as this ...

And He came up and touched the coffin; and the bearers came to a halt. And He said, "Young man, I say to you, arise!" The dead man sat up and began to speak. And Jesus gave him back to his mother.
— *Luke 7:14,15*

Choosing The Right Doctor

Anyone think that isn't important? Choosing the right doctor? Of course it is, and anyone who has ever been seriously sick or injured would be happy to testify just *__how__* important it is. The doctor you choose can mean the difference between life and death. Let's say that you have the best dentist in the world — but, if what you need is emergency open-heart surgery, you will die if you choose your dentist for the surgery. The same is true about where you will spend eternity one day. In our daily lives we can encounter all sorts of positive things and people that can help us. But … when the life and death subject is where you will spend eternity, it is critical that you choose the One who can actually take you there.

Do you know a doctor who can raise people from the dead? I do. His name is Jesus. I love the way Luke records the medical miracles of Jesus, because Luke was a doctor, too. And if he, as a doctor, had thought any of the miraculous healings Jesus performed weren't 100% authentic, he would never have recorded them as authentic. In fact, the verb here for "sat up" was used exclusively by the medical profession of Jesus's day.

What makes these verses so exciting and encouraging for you and me is realizing that Jesus is in the business, still today, of raising people from the dead. The young man here was raised physically from the dead, but there are all sorts of ways to be "raised from the dead." For us today, it doesn't have to mean returning to life only after you have died. If you don't believe that, ask anyone who had reached the point of not wanting to go on any more and then found new life in Christ. People can feel dead because a relationship ended. People can feel dead because their economic future collapsed at their feet. People can feel dead because every single thing they have tried to do has failed. The despair that brings, the death of hope that brings, can all be healed — you just have to choose the right Doctor. And His name … is Jesus.

Peter said, "I do not possess silver and gold, but what I do have
I give to you: In the name of Jesus Christ the Nazarene-walk!"
— *Acts 3:6*

You and the Lame Man

Peter and John were on their way to the temple to pray. And the man —
lame from birth — did indeed rise up and walk. Immediately. In fact, he
LEAPED up ... and kept on leaping with joy.

Through my professor of Church History, W.R. Estep, I learned one
day about a legendary medieval encounter between Thomas Aquinas and
Pope Pius IV. Walking through the Vatican one day the pope swept his
hand around at all the gold opulence that adorns the interior and said,
"No longer do we have to say, 'silver and gold have we none.'" To which
Aquinas replied, "Yes ... and neither can we any longer say, 'Rise and
walk.'"

Those words reach across almost 800 years and touch us today, don't they?
So often, the god we choose is the one we fold up in our wallets. The
truth is, if money was an effective god, wealthy people would never get
divorced, or commit suicide, and their children would all grow up perfect
and happy. The truth is, money is a paltry substitute for the real God
with the real power. The truth is, also, that we can choose to not let the
wrong god control our life. Jesus said, "All power and authority has been
given to Me — in heaven and on earth, and I am with you always ..."
Do NOT miss that last bit. "I am with you always." Always.

Stop for a minute and let that sink in. God may not use us to command
a physically lame man to rise and walk, but His power is always available —
always — to those of us who believe in His Son. What will you do with
the lame man on the wall? We walk past him just about every day. There
are all sorts of way to help someone "rise and walk," and God can display
His power and love through us is myriads of ways if we will let Him be
God instead of silver and gold. Who knows what God may be wanting
to do through you ... in the name of Jesus Christ of Nazareth...

"For God so loved the world, that He gave His only begotten Son, that whoever believes in Him shall not perish, but have eternal life."
— *John 3:16*

The Greatest Sentence Ever Written

Some have called John 3:16 the greatest sentence ever written — I agree.

1. Who loves the world? Some benevolent, intelligent leader of one of the countries of the world? No — the one and only God Himself.
2. Does He just sort of "like" the world, or look at it and smile? No — God SO LOVED the world. I have a sermon on the biggest word in the Bible. It is right here, and it is the word "so."
3. Does God play favorites? No — He loves the WHOLE WORLD.
4. Does God charge for His love? No — His Son was a gift.
5. Does God have a large family? No — The Son He gave was His only Son.
6. Was God's gift common and cheap? No — It was His Son ... the same Son who created the heavens and the earth.
7. Does God exclude anyone? No — God's offer is for "whosoever." I am so very grateful, personally, for that part because it includes even me.
8. Does God make us sacrifice for His gift to us? No — we need only to believe in His Son.
9. Does God short change us in the end in exchange for a life of faith in Jesus? No — everlasting life in heaven. John 3:16 is the greatest retirement plan the world has ever seen. In a single sentence.

In Him we have redemption through His blood, the forgiveness
of our trespasses, according to the riches of His grace which He
lavished on us.
— *Ephesians 1:7,8a*

The Treasure Chest

You could write an entire book on the beauty of just these two verses.
Space won't allow that, so here is a quick look at just a few of the
"diamonds" from God's treasure chest that shine from Ephesians 1:7,8.

1. If you are a Christian, your relationship with God for now and forever
   already exists. Note "have," not "WILL have." There's you a big
   diamond sitting right there on the top.
2. Redemption written in blood and total forgiveness, while being
   undeserving of either. Diamond #2 right beside the first one.
3. Did God do this for us grudgingly? Did we have to pry it out of
   God? Nope. To picture the riches of God's grace, imagine that two
   people have said they are going to offer you something to use for
   a ride to work. One shows up with a pogo stick and charges you for
   the ride. The other shows up with a Rolls Royce — as a gift. The
   Rolls is God's grace. There's diamond #3 for you, sitting right there
   beside the first two.
4. Was this grace toward us dripped sparingly on us, like trying to wring
   out a damp rag? Nope. To picture "lavished," put in your mind the
   most beautiful, clear, refreshing waterfall you can imagine. Now put
   yourself under it. THAT is "lavished." I will put that treasure chest
   up against a life without Jesus any day.

Finally, brethren, whatever is true, whatever is honorable, whatever is right, whatever is pure, whatever is lovely, whatever is of good repute, if there is any excellence and if anything worthy of praise, dwell on these things.
— *Philippians 4:8*

Whatever

If everyone could obey just this one verse ... what a wonderful world it would be.

He said, "Look! I see four men loosed and walking about in the
midst of the fire without harm, and the appearance of the fourth is
like a son of the gods!"
— *Daniel 3:25*

You Never Get A Second Chance
To Make A Good First Impression

This expression is almost a holy mantra in the business world. Great
expense and effort are poured into making a good first impression,
because you might not even get a second chance. We should be at least as
dedicated when it comes to giving a witness for the God we say we love.

Sometimes it isn't easy, though, is it? Standing up for God in the middle
of a Godless world. It was extremely difficult in the world of Daniel
during the time this experience before us took place. And Nebuchadnezzar,
King of Babylon, the one who was speaking here in Daniel 3:25 certainly
didn't make it any easier. You know, the same Nebuchadnezzar who
destroyed Jerusalem, razed it to the ground and took all its people captive
to Babylon. However, because of the stainless steel faith of three teenage
boys, he was changed in an instant after a supernatural encounter with
the Lord Jesus Christ (you really should read the whole story in Daniel
3:1-30). Let's look at it together.

The setting here:

1. The king erects a golden obelisk to himself and orders everyone to
   bow down to it.
2. Even though all the government leaders in the land obey, three courageous
   young men, knowing the cost was execution by fire, refuse to do it.
3. Their execution is ordered. The execution furnace is raised to 7 times
   its normal heat.
4. The soldiers escorting the young men to the furnace die from the heat
   as the three fall into the fire.
5. Not only do the three young teenagers not die, they walk around IN
   the fire — with the pre-incarnate Christ.
6. When they leave the fire, they are not hurt. The smell of smoke isn't
   even on their clothes.

7. Nebuchadnezzar is changed forever. (I wonder why ...)

Lessons of hope and encouragement for standing up for your faith:

1. You never get a second chance to make a good first impression. You never know who might be affected by your faithful witness for God and the Lord Jesus Christ. In this passage of scripture, three teenage boys changed the mind of a vicious king.
2. One of the most beautiful and most encouraging lessons of the entire Bible is here: we are never promised a life without "fiery trials," but — we ARE promised the presence of the Lord with us — always — in the midst of them.

And He got up and rebuked the wind and said to the sea, "Hush, be still." And the wind died down and it became perfectly calm.
— *Mark 4:39*

Captain to the Bridge!

We've all heard that shout many times in the movies, haven't we? There is a crisis on a ship and the call goes out, "Captain to the bridge!" The one in charge needs to take command of the situation.

So it was here with the disciples. Storm raging. Paralyzed with fear. And their Captain was asleep in the back of the boat. Jesus never worried because He knew there was no need to worry.

Hearing a very rude remark, "Are we to drown for all You care?" (in today's language), their Captain rises and takes command. To the wind and the waves His literal words were, "Silence! Muzzle!" They were commands, and the wind and the waves obeyed. The wind stopped. Instantly. The waves became like glass. Instantly. Anyone reading this who has had experience at sea knows that even when a storm stops, it takes a while for the sea to become calm. Not here. Not this time. Jesus is Lord — over everything.

He can do the same in your life, too. There are all kinds of storms: emotional storms, financial storms, physical storms, family storms, job storms. Jesus can calm them all as easily as He did the storm for the disciples. But ... a couple of things need to happen first. You have to let Him be the Captain, and — you need to make sure He is in your boat.

Jesus said to him, "I am the way, and the truth, and the life; no one
comes to the Father but through Me.
— *John 14:6*

One Way

If you are looking for a vacation that is truly exquisite in its beauty and
yet absolutely secluded, you might consider one of the more isolated
destinations in the Cook Islands in the South Pacific — Palmerston.
Everyone is welcome, but there is only one way to get there. By boat.
Several days by boat. You can't fly there, drive there, or hike to it.

A relationship with Almighty God is like that. Everyone is welcome, but
there is only one way to get there. Jesus identifies that way right here in
one of the most powerful statements in all of scripture …

The sense of the Greek is:

"I, and I alone, am the way"

"I, and I alone, am the truth"

"I, and I alone, am the life."

Not "I know the way" … He IS the way,

Not "I speak the truth" … He IS the truth,

Not "I have the words of life" … He IS the life.

You want to have a relationship with God? Look no further. A relationship
with Jesus IS a relationship with God. Some folks say this statement of
Jesus is "exclusive." I say it is INclusive. The opportunity for anyone to
have a heavenly future and a relationship with the living God — where
otherwise we would have no hope.

The words of Amos, who was among the sheepherders from Tekoa,
which he envisioned in visions concerning Israel in the days of
Uzziah king of Judah, and in the days of Jeroboam son of Joash,
king of Israel, two years before the earthquake.
— *Amos 1:1*

Local Boy Becomes A Prophet

From Genesis to maps we see a remarkable and beautiful pattern in the way God accomplishes His will. That pattern? Using the ordinary to accomplish the extraordinary. He did it again here, with Amos. He was not on the "Executive Board of Prophets," he had no diploma from the "Seminary of the High and Mighty Educated." Amos was, as we might say in Texas, just another ranch hand, or in Old Testament days, "among the sheepherders from Tekoa." If you read on, you learn that he was also a fig farmer. Not exactly the resumé one might expect for a prophet of the Almighty God.

But then, God has this thing about the way He acts: He does what He wants to do and He chooses who He wants to choose. He is almighty, He is sovereign — and He never makes a mistake. What does that mean to us? It means God can use you, too. Even if you feel like you are President of the Club of the Ordinary. Or even the "Less Than Ordinary." Your position — or lack of position — means absolutely nothing to the power or the plan of God:

If God can use Amos to do this — deliver a fearless prophecy to Israel.

If God can use Noah to do this — build something he had never built before ... for a flood that had never happened before.

If God can use David to do this — as a young shepherd boy, kill Goliath, then become Israel's most famous king.

If God can use crusty fishermen to do this — join the group of the first disciples of Jesus Christ.

If God can use Paul, the greatest persecutor of the first believers in Christ to do this — become one of the greatest champions of Christ who has ever lived —

Then ...

God can use you to do this — ___(you fill in the blank)___.

More than the sounds of many waters, than the mighty breakers of
the sea, the Lord on high is mighty.
— *Psalms 93:4*

In The Presence of Power

One of the most astounding and stunningly beautiful places in the
entire world is the mighty falls at Foz do Iguaçu in Brazil. I have had
the honor of going there several times. A poverty of language prevents
a proper description of the sight and feeling when you are standing
there. You can hear — and FEEL — the mighty power of the falls
rumbling long before you can see them. There are over 260 cataracts
stretching for more than 3 miles. As you approach the entrance, it
gets louder and more powerful ... then, as you descend into the area of
the falls themselves, embedded in the rock is a steel plaque with this
verse. I took this picture myself. The plaque itself gives our words of
hope and encouragement for today: "God is always greater than all our
troubles."

God, after He spoke long ago to the fathers in the prophets in many
portions and in many ways, in these last days has spoken to us in
His Son, whom He appointed heir of all things, through whom also
He made the world.
— *Hebrews 1:1,2*

Will The Real Last Days Please Stand Up

The long wait is finally over. The last days have arrived. All the modern
day "end-time prophets" can put their pens down. Enough already, with
trying to get rich writing books that tickle people's fascination with the
apocalyptic language in John's Revelation. According to God's own word,
right here in the book of Hebrews, we have ALREADY been in the last
days ever since Jesus came and was resurrected.

What all those authors are really trying to predict is what the Bible calls
"The Day of the Lord," or the end of the age. The SECOND coming
of Jesus. There is only one truly reliable source on the subject. It is the
Bible. Here is how God's own word says it will happen:
1. No one will EVER know when it is going to happen. (Matthew 24:36)
2. It will be a complete surprise. (Matthew 24:44)
3. Everyone — all at the same time — will see Jesus coming. (Revelation1:7)
4. Jesus will gather all believers and take us all to heaven. (1 Thessalonians
   4:16,17)
5. #4 will happen in the twinkling of an eye. (1 Corinthians 15:52)
6. Be ready. (Matthew 24:44) That's it.

What is beautiful about these verses in Hebrews in how God draws a line
between the "past days" and the "last days." In the former, He spoke
through messengers. In the latter He spoke through a family member.
His one and only Son, Jesus. His Son who is the appointed heir of all
things. And — and — and — when a person believes in Jesus, they
become heir to all those same things (Romans 8:17). How's THAT for
a little hope and encouragement for today?

And the next time you go outside and look up into that big, beautiful
heaven full of stars, remember — that same Jesus with whom you are
joint heirs ... He made all of it.

Blessed be the God and Father of our Lord Jesus Christ, who has
blessed us with every spiritual blessing in the heavenly places in
Christ ...
Ephesians 1:3

Shinsegae Centum City in the Sky

If I were to ask "What is Harrods?", the great majority of people would
know and immediately answer, "It's one of largest and most famous
department stores in the world in London, England." If I were to ask
"What is Shinsegae Centum City?", that same group would probably give
me a blank stare, even though at 3,163,000 square feet, it is over three
times the size of Harrods. It is in South Korea, and it is the largest
department store in the world.

I can't imagine anything that a person could want that they could not find
in a place as big as that. What if you could go there and get all your
heart's desires — all for free. The finest jewelry, the finest clothes, the
finest furniture ... on and on we could go. No matter what you want, you
can get the very best that money can buy, except you don't have to pay for
any of it. All because you know the owner. Sound inviting?

Well ... what if I were to tell you that there is a "Shinsegae Centum City
in the sky" that makes the one on earth in South Korea look like a small
town 7-11? Have a closer look at what God is doing here in this verse
of Ephesians. I don't know what would constitute a comprehensive list of
spiritual blessings, but I bet they are better than any earthly possessions —
and God Himself is giving them away. To you. And not just a few of
them — ALL of them. Every single one. All because you know His
Son. And what a store ... heaven itself. All the spiritual blessings it
contains, all for you. No wonder Paul is praising the Lord here. I say we
join him! What do you say?

but just as it is written, "Things which eye has not seen and ear has not heard, and which have not entered the heart of man, all that God has prepared for those who love Him." For to us God revealed them through the Spirit; for the Spirit searches all things, even the depths of God.
— *1ˢᵗ Corinthians 2:9,10*

You Have No Idea

Unless you are a microbiologist, you really have no idea how incredibly complex life is — even on the microscopic level (which, all by itself makes the notion of evolution the argument of fools). Unless you are an astronaut who has been to the moon, you have no idea what it feels like to look out of a spaceship window and see the entire earth with your own eyes from the vastness of outer space. And, unless you have already been to heaven, you really have no idea about "the things which God has prepared for those who love Him."

Because of God's revelation through the Holy Spirit, we know some of the facts of our future, but we still have no idea of the fulness of those facts. We know we have a Savior, but we have no idea of His risen splendor in heaven. We know He loves us, but we have no idea how much — and won't know — until we see Him face to face with our own eyes.

From God's revelation to John in the last book of the Bible, we can read about what awaits our arrival in heaven — an entire city and its streets that are so much more brilliant than gold that they appear as transparent as glass. An entire city that has no need of the sun because the glory of the Lord illuminates it, the tree of life from which man was banned in the garden now accessible once more, with a river as pure as crystal running beside it, the sound of heaven's choir of angels so mighty in their song that they shake the very foundation of heaven. And ... a place in which, for eternity, we will never again experience even for one second — the feeling of a tear in our eyes, the fear of death, or sadness, or any pain. In his revelation, John was a man grappling with the poverty of the written word, to describe something about which we can really have no idea until we, too, see it with our own eyes.

But — what we do know, my friend, is that all these things are coming. If you are one who loves the Lord, they are coming. In fact, God already has everything prepared — all that is missing is your arrival.

Then Moses stretched out his hand over the sea; and the Lord swept
the sea back by a strong east wind all night and turned the sea into
dry land, so the waters were divided. The sons of Israel went through
the midst of the sea on the dry land, and the waters were like a wall to
them on their right hand and on their left.
— *Exodus 14:21,22*

When Life Gives You Lemons

We've all heard it — "When life gives you lemons, make lemonade." And
we think: That's easy for someone to say when they are sitting there in
the shade, on the other side of the lemonade stand. Have you ever felt
like life was just one big lemon — or even a series of lemons? I know
I have. Lemonade in a glass is easy — just add lemon juice, sugar, water
and stir. Lemonade in life is different.

As Israel looked here at the Red sea in front of them and the Egyptian
army closing in fast behind them, it might have well-looked like "lemon
time" to them. In lemon times, however, we would do well to remember
that our God is the ultimate Lemonade Maker. He really is, isn't He?
We see it all through the Bible — Noah's worldwide flood, Joshua's
battle against huge armies of the enemy, saving Jonah in the belly of
a fish, Daniel's den of lions, the fiery furnace of Shadrack, Meshak and
Abednigo ... and on and on we could go. Time after time, in impossible
situations just like here at the Red Sea, God has turned "lemon time" into
"lemonade."

And He can do the same in your life. He is much better at it than we
are. Trust me, I've already tried it many times without God. The next
time the sea is in front of you and the enemy is closing in fast from
behind, here's the recipe for lemonade in life: all your lemons + all your
faith + all God's power.

Mix that together and watch what happens.

Love is patient, love is kind and is not jealous; love does not brag and is not arrogant, does not act unbecomingly; it does not seek its own, is not provoked, does not take into account a wrong suffered, does not rejoice in unrighteousness, but rejoices with the truth; bears all things, believes all things, hopes all things, endures all things. Love never fails;
— *1ˢᵗ Corinthians 13:4-8a*

I can't imagine a better day than Valentine's Day for this…

The Response of Love

(Adapted from 1st Corinthians 13)
Kelly Adkins

When love is faced with injustice –
love remains patient.

When love is faced with heartache –
love remains kind.

When love is in the presence of another's success –
love is never jealous.

When love is victorious –
love remains humble and never responds proudly.

When love is mistreated –
love does not behave rudely.

When love is presented with the wishes of another –
love is never selfish.

When love is faced with anger –
love remains peaceful.

When love is tempted to hold a grudge –
love never takes into account, a wrong suffered.

When love is tempted with the pleasure of sin –
love refuses to enjoy what is wrong, and always finds its joy
in the truth.

When love is given a burden –
love bears all things.

When love is asked to trust –
love believes all things.

When love is faced with despair –
love hopes all things.

Whatever the test, no matter how long –
love endures all things.
True love never fails.

> Then Jesus was led up by the Spirit into the wilderness to be
> tempted by the devil. And after He had fasted forty days and forty
> nights, He then became hungry. And the tempter came and said
> to Him, "If You are the Son of God, command that these stones
> become bread." But He answered and said, "It is written, 'Man shall
> not live on bread alone, but on every word that proceeds out of the
> mouth of God.'"
> — *Matthew 4:1-4*

The devil Made Me Do It

Wrong. The devil does not, and cannot, make you do anything. Not one single thing. He hasn't the power to do that. Jesus has all the power (Matt.28:18), remember? And even Jesus doesn't make you do anything. Everything we do is because we choose to do it. Is the devil dangerous? Absolutely. He can't touch us — but, he can tempt us. And therein lies the danger my friend ... when we give in to that temptation and choose of our own free will to do what we should not, even when we know better. Just ask Adam and Eve. That is how the devil destroys lives. And families.

The most beautiful, powerful, inspiring, and perfect example of how we should conduct our lives is always Jesus, and that is true right here, too — at the very beginning of His ministry, and at the weakest physical moment of His life up to that time. Jesus had just gone without food for 40 days ... and the devil tempted Him with using His power as God to turn stones into bread, which would have been easy for Jesus — and — no one was there to see. We can't go three days without hunger tearing us apart. Try to imagine 40. Yet Jesus remained strong and did not yield to the devil's temptation. How?

Look at the example and solution Jesus gives you and me: in the middle of what had to be raging hunger, and the temptation to use His power as God, He said instead, "Man shall not live by bread alone, but by every word that proceeds out of the mouth of God." What truly satisfies isn't the brief feeding of physical desires. What truly satisfies is the word of God. It is what protects us, too — against any temptation.

See how great a love the Father has bestowed on us, that we would be
called children of God; and such we are.
— *1ˢᵗ John 3:1*

What It Takes to be a Parent

Those of us who have actually been parents can compile that list really
fast, can't we? At the beginning there is the getting up every few hours
to feed the baby, in the middle of bone-crushing exhaustion. You learn
to change a diaper with one hand tied behind your back — and you
develop the super human skill of enduring the foulest smells imaginable
that can come from those same diapers. There are almost endless
financial sacrifices, starting with restructuring your budget to be able to
afford all those diapers. Then there is food, clothes, insurance, endless
school expenses. Then there are the emotional costs of trying to guide
your child through the process of "growing up." Then there is the most
difficult emotional cost of all, when one day it is time to watch someone
else take your "baby" and start a family of their own. And that is the
SHORT list, right? But who among us who have been parents would
say it wasn't worth all the effort and all the cost? That's because along
the way a love grows for your child so intense that there are no words
to even describe it.

God knows well, what it takes to be a parent. What it took for God
to be a parent, for you to be His child, cost Him the life of His only
Son. His love for you, His child, is so great that it left the apostle John
in a state of wonderment here in his first letter, just trying to describe it.
And God had that love for you in His heart before the world even existed
(Ephesians 1:4-8). And God would be the first to say that it was worth
all the effort and all the cost … to be able to have a loving relationship
with you, for you to be able to talk to Him, and walk with Him every day
of your life — to have the King of Kings and Lord of Lords to help you
and dry your tears and encourage you, no matter how difficult the trial.
And for the greatest joy of all — having you with Him in heaven for all
eternity. Your Heavenly Father loves you deeply, my friend.

Keep me as the apple of the eye; hide me in the shadow of Your
wings.
— *Psalms 17:8*

What A View

I absolutely love this little verse. So short, and yet so very beautiful. It
speaks to both the strong protection and the ever-watchful love of God.

The image of the protection of God here is one that is repeated several
times in scripture and it pictures a mighty bird protecting its young under
its wings. It is the imagery of a place we can be and always feel secure,
because it is God whose wings we are under.

To capture the imagery of the ever-caring, ever-watchful love of God,
David prays the words, "Keep me as the apple of your eye." When
someone is especially dear to us, many times we too, use this loving and
very familiar expression to describe how much they mean to us. If you
have ever wondered where the expression came from, now you know.

In King David's language of Hebrew, it goes still further. The "apple" is
the pupil; the part of the eye through which all images are captured. If
you could look into the eye of a person who is looking at a mountain
range, you would see the entire mountain range from beginning to end,
captured right on the pupil of their eye. Being in the "apple of God's eye"
means that you are especially dear to God and He sees your whole life
the same as the mountain range, from beginning to end. What a view!

"He found him in a desert land, and in the howling waste of a wilderness; He encircled him, He cared for him, He guarded him as the pupil of His eye.
— *Deuteronomy 32:10*

Lost And Found

In high-flown theological circles, this verse about God's love for Israel is in the middle of what is known as the "Song of Moses." But outside those circles — where you and I live — it could be called our song as well.

This verse could be called the "Song of (your name here)."

Here's the lost part: desert land, wasteland, howling wilderness. It is the picture of an absolute dead end, with no hope, and howling wild animals waiting just around the corner. It doesn't take much imagination to place some of us today into this picture. Sometimes life can take a nose dive, can't it? We can think we are sitting pretty, then life yanks the chair out from under us and leaves us feeling there is no hope, and afraid of the future around the corner. And life can be that way if you don't know the Lord — or at times, even if you *do* know the Lord.

Here's the found part: found, encircled, instructed, kept as supremely precious in the heart of God. There is no one so lost that God cannot find them. He has been finding His lost creation ever since He "searched" for Adam in the Garden of Eden. Then, the Almighty God who created the universe and eternity covers and encircles the one He finds. Then He gives that person all the instruction he will never need in life through His Holy Spirit and His holy word in the Bible. Then God places that person in the very center of His heart as His own child — and as a joint-heir of heaven with the Lord Jesus Christ.

Dear friend, you don't have to stay in the desert.

*Psalms 17:8 * Deuteronomy 32:10*

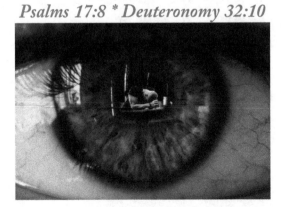

In the beginning was the Word, and the Word was with God, and
the Word was God.

****

And the Word became flesh, and dwelt among us, and we saw His
glory, glory as of the only begotten from the Father, full of grace
and truth.

****

He is clothed with a robe dipped in blood, and His name is called
The Word of God.
And on His robe and on His thigh He has a name written, "KING
OF KINGS, AND LORD OF LORDS."
John 1:1,14, Revelation 19:13,16

Snapshots

Too much comment here would only detract from the power of these
verses. Read each one several times, slowly, and honestly try to absorb
how deep the meaning of each goes. Three "snapshots" in the Bible that,
when taken together, paint a powerful and eternal picture of the fullness
of just who the Lord Jesus Christ really is.

The most amazing thing of all to me is that this same Lord Jesus Christ
is also my Savior.

"God is spirit, and those who worship Him must worship in spirit
and truth."
— *John 4:24*

A Spiritual Frac Job

Let me guess — everyone except my friends who have worked in the oil patch is saying, "Whaaaaat???" Well, "fracking" is an oil field term that is short for "hydraulic fracturing." It is a procedure that uses high-pressure injection of water and sand into rock formations that contain oil, but the oil doesn't flow. The process creates tiny fractures held open by the sand, so oil and natural gas can be extracted. It is a great illustration for many of us today, whose worship has "stopped flowing," and who need a frac job of spirit and truth so our worship can flow once again.

Maybe today, this little devotional has found its way to someone who has honestly searched for God, but who has looked in all the wrong places, false religions, crystal vibrations or cold cathedrals. Or ... perhaps someone who has attended church, maybe even for years, and now it all seems a bit dry and unfulfilling. You can attend a church so beautiful that it gives you goosebumps, sing hymns that give you goosebumps, hear sermons that give you goosebumps. But — goosebumps don't satisfy the soul in the valley of the shadow of death spoken of in Psalm 23 and are gone before you leave the church parking lot. Has anyone else been in that same parking lot with me?

Soul-satisfying worship that warms you to the marrow of your bones and to the center of your heart — and doesn't dry up in the church parking lot, comes only from worshipping the one true God the one right way — in spirit and truth. From the lips of Jesus Himself, here by an old water well in Samaria, we learn that true worship isn't found in a place, or a religion, or a song. Those things can help, but they do not create worship. Emotion can be felt in those things — and — worship is often very emotional, but ... emotion is not worship. In an old church with broken windows, with an out-of-tune piano, with no one singing on key and with a boring sermon, worship can still happen. Because worship doesn't depend on any of that. Worship can happen sitting on a tractor or cleaning out a dirty frac tank. I know because I have done it in both those places. True worship depends on just you.

We often forget that we are spiritual beings — that part of us that never dies, even when the physical part does. Allow yourself to experience a "spiritual frac job" — in spirit and truth. Come to God with that part of you — the spiritual part — hiding nothing, truly wanting to meet with God with all your heart — and you will find that He has been there, waiting for you the whole time.

"Give and it will be given to you. They will pour into your lap a good measure — pressed down, shaken together, and running over. For by your standard of measure it will be measured to you in return."
— *Luke 6:38*

Food For Thought

First item on the menu: Misinterpretation. These often misused and misinterpreted words spoken by Jesus are not talking about God rewarding those who give generous donations of money to the church ... or any other worthy cause for that matter. Even a light reading of the context (before and after this verse), shows that Jesus is talking about how God compensates us for the way we treat others. Food for thought.

Second item on the menu: Our attitude. In my years of ministry, I stopped counting long ago, how many people I have encountered who had negative things to say about God: "doesn't answer my prayers," "doesn't even exist," "if He loves me, why doesn't He give me a better job," "doesn't care about my hurt." And then I ask them, "Well, when was the last time you really and truly gave your best effort at being the Christian you say that you are?" Their reactions range from sudden shock, that I would suggest they actually give something of their life to God for Him to give something to them — all the way to outright indignation that I would ask such a thing.

I have also encountered many people who faithfully, year after year, have actually done their best to give their best to God and love everyone around them. These folks had problems from time to time too, just like the first group I mentioned. Sometimes problems that hurt all the way to the bone and the heart. Know how many of them I ever saw keep a negative attitude about God? None. Zero. Food for thought.

Third item on the menu: Try it — you might like it. Even when those two nasty neighbors known as "confusion" and "hurt" sometimes seem to buy a house on the street of our lives, for this second group of folks, hope and encouragement in God never seem to disappear — because they actually live the truth of these fabulous words of Jesus in this verse of scripture. He isn't talking about giving the best of your money here. Want to see the best of God? Give Him the best of yourself, and watch what happens. Food for thought.

Then Elisha prayed and said, "O Lord, I pray, open his eyes that he may see." And the Lord opened the servant's eyes and he saw; and behold, the mountain was full of horses and chariots of fire all around Elisha.
— *2ⁿᵈ Kings 6:17*

An Eye-Opening Experience

Ever had one of those? An eye-opening experience? Most of us have, although maybe not on the scale of what happened here to Elisha's young helper. This is one of my very favorite places in all of scripture (I know I keep saying that), but of all the places of hope and encouragement in the Bible, this is surely one of the crown jewels.

The king of Syria had sent what the Bible describes as a "great army" to kill Elisha and his young helper. When they awoke that morning, all the young man could see was that army — large enough to encircle them, AND the entire city. He was scared out of his wits, and with good reason. It was one of those "entire life flashing before you" moments. I'm sure he was quite sure he was about to die — but then Elisha prayed a one-sentence prayer for him to be able to see ...

In our own times of trouble, sadness, despair, fear of the imminent or even the unknown, what that young man saw that morning is something we need to always remember. There is a spiritual reality stronger and mightier than all of our troubles and fears put together. The power of God to protect us and watch over us may be unseen, but it is also unmatched. Whatever life or the devil throws at you today — or any day — is no match for what God keeps in the mountains around you!

He is the image of the invisible God, the firstborn of all creation.
For by Him all things were created, both in the heavens and on
earth, visible and invisible, whether thrones or dominions or rulers or
authorities-all things have been created through Him and for Him.
— *Colossians 1:15,16*

Who Is Jesus, Really?

Who is Jesus, really? This verse leaves no doubt at all. All of the religions/
cults/sects who say they believe in God, but who think that Jesus is less
than God have a whole host of difficulties to explain in order to maintain
their position. Colossians 1:15,16 is one of them.

In the fullness of the original language, this verse is saying to us that
when you look at Jesus, you are seeing none other than the Almighty
God. It follows then, that it is saying to us as well that Jesus has existed
from eternity (as verse 17 actually, specifically states). It is saying to us
through the word "firstborn" that all creation is under the authority of
Jesus. It is saying to us that it was Jesus who said "Let there be light,"
and "all things" means He created everything else too. Jesus did it all, and
it was all according to His purpose from the very beginning.

Our God IS God, and His name is Jesus — A.K.A.: Jehovah, King of
Kings and Lord of Lords, and the Great I AM.

Then David said to the Philistine, "You come to me with a sword,
a spear, and a javelin, but I come to you in the name of the Lord of
hosts, the God of the armies of Israel, whom you have taunted.
— *1ˢᵗ Samuel 17:45*

Slapping a Giant With a Slingshot

Sometimes it isn't smart to "spout off" about your enemy. John Sedgwick
was a Union Major-General in the America Civil War. What made him
immortal in history, however, were his last words. Receiving some very
long range Confederate sniper fire, some of his men were diving for cover,
to which he responded: "I am ashamed of you! They couldn't hit an
elephant at this dist ..."

One of the most famous "spouting off" instances in the entire Bible is this
event right here, recorded in 1ˢᵗ Samuel. Turns out that the chihuahua
CAN bite the heel of the hound, if his friend the Mastiff is walking
beside him. Goliath was close to 9 feet tall, with weapons and armor
approaching 200 pounds. The skinny little shepherd boy named David
who stood in front of him had no armor at all. All he had was a slingshot
and a stone. Turns out that was all he needed. "In the name of the
Lord of hosts" one stone and one swing was all God's skinny little servant
needed to bring down the mightiest warrior of the Philistine army. And
God can use you too ... in exactly the same way.

Today, just like when He chose David, God doesn't need "big," God
doesn't need "powerful," God doesn't need "important." I sure am glad,
too, because I'm not any of those things. You may feel the same way,
and that compared to others around you, all you have to offer God is
a slingshot and a stone.

Take heart dear friend — in God's hands, a person with a slingshot and
a stone is a lethal weapon.

... God, who has saved us and called us with a holy calling, not
according to our works, but according to His own purpose and grace
which was granted us in Christ Jesus from all eternity ...
— *2ⁿᵈ Timothy 1:8c,9*

Plan "A"

"Fall back" is a popular expression used today for a second plan held in
reserve, a "Plan B" if you will, in case the first plan doesn't work out. God
has never needed one.

Every phrase here is a shout of effusive praise from the apostle Paul for
God's plan of salvation — a salvation carried out by the infinite power
of God. We didn't choose Him — He chose us. Jesus said the same in
John 15:16. And as much as we never deserved it, He saved us, and loved
us, and called us anyway — a choice born in the depths of God's own
grace. It was not because of anything we ever did, or ever will do. It was
entirely His plan, His grace — given freely to us in Jesus.

The entire Old Testament history of God's interaction with Israel was but
a piece of His plan. God's plan and love for you has been in place much,
much longer. "In the beginning" of Genesis 1:1 was when time began.
It was even before that. Ephesians 1:4 reveals that it was "before the
foundation of the world."

Your salvation and eternal life through faith in Jesus was never a "Plan B."

and he said, "Listen, all Judah and the inhabitants of Jerusalem and
King Jehoshaphat: thus says the Lord to you, 'Do not fear or be
dismayed because of this great multitude, for the battle is not yours
but God's ...
— *2nd Chronicles 20:15*

The Stand In

A "stand in" is someone who takes another person's place. It is a very
common practice in the film industry, especially when a scene calls for
a dangerous stunt. A stuntman will, many times, be a "stand in" for the
actor in that scene. God is one of the greatest "stand ins" in all of history.
Every time He does it, it is spectacular. Here in 2nd Chronicles is no
exception.

The setting: a massive, imminent invasion of Judah. Even the king was
afraid.

Action taken: the king AND the people from all the cities physically
came together and sought the Lord's help.

Result: Enter the "Stand in." The Lord helped. Boy howdy did He help.
On the day of the invasion, for some strange reason the invading armies
turned on themselves and destroyed each other — to the last man. God's
people didn't have to raise so much as a finger, much less a sword. You
can read all about in in verses 1-25.

But, what is really thrilling is how this verse speaks so powerfully to us
today. First of all, take note that its message is good for entire nations
(all Judah), or, individual people (inhabitants of Jerusalem), or, kings and
presidents (King Jehoshaphat). All of us have had battles in our lives,
haven't we? Sometimes those battles can be heartbreaking and spirit-
crushing. The question is this: how many of those times did you fight
the battle yourself ... and — how many times did you give the battle
to God and let Him do the fighting? Your Stand In. If you will give
your battles to God, your anxiety, and stress, and fear, and hopelessness
are all impaled on the mighty sword of the Lord. He has never lost
a fight. Ever.

Pure and undefiled religion in the sight of our God and Father
is this: to visit orphans and widows in their distress, and to keep
oneself unstained by the world.
— *James 1:27*

Choosing The Right Religion

Choosing which shampoo to buy in the past used to be dead easy: choose for oily, dry, or normal hair, and with dandruff control, or without it. Nowadays it seems like there are about 50 different choices and you have to be a dermatologist to even understand what some of the labels say. It sort of feels that way, sometimes, trying to choose a religion or a denomination, or even a church. With all the choices out there it can often seem like a very confusing, and even frustrating task.

It is an important, personal choice because Christian religion is more than just theology. It is also living an obedient, active Christian life, the way Jesus said to live it. And that is true, whether you are talking about a person, or a church. In your quest to "do" religion, or choose a church that does it right, note well the sharp focus James brings to the type of religion that is pleasing to God. Want a "well done" from God? To arrive at that point, the formula is not complicated. Make sure your religion and the religion of your church includes these two priorities:

1. Ministry that cares for those unable to care for themselves.
2. A Christian life or church that shares the gospel in the world, while not allowing the sinful ways of the world to have a place inside it.

Hope and encouragement, your spiritual health and your Christian growth will benefit greatly from those two things.

> And He said to them, "Come away by yourselves to a secluded place
> and rest a while."
> — *Mark 6:31*

Take A Load Off

Even God felt it was important to rest. He worked for six days and rested on the seventh. His attitude didn't change when He put on human flesh and came to earth as a man. That's why Jesus said what He did here to His disciples. He tells them how to rest in four little, but very important phrases. It would change the lives of countless people today if they would pay attention to it. Even Jesus took His own advice.

Life is a busy place, isn't it? In our text here (if you read on a bit), the disciples didn't even have time to eat. Been there. Done that. And I bet you have too, am I right? Rest — according to Jesus Himself — is not only important, it is essential. It is more than just a good idea.

We don't need a book on the psychology of rest. Jesus tells us how to do it in about 5 seconds. The important thing is to actually do it.

"Come aside" — spend some time apart from the normal list of things that keep you busy.

"By yourself" — spend some prayer time, devotional time, hobby time, or just pure rest time, apart from the people who surround your life, even those who love you. "By yourself" means exactly that ... by yourself. It doesn't mean to NOT do things together with people you love, but time alone is also important.

"To a deserted place" — You can't rest in Grand Central Station. I bet I don't need to explain that.

"and rest a while." How long? Until you feel rested. The very best way I know to do that is to come to Jesus during "rest time." In Matthew 11:28 Jesus says, "Come unto Me, all who are weary and heavy laden, and I will give you rest."

Jesus said it. That makes it important. And true.

"Come now, and let us reason together," says the Lord, "Though your sins are as scarlet, they will be as white as snow; though they are red like crimson, they will be like wool."
— *Isaiah 1:18*

An Offer You Can't Refuse

It would be hard to deny that Hollywood has dumped a lot of trash into our lives and living rooms. However, it is also true that it has provided some of the most unforgettable quotes in history. From the very short, "I'll be back." of Arnold Schwarzenegger in The Terminator, to the endearing, "My Mama always said life was like a box of chocolates; you never know what you're gonna get." of Tom Hanks in Forrest Gump ... to the gut-chilling, "I'm gonna make him an offer he can't refuse." of Marlon Brando in The Godfather.

The Almighty God has tried — and is still trying — to reach out to mankind with that same offer, except from a positive perspective. One of the most unforgettable examples is this verse from Isaiah. God says to everyone here, "Let Me make you an offer you can't refuse. Although the sin of your life drips crimson as blood, I will make your life white as snow." For all who are outside a relationship with God, or who need to renew their relationship with God, He is saying, "Regardless of what you have done before, I can make you a new person and give you a new life — starting right now." Doesn't that sound to you like an offer you can't refuse?

> for we cannot stop speaking
> about what we have seen and heard."
> — *Acts 4:20*

Being Just a "Normal" Christian

Many times devotional thoughts of hope and encouragement from scripture pick us up when we are down, or discouraged, or when we have "messed up," or we are lonely, or without an answer for a problem or a trial in our lives. But — what about the trial of being just a "normal" Christian? This devotional thought is for that person.

Unfortunately, life — and even churches — can have people who either make fun of, or actively discourage a person who has a sustained, extroverted, joy-bubbling witness about Jesus in their lives. I have always thought that kind of discouraging person was a bit strange, if not downright sad. There are actually folks who come to church and just sit and never do a thing for Jesus. If you are a new, or growing Christian, don't get anywhere near this group. It is almost as if they feel they are doing the Lord a favor just by showing up. This is what I would call <u>AB</u>normal Christianity. If those same people were saved from a burning house, or experienced life-saving heart surgery, they would talk about it for the rest of their lives. And yet — when it comes to Jesus, who has done something far better than that in their lives, they are strangely silent.

Normal Christianity is what we see in this verse. Embrace it and do your best to emulate it. Peter and John saw Jesus in action and it was impossible for them to keep quiet about it. When they were admonished — by church leaders — to not be so vocal about it, this verse was their response. Let it be your response too.

Keep right on bubbling over for Jesus. Keep right on being normal in your Christian walk.

"...but whoever drinks of the water that I will give him shall never thirst; but the water that I will give him will become in him a well of water springing up to eternal life."
— *John 4:14*

Ever Been Thirsty?

You are working in the back pasture and you run out of water. You are in the hospital with nothing but those ice chips. You are on the hiking trail and suddenly your water bottle looks about the size of a thimble. Or ... here's one for all of us, I bet: You eat a huge, salty meal and can't get enough to drink afterward.

There are many ways to be thirsty, however, and Jesus knew that in a conversation He had with a Samaritan woman at a well of water. Today we thirst for money, thirst for recognition, thirst for companionship, thirst for position, thirst for success, thirst for love — it can be a long list, can't it?

Jesus is still at the well, waiting perhaps for you today, with the same offer that He gave to this Samaritan woman. He is the answer to all your thirst. He sees our lives today that are as parched as the Mojave Desert, or perhaps lives that are stuffed full like that huge salty meal ... but, no matter how full you are there is still that thirst that only a drink can satisfy. And, contrary to all our water bottles here that eventually and inevitably become empty, Jesus says to you:

"Drink the water that I give you and you will never thirst again — and — it will become in you a fountain of water springing up to everlasting life."

> For momentary, light affliction is producing for us an eternal weight
> of glory far beyond all comparison,
> — *2nd Corinthians 4:17*

Point of View

Many times in life what we think about something, or someone, depends very much on our point of view. It is very important when we consider a question that gets asked many times every day — especially by people who don't put their trust and faith in God. The question is: Why does God allow disasters and suffering? It is answerable, but not tritely, nor briefly, especially in a short devotional. We can however, throw a little light on it perhaps.

First of all, our point of view can cause difficulty for our perception. The trial, or problem, or heartache we are experiencing might not seem momentary OR light at all to us. From our point of view it might seem endless and intense. Remembering that we can never plumb the depths of God's ways, let's look together at a famous analogy ...

A hunter came upon a bear caught in a trap in the woods. The hunter, wanting to help the bear, tries to approach him, but the bear won't allow it. The hunter, determined to help, shoots a dart full of drugs into the bear. The bear is now completely convinced that the hunter wants to hurt him. The drugged animal, now semi-conscious, watches as the hunter actually pushes the bear's paw further into the jaws of the trap in order to release the tension. The bear has all the evidence it needs to conclude that the hunter is evil. But the bear has made its judgment too soon, before the hunter frees him from the trap.

At various times in our lives, God may seem unfair to those of us trapped in time, but we make our judgment too soon. One day, perhaps not until we get to heaven, we will understand what the Hunter was up to in our lives. Until that time, God says, "Trust Me. I have numbered every single one of your days even from your mother's womb. I love you and I have a plan for your life — even though sometimes, in the cold fury of the middle of the storm, your point of view makes it difficult to see what that plan is.

Then David the king went in and sat before the Lord, and he said,
"Who am I, O Lord God, and what is my house, that You have
brought me this far?
— *2nd Samuel 7:18*

Remembering Who The Real King Is

Here is one of the greatest snapshots of humility in all the Bible. David, the king of all Israel, had just been told through Nathan the prophet that his house and his kingdom would endure for eternity (v.16). This verse is the beginning of his response.

Did David strut around like "It's about time someone showed some proper respect for who I am and what I've done!?" Nope. Did he use his power to start "hammering down" on those further down the ladder because of the success he had just been promised? Nope. The king of the entire nation of Israel went in and sat before the Lord and laid bare a heart full of humility and gratitude. And recognition ... recognition that there was absolutely nothing about who he was, absolutely nothing about what he had accomplished that deserved the grace he had received from the Lord. David never lost focus on who the real King was, even though he made his share of very big mistakes.

As we go through this life trying, trying, trying to move ever upward on the "ladder of success," wouldn't we do well to learn from what king David did here? No matter who we become, no matter how far up the ladder we go, when success or position comes our way, wouldn't we do well to go in and sit before the Lord and say, "Who am I, O Lord God, and what is my house, that You have brought me this far?"

He who testifies to these things says, "Yes, I am coming quickly."
Amen. Come, Lord Jesus.
— *Revelation 22:20*

Unexpected Arrival

This phrase has been used many times to describe the birth of a baby that wasn't supposed to happen, or a relative or friend that showed up unexpectedly for a visit. Using it for when Jesus comes back may seem a little strange, however, considering how many times it is mentioned in the Bible. Even though Jesus Himself says it will come like a thief in the night. Even though no less than three times in this last chapter of the Bible He says that He is coming quickly.

What we have to remember, is that the concept of "quickly" in eternity is much different than our concept of "quickly" in our daily lives. This difference creates a real danger when we go about each day of our lives, believing that we have plenty of time to decide what to do with Jesus — when nothing about our lives creates within us an imminent sense of urgency. The devil loves it when we feel that way, and it is a very dangerous way to live. If it was possible, for example, to ask someone who lost their life in a car accident about it, they would tell you that their arrival in the presence of Jesus was very quick and very unexpected.

For all of us who are Christians, it doesn't matter because we know what is waiting for us in eternity. In the language of today we could say with John here: "Woo hoo!!!" Bring it on, Lord Jesus!!" Why? Because we are ready, even though He will come when we don't expect it. However ... for anyone who might be reading this and who is still delaying a decision about Jesus, thinking there is always "tomorrow," I offer this interesting little poem that a friend of mine let me share —

Time is short.

Hell is hot.

The King is coming ...

Ready or not.

Jesus said to them, "I am the bread of life; he who comes to Me will not hunger, and he who believes in Me will never thirst."
— *John 6:35*

Sweet Satisfaction

These are some of the most encouraging words in all the Bible. They are the words of Jesus Himself. You may know what it is like to be truly hungry and thirsty. I know I do. However, Jesus isn't talking about filling our stomachs here, or slaking a physical thirst. He is talking about something much, much better. For those who come to Jesus and believe in Him, it doesn't matter what this old world throws at them. You can go through any trial, you can endure any hardship or loss — and remain above it all.

No hunger for money, or success, or things because what we have in Jesus is better than all of that. No thirst for fame or relationships, no thirst of loneliness ... because what we have in Jesus is better than all of that. There is a satisfaction in Jesus that transcends all of it. It is the comfort of having the King of Kings and Lord of Lords as our Brother, having God as our father, and having the Holy Spirit as our guide in all of life. Jesus is offering here a serenity, a tranquility, a fullness of the soul and spirit that nothing can touch. Real life, real satisfaction, Jesus style.

For I am confident of this very thing, that He who began a good
work in you will perfect it until the day of Christ Jesus.
— *Philippians 1:6*

Be Patient, God Isn't Finished With Me Yet

That is more than just a catchy phrase on a bumper sticker. It is a spiritual
truth ablaze with hope and encouragement. Should you feel conviction
about your sin? Absolutely. But — you should NEVER feel guilty
because you are not perfect. The devil loves to beat us up with guilt —
don't let him do it. Instead, rejoice because you have forgiveness in Jesus
Christ. And until the day we see Him face to face in heaven, here in the
midst of our imperfection is this fabulous promise from God's word. God
never abandons anyone as an unfinished product ... including you.

If you are a child of God, He started something good in you, and He will
finish the job.

Then God said, "Let Us make man in Our image, according to Our likeness ..."
— *Genesis 1:26*

Spiritual Genetics

I know, I know ... sometimes human beings (maybe even you and me from time to time) sure don't look much like God, right? Where's the hope and encouragement in that? Well, there wouldn't be much — if that was where the story ended. But it doesn't end there, thank goodness.

First of all, if you are a Christian and have had your sins and past taken away by the blood of Jesus, this is exactly how God sees you: in His image — even at this very moment (Hebrews 10:14). Even though you still make mistakes sometimes. What Jesus did for you had very powerful — and permanent — results.

Second, don't forget, we will not be trapped in these weak, prone-to-sin bodies forever. And when we do leave this place and these sin-disfigured bodies for our home in heaven, the Bible tells us we will be like Jesus. Just the sight of Jesus will transform us to be like Him (1st John 3:2). Then we will see ourselves exactly the same way God has seen us ever since the moment we trusted Jesus as our Savior — perfect — and "in the image of God," just the way He designed man in the first place, right here in Genesis 1:26.

The Lord is my shepherd, I shall not want. He makes me lie down in green pastures; He leads me beside quiet waters. He restores my soul; He guides me in the paths of righteousness for His name's sake. Even though I walk through the valley of the shadow of death, I fear no evil, for You are with me; Your rod and Your staff, they comfort me. You prepare a table before me in the presence of my enemies; You have anointed my head with oil; my cup overflows. Surely goodness and lovingkindness will follow me all the days of my life, and I will dwell in the house of the Lord forever.
— *Psalms 23*

The Shepherd in the Sky

I am going to use a little bit different format for our time together in this psalm. Hopefully it will be a blessing as I try to show you something really beautiful. Many, MANY times the Bible is like a diamond that sparkles differently as you turn it in the light of how you read it. Let's put that to the test with the 23rd psalm, ok? We will read it together three times — and it will appear different each time. Do it slowly and reverently and watch what happens to your heart. Trust me.

First time — emphasizing who the Shepherd is.

The **Lord** is my shepherd, I shall not want. **He** makes me lie down in green pastures; **He** leads me beside quiet waters. **He** restores my soul; **He** guides me in the paths of righteousness for His name's sake. Even though I walk through the valley of the shadow of death, I fear no evil, for **You** are with me; **Your** rod and **Your** staff, they comfort me. **You** prepare a table before me in the presence of my enemies; **You** have anointed my head with oil; my cup overflows. Surely goodness and lovingkindness will follow me all the days of my life, and I will dwell in the house of the **Lord** forever.

Second time — emphasizing how the Shepherd cares.

The Lord is my **shepherd**, I **shall not want**. He makes me **lie down in green pastures**; He **leads me beside quiet waters.** He **restores my soul**; He **guides me in the paths of righteousness** for His name's sake. Even though I walk through the valley of the shadow of death, **I fear** no evil, for **You are with me**; Your **rod** and Your **staff**, they **comfort me**. You **prepare a table** before me **in the presence of my enemies**; You have **anointed my head with oil**; my **cup overflows.** Surely **goodness and lovingkindness will follow me all the days of my life**, and I **will dwell in the house of the Lord forever**.

Third time — emphasizing who the Shepherd cares for.

The Lord is **MY** shepherd, **I** shall not want. He makes **ME** lie down in green pastures; He leads **ME** beside quiet waters. He restores **MY** soul; He guides **ME** in the paths of righteousness for His name's sake. Even though **I** walk through the valley of the shadow of death, **I** fear no evil, for You are with **ME**; Your rod and Your staff, they comfort **ME**. You prepare a table before **ME** in the presence of my enemies; You have anointed **MY** head with oil; **MY** cup overflows. Surely goodness and lovingkindness will follow **ME** all the days of **MY** life, and **I** will dwell in the house of the Lord forever.

God really is our "Shepherd in the Sky."

"Blessed are the poor in spirit, for theirs is the kingdom of heaven."
— *Matthew 5:3*

Poverty That Makes You Rich

Poverty has a universal reputation for being a bad thing, and it is. It is a horrible thing which can destroy families, hope, and self-respect. There is one "poverty" however, that is good. In fact, it is essential for the person who wants to be right with God. This is the person described by Jesus here, as "poor in spirit."

We say ... "*What*??" All the rest of the "beatitudes" Jesus mentions in His sermon on the mount (Matthew, Chapters 5–7) are relatively easy to understand, but this — we need to be POOR in spirit? This first "blessed are ..." statement confuses many people. Wouldn't it be better to have a strong spirit, a courageous spirit? Isn't that what is taught and preached to us? It would be, but that isn't the kind of spirit Jesus is talking about here.

It is easier to capture the idea if you substitute the word "humble" for the word "poor." Literally this word means "to crouch or cower as one completely helpless." It pictures a beggar in absolute poverty, totally destitute and dependent on others. And what Jesus is teaching here is that those who come to God confessing they are completely spiritually empty, having no righteousness or hope of their own outside God's mercy, are the very ones who will be joyously favored (blessed), and who will inherit the kingdom of heaven. Not a bad trade, wouldn't you agree? My mess of nothing in return for God's love, and favor, and the kingdom of heaven.

A good way for a new Christian to start their walk with God. A good way for a mature Christian to renew their walk with God.

And behold, an angel of the Lord suddenly appeared and a light
shone in the cell; and he struck Peter's side and woke him up,
saying, "Get up quickly." And his chains fell off his hands.
— *Acts 12:7*

Roadside Assistance

Not everyone has had their car break down in the middle of the night in
the middle of nowhere, but those of us who have, know from experience
the fabulous feeling of seeing the approaching headlights of roadside
assistance. The apostle Peter never had a car, but he for sure felt the pure
joy of roadside assistance. In prison.

As we see here, there are all sorts of ways to feel "broken down in the
middle of the night in the middle of nowhere." It doesn't have to involve
a car. Being stuck in a dead-end job that can't pay the bills can feel like
a prison, being addicted to drugs can feel like a prison, having friends turn
their backs on you when you need them most can feel like a mighty dark
and lonely stretch of life's highway. But take heart — roadside assistance
is closer than you think.

God's light can, and does, shine anywhere — in prison, or in the middle
of life's darkest and loneliest highways. And whatever your chains are,
they can fall off too, just like Peter's. The key is a personal relationship
with the Lord Jesus Christ. In case you didn't notice, Peter was sleeping
so soundly that the angel had to whack him on the side to wake him
up. He wasn't worried — even in prison. When you have Jesus as your
Savior, you don't have to worry either ... no matter how stuck out you are
in the middle of the night.

Roadside assistance is only a whispered prayer away.

My God sent His angel and shut the lions' mouths and they have
not harmed me, inasmuch as I was found innocent before Him;
— *Daniel 6:22a,b*

Concentrated Comfort

Anyone who has had their hope ripped out, anyone who has had their heart
ripped out, anyone who has been unjustly accused and had their life and
future destroyed — even by someone who is supposed to love you — can tell
you that there are many types of lions in this old world. Sharing honestly
and openly, I will tell you that each one of these things has happened to
me, and my bet is that they have happened to some of you, too.

My encouragement to you today is that there is more comfort in God
than there is hurt in the world, and I share this verse of scripture with
you today as one I have gone to many times when it feels like I have
been left — or thrown — in the lion's den. Can we look together at its
concentrated comfort?

First, it doesn't matter who has hurt me, or who my enemy is — my God
can send His angel to help me. Not "angels"… angel — just one, and it
is more than sufficient. As spoken by Daniel here, that can mean just
one of three things: the archangel Michael, the archangel Gabriel — or
the preincarnate Lord Jesus Christ. It is used all three ways in the Old
Testament.

Second, God is imminently powerful enough to close the mouths of any,
and all, of the lions in your life no matter what, or who, they may be.

Third, God is imminently powerful enough to keep you from all harm, no
matter how much someone or something may want to hurt you.

Fourth, and best of all is the reason — " inasmuch as I was found innocent
before Him." Why is this such beautiful comfort when we all know that
all of us are so far from really being innocent? It is a truth you will see
embedded throughout this book of devotionals — it is beautiful because
the way God sees us from eternity does not depend on us. It depends on
the blood of Jesus Christ. The blood that has taken away not just some
of our sin — it has taken away all of it. God looks at you through the
sacrifice and the blood of His Son — and sees perfect innocence.

"Blessed are those who hunger and thirst for righteousness, for they shall be satisfied."
— *Matthew 5:6*

Pig Out

Want to know the one place in the Bible where gluttony isn't a sin? Here it is. Eat and drink all you want. Jesus even promises blessings here for the ones who do. A popular way of saying this today is "go hard after God."

For many of us in this day and age it seems we are busy all the time, and we must choose wisely how we spend our time, lest we waste it. There is always some other thing we could be, or should be doing. What Jesus tells all of us in this verse is never a waste of time — no matter how busy our lives are. Looking for some hope and encouragement? Here it is in overflowing abundance. In fact, Jesus promises us two things for hungering and thirsting after God:

Promise #1 — Blessed — a favored, spiritual happiness that comes from God to you.

Promise #2 — Satisfied — literally, stuffed full, like a calf being fattened on purpose in a stall.

So — go ahead. Pig out. Have a heapin' helpin'. Hunger and thirst for righteousness, go hard after God, and then keep coming back for more. You won't be sorry.

These words, which I am commanding you today, shall be on your
heart. You shall teach them diligently to your sons and shall talk
of them when you sit in your house and when you walk by the
way and when you lie down and when you rise up. You shall bind
them as a sign on your hand and they shall be as frontals on your
forehead. You shall write them on the doorposts of your house and
on your gates.

— *Deuteronomy 6:6-9*

God's Lesson Plan

Here's something we have all heard a thousand times: "I have to let my
children decide for themselves about their beliefs." That's not much of
a lesson plan for the lives of our children, is it? Any good teacher will
tell you that it is impossible to educate a class without a good lesson plan,
and the same is true of our children.

If we are going to consider ourselves followers of the God of the Holy
Bible, the attitude about not helping our own children develop the right
beliefs is not an option for us. That attitude is the coward's lazy way
out of not spending the physical and emotional energy needed, to follow
God's lesson plan for the lives of our children. His plan is a powerful, time
consuming command. Don't let that word get by you — it is a command.
It is not advice. Not following the lesson plan is being disobedient to
God, and paving the future of our children with disaster. We owe our
children — and God — a passionate attempt to teach them what God
says is right. Without compromise. And sometimes — in fact, a lot of
times — it isn't very easy. But — the plan never describes the lesson as
being easy, does it? Just very, very thorough and diligent in every aspect
of our daily life.

In the end, we can never guarantee that our children will never make
a wrong decision, but that isn't our responsibility. Teaching them what
God says is right, on the other hand, is. It is the legacy of hope and
encouragement ... and it is our responsibility to see that the generations
following know where to find it, Who offers it, and how to have it.

A friend loves at all times....
— *Proverbs 17:17a*

My Friend

I am a big fan of western movies, and one of my all-time favorites is "Tombstone" — and one of my favorite scenes in the movie is where the "good guys" are pinned down by the "bad guys" at a small river. Doc Holliday (who is dying with pulmonary tuberculosis) is coughing up blood, and Turkey Creek Jack Johnson asks him, "Why are you even doing this, Doc?" Doc says, "Wyatt Earp is my friend." Johnson responds, "Heck, I've got lots of friends.", to which Doc simply replies, "I don't."

I think one of the reasons I like that movie so much is because the relationship between Wyatt Earp and Doc Holliday reminds me of what real friendship should be like: an unshakeable bond that remains, even knowing each other's faults and shortcomings. Today, unfortunately, the term "my friend" gets passed around and handed out almost like a party favor, when the truth is that a real friend has much more value than that, and can be very rare.

You may feel like you are not in the "popular circle," and like Doc, you feel that you don't have many friends. Take heart, soldier, real friends don't grow on trees. Real friends look like this: They don't run for cover when a little rain comes — or even a storm. They stay at your side even when you are at your worst. Because a real friend loves at all times — and that kind of friend is very rare and very precious.

To have a friend like that, you may need to *be* a friend like that. If you want a good example to follow, take a long look at the best example of all — the Lord Jesus Christ. In your own life, there is never a day, never an hour, never a minute, never a second ... day or night, awake or asleep, rain or shine, good times or bad times, on the mountain top or in the valley, at your best or at your worst ... that Jesus does not love you. Because a real friend loves at all times.

So the woman left her waterpot, and went into the city and said to the men, "Come, see a man who told me all the things that I have done; this is not the Christ, is it?"
— *John 4:28,29*

Meeting Jesus at the Water Well

The term "water well" would be greeted by many people who grew up in the city today with a blank expression. You just go to the sink, turn on the faucet, and out comes the water. However, for those of us who grew up in, or still live in the country, the term "water well" has huge importance. Your garden depends on it. Livestock depends on it. Your family depends on it. If it goes dry, or if it stops working properly, things can get serious in a hurry. One thing is pretty certain, though, if you were to go to your water well to either turn it on, or to get some water, you probably wouldn't be expecting to find Jesus waiting for you there and asking you for a drink. However, that is exactly what happened here in this famous event in the Bible. It was an encounter between the King of creation and a woman of the streets — at the water well. You can read the whole thing in about two minutes — verses 7 through 29.

If you don't know Jesus yet, this can be a beautiful passage of hope and encouragement for you. This woman had no idea who Jesus was either, when she arrived at the well. That didn't surprise Jesus, nor did it make any difference to Him. He loved her just the same, just as she was. If, like this woman, you have a past you are not proud of and you think you are beyond the reach of Jesus's love — think again. He will meet with you too, at the well of living water, the well of eternal life, if you will only believe in Him.

If you already know Jesus, but hope and encouragement seem more like faded memories today instead of something you wake up with every day, may I suggest something? A change of priorities in your life. That is exactly what happened to this woman. One minute her priority was drawing a bucket of water from a well, the next — she was consumed with sharing the love inside her that came from Jesus. What do you suppose would happen to your hope and encouragement if you left your own bucket of priorities at Jesus's feet and made the excitement of sharing His love in your life your priority instead?

"The Lord is my strength and song, and He has become my
salvation; this is my God, and I will praise Him; my father's God,
and I will extol Him.
— *Exodus 15:2*

The Here And Now

We've all heard it a million times, haven't we? The classic response to
a dreamer: "Get your head out of the clouds, you live in the here and
now." Well, these words from Exodus, some of the earliest in the written
history of man, poke a finger straight in the eye of all who think that the
dividends of the Christian faith are "out there" somewhere in the misty,
invisible future. The excitement of the Christian life is in the here and
now.

From the second book of the OLD Testament, just look at the present
tense excitement! Did you ever think verb tenses could be exciting? And
this is only one place of many in the Bible that tell this truth.

1. The Lord IS my strength — not might be, not will be. IS ... right
   now, as in this very moment.
2. The Lord IS my song — not might be, not will be. IS the source of
   joy in my life ... right now.
3. He HAS BECOME my salvation — not waiting to save me some
   day. I already have it ... right now.
4. He IS my God — not "can be," not "will be" — IS ... right now, as
   in this very moment.

Praiseworthy? It is in my book. In fact, the word "extol" here means to
beautify, or adorn with praise.

For those who have Jesus as their personal Savior, Christianity is not a "pie
in the sky when you die" kind of life. It is a "steak on the plate while you
wait" kind of life. Present tense. Right now. We have a beautiful hymn
about when we leave this life called "The Sweet By and By," and what it
says is true, but — there is also "the electric here and now."

... just as it is written, "Things which eye has not seen and ear has not heard, and which have not entered the heart of man, all that God has prepared for those who love Him."

— *1ˢᵗ Corinthians 2:9*

Let Your Imagination Run Wild

This is such a fantastic little verse. I mean, absolutely fantastic. Especially during a time when one might be tempted to wonder if it is all "worth it" — this lifestyle of following Christ, especially when there is so much "eye candy" out there in the world, and "magnetism" toward the things that appeal to our human nature.

During times like that, this little verse appeals to your spiritual side and says, "Let your imagination run wild." Go ahead. Spend some time trying to think of the most beautiful thing you have ever seen, and the most beautiful image of eternity that your mind's eye can create. Got it? Now chuck it out. It's not even close to what God has prepared for those who love Him.

Try again. Then do the same exercise with your ears and the most beautiful sound, or music you have ever heard, or the most precious conversation. Do the same exercise with your heart and the most beautiful, exhilarating emotion and joy you can imagine. Let your imagination run wild over and over.

When you are done, let it sink in that no matter what you imagined, you didn't even come close to understanding the infinite beauty that God has prepared for you. No one ever has. Your eye has never seen it, your ear has never heard it, your heart has never felt it ... but it is there, already prepared — waiting just for you.

"If anyone wishes to come after Me, he must deny himself, and take
up his cross daily and follow Me."
— *Luke 9:23*

Old Habits Die Hard

I don't really need to list them, do I — our own personal lists of bad
habits? We all have them, and for many of us a number of items on the
list could be considered "current." Correct? However, the fact that they
are current doesn't mean that we want to continue doing them, does it?
We want to stop, but we don't. Why? Because old habits die hard.

Fortunately, for the frustrated Christian, Jesus understands that and gives
us wonderful encouragement here. If you truly desire to "come after"
Jesus, He says that it involves a deliberate, personal decision to say "no"
to that part of us that wants to participate in our own selfish habits and
pleasures. The part of us that puts "me" before Jesus. BUT — (and it is
here where Jesus shows us such tender compassion and understanding) —
the "putting to death" of the old you that still enjoys the old ways requires
daily diligence. Some may not see that as compassion and patience, but
I do. Jesus doesn't demand that we become instantly perfect, or perfect
at all, for that matter. Why? Because old habits, and sometimes old
problems, die hard.

Jesus understands. His invitation to "follow Me" is in the midst of our
struggle with our old ways. Perfection is not the requirement to be
a disciple. You can pick up your cross daily and still follow the Lord
Jesus Christ. By His own invitation. Jesus doesn't demand perfection —
what He does demand (and deserves) is perseverance. His requirement
is to keep trying. He doesn't offer a "magic pill" or an "abra-cadabra"
magic spell to change us, to give us a perfect life with no problems or
challenges. How could Jesus measure devotion if He did something like
that?

"… but I say to you …"
— *Matthew 5:44*

The Road Not Taken

Robert Frost was one of the most beloved poets in American history. "The Road Not Taken" is the title of one of his most popular poems. It is about the choice between two paths encountered in the woods. These words of Jesus are about that same thing — making one of two choices.

In verses 21 through 48 (about 3½ minutes worth of reading) no less than 6 times, Jesus unmistakably presents two paths and leaves the listener with a choice. He does it with the words, "You have heard … but I say to you …" It is a choice between the popular notion that the world, or even religion, teaches — and the high road that Jesus teaches.

Our lives today can many times seem like a walk in thick woods, or even a forest. We are faced many times with a choice between two paths: the world … or Jesus. The world will always make its choice seem easier and more attractive. The devil isn't stupid. If you want to take the right path, no matter what the world puts in front of you, measure all your choices against "… but I say to you …" the teachings of Jesus. You can always find God's way in the Bible between Genesis and maps.

Many times the path that Jesus paints in your woods may not seem like the easiest path. But it is always, always, always, the right one to take.

"I love You, O Lord, my strength." The Lord is my rock and my
fortress and my deliverer, My God, my rock, in whom I take refuge;
my shield and the horn of my salvation, my stronghold.
— *Psalms 18:1,2*

You're My Everything

Perhaps you know this beautiful old love song, "You're My Everything,"
made popular by The Temptations. It may be only a love song, but the
truth is ... there actually IS someone who is our everything. It is the
Lord of heaven and earth.

We are not always strong, but He is: He is not only our Foundation, He
is a foundation of solid stone. Not only do we stand on the Rock, He
is our Fortress as we stand on the Rock. Not only is He our Fortress
surrounding us, He is the Army that fights for us and the Shield that
protects us. Not only is He our Champion who fights for us — our
victory and eternal salvation rest secure in His own strength. And if you
want to know the word picture for "stronghold" as it is used here, imagine
the Lord God Almighty holding you in one hand — and covering you
with the other.

Our part? Just love Him.

> Behold, I tell you a mystery; we will not all sleep, but we will all
> be changed, in a moment, in the twinkling of an eye, at the last
> trumpet; for the trumpet will sound, and the dead will be raised
> imperishable, and we will be changed.
> — 1st Corinthians 15:51,52

Presto Chango

Used originally as a magician's command, this "word" actually has its own definition in Webster's Dictionary: "a sudden transformation as if by magic." It could certainly be applied to what happens when the Lord Jesus Christ returns to Earth, as the apostle Paul describes it here.

Opinions of the exact circumstances that surround the second coming of Christ are almost as numerous as the stars in the sky. Two things, however, are certain: it will be VERY fast, and it will be VERY transforming for us all. May I share with you, a really special opinion about what might happen that you may have not heard before? It is special to me because I believe the Lord Himself put the thought in my heart. I have never read it anywhere else. Ok, here goes … stay with me …

When we die, our experience of eternity begins, right? In eternity there IS no clock, or any sense of the passing of time because it simply doesn't exist anymore, right? With the Lord a day is like a thousand years and a thousand years a day (2nd Peter 3:8). SO, then —

Let's imagine for a minute that you and I are having a conversation over coffee on the patio one day and as fate would have it, a bolt of lightning strikes the table and we both die at the same time. Instantly we are in the presence of the Lord … BUT …

Since in eternity we don't feel any sensation of the passing of time, it will seem to you and me like EVERYone is arriving in the presence of the Lord all at the same time, the same way we just arrived. Think about it for just a minute … instead of looking at it from the perspective of Christians who are alive at the moment, if you look at it from the perspective of a Christian who has died, that might just be exactly what the second coming of Christ will seem like. And we will ALL be changed — in the twinkling of an eye.

Pretty cool, isn't it?

'As for the promise which I made you when you came out of Egypt,
My Spirit is abiding in your midst; do not fear!'
— *Haggai 2:5*

Nothing Changes

We use the phrase "nothing changes" just about all the time in a negative way, don't we? I have used it that way, haven't you? Well, it isn't negative when it is applied to the Lord God. In fact, it is incredibly positive and encouraging.

This little verse tucked away in the little book of Haggai was a word of encouragement from God Himself to Israel when they had become discouraged in the rebuilding of their temple. Don't we need that same encouragement today? In our walk with the Lord, life's struggles can make the day when the preacher lifted us out of the waters of baptism seem as far away as the memory of crossing the Red Sea seemed to Israel. Perhaps a crushing defeat in your life or weakness in the flesh has left little to recognize of the temple you once built in your heart for the Lord long ago.

It doesn't matter. Why? Because nothing changes with God. Do we hurt God? Do we disappoint God? Do we cause Him to have to "remap" our journey over and over because of our mistakes? The answer to every one of those questions is "yes." But — the beautiful thing about God is that He keeps His promises to us, even when we don't keep ours to Him … just like He did with Israel here in the book of Haggai.

If mistakes have destroyed your temple and you are tempted to become discouraged in rebuilding your relationship with God, He would say to you today, "The promise I made when you first came to Me still stands. My Spirit is abiding in your midst; do not fear." Nothing has changed.

Beloved, now we are children of God, and it has not appeared as yet
what we will be. We know that when He appears, we will be like
Him, because we will see Him just as He is.
— *1ˢᵗ John 3:2*

A Diamond in the Rough

If you have never had the thrill of meeting the world's largest cut diamond,
and arguably one of the most beautiful, allow me to introduce you to the
Cullinan 1, the 530 carat diamond in the Sovereign's Scepter which is
part of the Crown Jewels of the English monarchy. Known as "The Star
of Africa," it is about half the size of a woman's fist. Seeing it in person
will take your breath away. Just ask me. I've seen it.

However, the diamond John places in our hands in this verse makes the Star of Africa look like a dried Bermuda grass seed by comparison. "Now" he says — as in right now — we are children of God. None of us, of course, are what we would like to be. All of us would like to change some things about ourselves today if we could. Your imperfections, however, don't change one bit the fact that you are still a child of God. A "diamond in the rough," but still a child of God.

But, there is better news yet. "Today" isn't the end of the story. The end of the story is seeing Christ in person. It will do far, far more than merely take your breath away. It will take your old self away. Just seeing Jesus in person will transform you — into the very likeness of Christ Himself.

Sorry Cullinan 1 You are beautiful, but you are not as beautiful as that.

For this reason I also suffer these things, but I am not ashamed; for I know whom I have believed and I am convinced that He is able to guard what I have entrusted to Him until that day.
— *2ⁿᵈ Timothy 1:12*

I Am Not Ashamed

This four-word sentence was also the title of a profoundly touching movie (I'm Not Ashamed) about Rachel Scott, the first student killed in the 1999 Columbine High School tragedy where 12 students and one teacher lost their lives. Rachel's last words were words affirming her belief in God to the boy who shot her. I think the apostle Paul would have liked Rachel a lot. Neither were perfect, but both were profoundly committed to God because of His saving grace in their lives.

Defending their faith cost both Rachel and Paul their lives. No one could shut Paul up, not even in prison, which is where he wrote this letter to Timothy. His consuming passion was to share the hope, the saving power and the unfathomable love of the gospel of Jesus Christ. In pursuit of that passion it never mattered to Paul what they did to him, he always kept going — unashamed. Can we say the same today?

The reason for Paul's resolve, and Rachel's resolve is what gives us hope and encouragement even today, that we CAN be the same. Where did that steel-hearted resolve come from? It came from a real, personal relationship with the risen Lord Jesus Christ. What drove Paul was that He knew Christ. Not "knew about," not "heard of," not "remembered." Knew, personally.

The genuineness and depth of that relationship utterly convinced Paul that there was no hell on earth, no fury from the dark side, no snare from satan that could even scratch the power of God to keep safe, Paul's deposit of his faith — Paul's deposit of his life — in the Lord Jesus Christ. It is the same relationship Jesus offers to us all.

Let the peace of Christ rule in your hearts ...
— *Colossians 3:15a*

In The Catbird Seat

It might surprise some to know that there really is a catbird, but "in the catbird seat" is a uniquely American expression, meaning a position of great favor, advantage or prominence. In baseball, for example it could be used to describe a batter up 3 balls to no strikes on a pitcher. In politics it might describe a candidate ahead 40 percentage points in the polls.

If you are searching for hope and encouragement, giving the peace of Christ the catbird seat in your life is one of the smartest moves you can make. Notice that it does not say here, "*have* a place in your hearts," it says "*rule* in your hearts." It is the difference in sitting on a footstool or a throne that are in the same room. The peace of Christ is a peace that forgave enemies and betrayal, remained calm in the middle of raging storms, loved in the face of rejection, accepted the will of God even when the difference was life or death.

Put that peace — the peace of Christ — in the catbird seat of your heart and see what happens.

"On the next day the large crowd who had come to the feast, when
they heard that Jesus was coming to Jerusalem, took the branches
of the palm trees and went out to meet Him, and began to shout,
"Hosanna! Blessed is He who comes in the name of the Lord, even
the King of Israel." Jesus, finding a young donkey, sat on it; as it is
written, "Fear not, daughter of Zion; behold, your King is coming,
seated on a donkey's colt."
— *John 12:12-15*

Motorcade for the King

This "motorcade" without motors on our Christian calendar is known
as Palm Sunday. And even though we call it "the triumphal entry," it
signaled the beginning of the end for Jesus and His time as a man on
this earth. Just a few more days and He would be dying on that cross
for you and me. But what was the beginning of the end for Jesus was
the beginning of the beginning for us. The light of hope through the
death and resurrection of Jesus Christ that all the darkness of hell cannot
extinguish.

I love these verses however, more for how they speak to us about the
unexpected. The Jews consistently got it wrong about who Jesus was ...
and is. To the end, they thought He would be their Conquering King
who would save them from Rome. And NO one expected Jesus to ride
into Jerusalem on a "triumphant donkey." It is difficult even today, for
those who don't know Jesus, to picture it or accept it.

What is so beautiful about these verses for us is this: Jesus still arrives
in our own lives today in unexpected ways. Leave the picture of Jesus
in the book of the Revelation and His second coming for just a minute,
and open your heart for all the different ways Jesus can make a triumphal
entrance into your heart today. To name just a few: through something
you see in the Bible, through looking into the night sky and realizing that
only God could do that, through the quiet comfort of the Holy Spirit, ...
or through the love of a friend.

"Father, if You are willing, remove this cup from Me; yet not My
will, but Yours be done."
– *Luke 22:42*

The Moment of Truth

We all go through them from time to time, don't we? Those testing,
proving moments of truth that define our character and what our integrity
is made of. I sit here with tears in my eyes grasping for words that would
do justice to the beauty, majesty, hope and love for you and me contained
in this one sentence from the gospel of Luke.

It was the moment of truth for Jesus.

The plea of Jesus here goes way beyond the physical agony of dying on
the cross. The Father and the Son had known unbroken communion and
perfect oneness for all eternity. That was about to change in a few hours
when Jesus would cry out, "My God, My God, why have You forsaken
Me?"

That was the moment when God turned His back on His Son, and Jesus
died alone ... completely alone on that cross, with the weight of the sin
of the entire world on His shoulders. Why? Because that is the cost of
sin — separation from God, and not just for a few minutes in death ...
it is separation for eternity. And the perfect, sinless Son of God felt
that separation as He paid for our sins. That is the cup Jesus asked the
Father to remove if it could be His will. The weight of our sin, and
eternal separation from His Father. And God said, "No." And a Father
watched His only Son die while He was crying out to Him ... Why?
Because He loves us. Including you and me. The cost of that love was
the life of His only Son.

The next time you are facing a moment of truth in your life, take courage
and hope from the way the Lord Jesus Christ faced His own moment
of truth — when your eternity in heaven hung in the balance, and He
showed you how much He loves you.

> And being in agony He was praying very fervently; and His sweat
> became like drops of blood, falling down upon the ground.
> *– Luke 22:44*

Sweating Blood

Sweating blood — a common expression used as an exaggeration to describe a condition of fear or nervousness, right?

Jesus sweating blood, however, was not exaggeration, poetic license or colorful writing to make a point. It is known as ***hematidrosis*** — the extremely rare medical condition of actually sweating blood. And, of the four gospel writers, the only one who was a physician (and who would have scoffed at this description were it not true), Luke, is the only one who recorded it happening. Now, for anyone thinking that being a doctor in Jesus's day didn't qualify Luke to make this medical observation, other instances are also mentioned in the writings of Aristotle, Theophrastus and Da Vinci. It is caused by elevated stress and intense emotional agony. The word in the original Greek for "great drops" here (and only here in the New Testament) is "thromboi," from which we get our word, "thrombosis."

What's the point? The point is how much Jesus loves you — and how much we should avoid "romanticizing" what happened here in the Garden of Gethsemane. It really, physically happened. At the end of Jesus's 40 days of temptation in the wilderness by the devil, the Bible tells us that the devil "departed from Him until a more opportune time." I personally believe that right here was that time. From here, until Jesus with His last breath shouted in victory, "It is finished." The weight of the horror and punishment of the sin of the world was on Jesus's shoulders, and heart. That includes my sin, and your sin ... and the agony of it came crashing down on Him here, in the Garden of Gethsemane.

I want to invite you to join me in a little exercise that I do from time to time. Put yourself in the scene here with Jesus and His disciples. You turn to your left and you see Jesus's most trusted disciples sleeping when He needed them the most ... they were not suffering at all for your sins. On your right you see Jesus. He is prostrate on the ground experiencing an emotional agony that is causing blood to fall like great drops of sweat from His face. Now ask yourself, "I wonder which one of those drops is falling from Jesus's face ... because of me?"

Jesus loves you with an intensity you can't even begin to imagine. The next time you are passing through a hard time and you begin to think no one cares, return to the Garden of Gethsemane and spend some time there with Jesus ... watching Him care deeply for you the night before He died.

When they came to the place called The Skull, there they crucified Him and the criminals, one on the right and the other on the left. But Jesus was saying, "Father, forgive them; for they do not know what they are doing."
— *Luke 23:33,34*

The Substitute

Substitute — "to take the place of" (Merriam-Webster Dictionary). At various times in my life, God has taught me some very powerful lessons that changed my heart and life forever. One of those times involved this word and was years ago when my son was very small and only just learning how to run.

One day I was standing on the raised cement "patio" area at the back of our house in England, and my son started running/waddling toward me from the back of the yard. He did not know that what he was doing was about to result in a great deal of pain. Just before he reached me, he tripped and fell, hitting his little head full force on the edge of the concrete. It opened a big gash just over his eye. He had never been hurt like that before, and he was crying and very afraid of the pain.

I scooped him up quickly and while his mother was getting some ice ready in a cloth, I sat in a chair, hugging him tight, reassuring him and kissing him on his forehead. I saw my son's blood all over the front of my shirt and I felt so very helpless. My eyes teared up and I wept as I thought, "Oh dear God, I'd give anything if I could just take his place and take this hurt for him." — and that's when God let me see it — a little glimpse of His heart. What I wanted so very much to do for my son, but could not, God DID do for me — and all of us. Holding us tight with His love, He took our place, He took our pain, and exchanged our blood for His own ... on that old rugged cross.

One of the criminals who were hanged there was hurling abuse at Him,
saying, "Are You not the Christ? Save Yourself and us!" But the other
answered, and rebuking him said, "Do you not even fear God, since
you are under the same sentence of condemnation? And we indeed
are suffering justly, for we are receiving what we deserve for our deeds;
but this man has done nothing wrong." And he was saying, "Jesus,
remember me when You come in Your kingdom!" And He said to him,
"Truly I say to you, today you shall be with Me in Paradise."
— *Luke 23:39–43*

Decisions, Decisions.

Every day of our lives we are faced with decisions. Some of them require
almost no thought at all, like whether or not to accept an invitation to
a delicious steak dinner, or whether or not to stop at a red light. Others
require a much greater degree of consideration, like which professional
direction to follow in life, or who you decide to marry.

One of the decisions which all of us will make is infinitely, and eternally,
more important than others. It is the decision you make about Jesus. Just
as it was with the two men who hung on either side of Jesus on the day
He was crucified, the decision you make about Him can define your hope
and joy and peace for the rest of your life. And it will definitely define
where you spend eternity. I choose Paradise, how about you?

When the sixth hour came, darkness fell over the whole land until
the ninth hour. At the ninth hour Jesus cried out with a loud voice,
"ELOI, ELOI, LAMA SABACHTHANI?" which is translated, "MY
GOD, MY GOD, WHY HAVE YOU FORSAKEN ME?"
— *Mark 15:33,34*

What's So Good About Good Friday?

The only language in the world that designates the day of Jesus's crucifixion
as "Good Friday" is English. In the "Romance Languages," which includes
Portuguese (the language of Brazil, where I serve) it is known as "Holy
Friday" (Sexta-feira Santa). In German, "Mourning Friday." In Russian,
"Passion Friday." Many linguists believe that "Good Friday" comes from
the fact that long ago, "good" was also translated "holy."

All that being said, what's so good about it, then? Especially considering
this agonizing cry of Jesus. Well ... out of that unspeakable agony and
pain that Jesus Christ endured that day, comes more good than a simple
devotional can explore, but we can give it a pretty good snapshot.

Out of the horror of Jesus's crucifixion, comes the dawn of our hope past
this life. What we can never do — pay the cost of our sin — Jesus did
do, with His own life. The death that we deserve, He took upon Himself.
An eternity we could never deserve — heaven — we have, because of
what Jesus did for us on the day we call "Good Friday." Jesus had been
one with the Father from eternity past. That union was broken here, for
the only time in eternity ... for you and for me. The feeling of separation
from God, not just for a few minutes while He died — but, for eternity.
That is what Jesus felt on the cross, because that is the penalty of sin.
And Jesus suffered that penalty for you and me ... so we wouldn't have
to. The feeling of that separation is what made Him cry those awful
words, "My God, My God, why have You forsaken Me?" It also creates
an incredible comfort for you the next time something has crushed you in
the heart and you cry out "Why?" — as you remember that Jesus knows
and understands how you feel because He too, asked that question one
day. The day we call "Good Friday."

"It is finished."
— *John 19:30*

Victory

Here it is — the greatest shout of victory in the history of creation.

For a person who doesn't know Jesus as Savior it is easy to look at this sentence, to look at Jesus beaten almost beyond recognition, breathing His last on the cross, and think that the enemies of Jesus had won, that the devil in the end had come out on top. That belies a careless reading of Jesus's last words.

Note carefully that Jesus did **NOT** say, "I am finished." Jesus did **NOT** say, "My life is finished." He said, "IT is finished." Big difference. In the Greek it is just one word, "Tetelestai!" — "Finished!!" In the language of today the sense would be, "Mission accomplished!!" If there is a greater place in all of scripture for hope and encouragement for you and me, I have yet to find it.

Mission accomplished — power of death, defeated.
Mission accomplished — power of the grave, defeated.
Mission accomplished — power of satan, defeated.
Mission accomplished — cost of my sin and your sin, paid in full.
Mission accomplished — my path and your path to God, laid open.
Mission accomplished — battle for my soul and your soul, won.

The angel said to the women, "Do not be afraid; for I know that you are looking for Jesus who has been crucified. He is not here, for He has risen, just as He said. Come, see the place where He was lying.
— *Matthew 28:5,6*

See For Yourself

This year, 2021, Easter falls on today — April 4, but regardless of which day it falls on, what never changes is the fact that Jesus Christ rose. Alive. Yes. He did.

The visible and irrefutable event that grounds our Christian hope in recorded history, and against which no skeptic can mount a cogent rebuttal of any logical credibility: it is the bodily resurrection of the Lord Jesus Christ. Oh — they'd like to, but there are some insurmountable difficulties …

1. Difficulty #1 — the empty tomb. No one — not even the enemies of Jesus, tried to deny the fact that on that first Easter morning His tomb was open, and that it was empty.
2. Difficulty #2 — the moved stone. 1.5 to 2 ***tons***. Moved uphill? And silently? With an elite detachment of Roman guards in front of it?
3. Difficulty #3 — The missing guards. What happened to the guards who were charged at the cost of their lives if they failed in their task? (Method of execution: being burned to death on top of their personal

effects.) Do you seriously believe that they ALL fell asleep under penalty of death, and let a group of cowardly disciples who all ran away when Jesus needed them the most, silently steal the body of Jesus?

4. Difficulty #4 — The missing body. The clothes were still there, still in the form of a body — but the body was gone. Even the enemies of Jesus didn't deny it.

5. Difficulty #5 — The witnesses who saw Jesus AFTER His resurrection. Paul would later write: "If you don't believe me about the ascension of Jesus into heaven, ask the more than 500 eye witnesses who also saw it, most of whom are still alive today."

... and there is much, much more ...

But these words appeared to them as nonsense, and they would not believe them. But Peter got up and ran to the tomb; stooping and looking in, he *saw the linen wrappings only; and he went away to his home, marveling at what had happened.

— Luke 24: 11,12

He has risen

There are a couple of things that make the Christian faith incomparably beautiful and authentic — one of those things is the written account of its history ... we call it the Bible. Even by secular historians, it is acknowledged to be one of the most compellingly honest and accurate historical documents ever written. These two verses are wonderful examples, where there is no attempt to cover up raw lack of faith.

An accusation of madness and refusal to believe that Jesus had risen from the dead would be easy for readers of the Bible today to accept — had it been the reaction of the crowd in Jerusalem. But it wasn't. This was the reaction of Jesus's own disciples. Before condemning them, however, put yourself in their shoes. They had put all their hopes in Jesus as being a conquering Messiah, and then had to watch as Roman guards pulled his bloody, dead and mangled body from a cross. Be as honest as the scripture. Had you been the one who discovered the empty tomb, how easy would it have been for you to believe that Jesus, as a piece of lifeless, human wreckage — that you saw with your own eyes — disappeared in victory, from a grave protected by the equivalent of the Navy SEALS of the Roman Guard?

Beautiful and authentic thing #2 about the Christian faith — the bodily resurrection of the Lord Jesus Christ. It can be difficult for some to believe — but — it cannot be denied. It can be rejected, but it cannot be denied. Even Jesus's enemies on that first Easter morning didn't try to deny that His tomb was open — and it was empty. They **_did_** not deny it because they **_could_** not deny it ... and it is still true today. Jesus Christ has risen indeed!!!!

"Why do you seek the living One among the dead? He is not here,
but He has risen.
— *Luke 24:5b-6a*

Together Again

Who would have thought that the title of a beloved old country song
could so completely capture the theme of Easter? It also describes what
happened to me a few years ago when my sister came to visit me here
in Brazil. It began the first visit I had had from family in Texas since
I moved to Brazil to do mission work. It had been a seven year wait.
That is a long time to never have a visit from anyone in your family. The
feeling of being reunited was overwhelming and beyond words. When
she came through those doors at the airport, unashamed tears of joy
flowed freely. Together again.

When Jesus left that tomb, victorious, on that first Easter morning it
marked the reunion of the Father and the Son. An eternal relationship
broken only by the price Jesus paid to give all of us the opportunity
to escape the eternal cost of our sin. When Jesus left that tomb, that
separation with His Father ended. Together again.

Ever since the beginning of time, when man first chose through his sin
to separate himself from the God who created and loved him, God's plan
has been to restore that relationship. God paid the ultimate price for that
reunion with man through the death of Jesus Christ on that cruel cross.
Why did He do it? Because He loves us. All of us. With a love that is
impossible for us to even imagine. I got a taste of it though, when I saw
my sister coming through those doors at the airport. Easter is about God
giving the ultimate sacrifice … doing whatever it took … to give all of us
the opportunity to be with Him for eternity when we leave this world.
To walk out of our own tomb and be with God. Together again.

and as the women were terrified and bowed their faces to the ground, the men said to them, "Why do you seek the living One among the dead? He is not here, but He has risen.
— *Luke 24:5,6a*

Endgame

I personally don't have time for video games, but I have become familiar with some of the words they have added to our vocabulary. One that I really like is "endgame," and it is in the mind of the writer of the game from the very beginning. It is the solution. It is the final steps you take to win the game.

Easter is the greatest endgame ever written. The bodily resurrection of the Lord Jesus Christ. It is an event Christians around the world celebrate every year. And with good reason. In Brazil where I serve, it is called "Páscoa," in Afrikaans "Paasfees," in Irish "Cásca," in Polish "Wielkanoe," but whatever the language, the resurrection of Jesus is the greatest endgame ever written. Easter isn't about some ridiculous, make-believe rabbit hiding colorful eggs. It is the defeat of satan, who was powerful enough to take a third of the angels with him when God cast him out of heaven. Easter is victory over death and the grave. It is the path and the visible proof of eternal life for us all. And it was in the mind and heart of God, the Author of everything, from BEFORE the beginning.

In a video game, you can choose not to win even though the solution for winning, the "endgame," is written right there in front of you. I don't know a single person who does that, do you? The only difference here is that Easter is not a game. Eternity is for keeps. There is no "reset" button once you are there. You have the "endgame," the key to victory written right in front of you. The only question is, what will you do with it?

"Go therefore and make disciples of all the nations, baptizing them in the name of the Father and the Son and the Holy Spirit, teaching them to observe all that I commanded you; and lo, I am with you always, even to the end of the age."
— *Matt.28:19,20*

Marching Orders

Here it is — the passage of scripture we enshrine as "The Great Commission." It is not the Great Suggestion. It is a command. Jesus's command to each one of us. What's so great about the Great Commission? Well, I'm glad you asked.

1. It is great because of the <u>Speaker</u>. Spoken by none other than the Son of God, risen Lord, living Lord, reigning Lord, King of Kings and Lord of Lords — and we could go on ...
2. It is great because of its <u>scope</u>. All nations. No discrimination as to race or place.
3. It is great because of its <u>purpose</u>. Eternal life in heaven for all who will listen.
4. It is great because of <u>who is commanded</u>. Us. It is a commission for all of us, not just the "professionals." It is OUR task, OUR privilege, OUR joy to tell people about the love of Christ and the hope we have in Him.
5. It is great because of its <u>timing</u>. The very last command of Jesus, the last words He spoke on this earth. In the legal world, last words carry great weight and value. They do here too.
6. It is great because of its <u>partnership</u>. Jesus ... and us. The One with all the power is with us — all the time. We never have to do ANYthing alone. Ever.

The grass withers, the flower fades,
but the word of our God stands forever.
— *Isaiah 40:8*

Got God's Word?

It was 1993. At the writing of this devotional it is now 2020. It hardly seems possible that it was 27 years ago when the California Milk Processor Board, with the help of the advertising agency Goodby, Silverstein & Partners launched an advertising strategy so effective that in just a few years, 91% of surveyed adults in the U.S. said they were familiar with the campaign. It was their "Got Milk?" series of advertisements. Many reading this will, no doubt, remember it. Today, however, it is almost forgotten because for all its popularity, it didn't cause people to buy more milk.

In a world where everything is transient and temporary, it is possible for you to have something that neither time nor circumstances can dent or destroy. Got God's Word?

Through not just 27 years, but thousands of years, many have tried to denounce God's word. Have tried to silence its truth and its power. Have tried to destroy it. They have all failed. It is still here, and it is still changing lives ... still today.

> I call upon the Lord, who is worthy to be praised,
> and I am saved from my enemies.
> — *Psalms 18:3*

The Cure-All

Got enemies? ——————→ Got the cure?

Enemies come in all sorts of forms, shapes and sizes. The Cure is the same for every single one of them.

> "... and the one who comes to Me
> I will certainly not cast out."
> — *John 6:37*

The Lord's Welcome Mat

Welcome, bem-vindo, croeso, willkommen, 歡迎, ' ahlaan bik, benvenuto, gratissimum, добро пожаловать, welkom, tere tulemast, wamukelekile, אבה ן ורב.

This is a very small sampling of all the different ways to say "welcome" around the world. How small? Well, most credible estimates list over 7,000 living languages — with some places like the unexplored Amazon here in Brazil, and the highlands of New Guinea still unknown — and the Lord is fluent in every single one of them. Even the "undiscovered" ones. And in each and every one of them He says, "the one coming to Me, I will certainly not cast out."

When you come to the Lord Jesus, you will never see a mat at the door that says "go away," or "not interested," or "closed until further notice," or "no overweight people allowed," or "caucasians prohibited," (or any other ethnic group), or perhaps more importantly for us — "all sinners excluded."

What is so, so, so beautiful about the love of Jesus is that it doesn't matter what color you are, what race you are, what nationality you are, what you smell like, what you look like, how rich or how poor you are ... or how long the list is of every single mistake you have made in your entire life. When you come to the Lord Jesus, His welcome mat will always say, "(your name), the one coming to Me, I will certainly not cast out."

But you are a chosen race, a royal priesthood, a holy nation, a people
for God's own possession, so that you may proclaim the excellencies
of Him who has called you out of darkness into His marvelous light.
— *1ˢᵗ Peter 2:9*

A Privileged Character

These are people who, mostly without earning it, enjoy a special position,
or right, or advantage. Entire royal families are full of them. We've all
seen them in the various arenas of our lives, too ... maybe even been
a little jealous of them from time to time. Maybe it was a person where
you work who got a promotion that you deserved, but they got it instead
because they were friends with "the boss." Maybe a classmate who enjoyed
grades he didn't deserve because he was the "teacher's pet."

Have you ever thought of yourself as a privileged character? You should. A
very, very special and positive type of privileged character. Even though we
could never deserve or earn the forgiveness and eternal life we can have with the
Lord Jesus as our Savior, we have it. We get to call the Creator of the universe
"Father." The Holy Spirit is our constant companion and guide. We don't
deserve any of it, yet just look at the privileged position we have in God's eyes:

1. Chosen — hand-picked by God Himself.
2. Royal — you will never be a "commoner" in God's eyes because you
    are a child of the King.
3. Holy — because God Himself, and God alone, is holy.
4. Special — God's own possession, unique in all the world.

And by His own initiative He has removed you from the night without
a light and has placed you in the light without a night. In one fell swoop
of God's grace He took you from eternal death to eternal life. As the
most privileged characters the world has ever known, "proclaiming the
praises" of our great God should be one of the most joyful and repetitious
activities of our lives. Amen?

... for the battle is the Lord's
and He will give you into our hands.
— *1ˢᵗ Samuel 17:47b*

Let's Get Ready To Rumble

Ok guys (girls, you are next) — you are ringside, forced into a fight you didn't even ask for, against that one person who absolutely turns your knees to jelly. Right when the ring announcer calls your name to enter the ring, Mohammed Ali in his prime jumps into the ring and says to you, "Relax, I've got this." Tell me you wouldn't be relieved. Girls, same scenario — with Ronda Rousey (famous MMA Bantamweight Champion in the past), a young lady who even GUYS are scared of. She says the same thing to you. I saw one of her fights on TV — it lasted all of 34 seconds. Is there any one of us who would tell either of these two champions, "No, no ... never mind, I can do this myself."? My guess is, no.

There are battles and challenges in life that can be much more scary, dangerous or crushing than what I just described. And — we never have to say, "No, no, never mind, I can do this myself." Why? Because just like David facing Goliath here, we have a Champion much greater than any earthly champion Who will fight for us if we will just let Him get in the ring. We too, however, have a part in the battle that is our responsibility. Our command is to put on the full armor of God (Ephesians 6:11) — but never ever forget — if you will let Him into your fight, "the battle is the Lord's, and He will deliver your enemy (whoever, or whatever it is) into your hands."

For the Lord Himself will descend from heaven with a shout, with
the voice of the archangel and with the trumpet of God, and the
dead in Christ will rise first. Then we who are alive and remain will
be caught up together with them in the clouds to meet the Lord in
the air, and so we shall always be with the Lord.
— *1ˢᵗ Thessalonians 4:16,17*

Exodus #2

If you want some inexpensive entertainment, just ask someone, anyone,
their opinion of the second coming of Christ. Especially if that person
holds him/herself out as an "expert" on the Bible. You will get almost as
many different opinions as there are different bathing suits on the beach.
You will get opinions on what happens to us when we die, soul sleep,
eschatology, the rapture, the world post-rapture ... and on and on.

Even though I studied diligently to obtain a Master's degree in Theology
from Southwestern Baptist Theological Seminary, I put the needle of all
our high-flown opinions about the second coming of Christ just slightly
above the mark "insignificant" on the dial of eternal events. What IS so
significant, and powerful about these two verses of scripture is this ...

The first exodus of God's children — what the Lord did through Moses at
the Red Sea — was one of the most astounding events of human history,
but, it will look like a crossing guard helping pre-schoolers across the
street compared to exodus #2 — the one the Lord Himself leads when
He takes ALL His children home.

There is an appointed time for everything. And there is a time for
every event under heaven. A time to give birth and a time to die;
a time to plant and a time to uproot what is planted. A time to
kill and a time to heal; a time to tear down and a time to build up.
A time to weep and a time to laugh; a time to mourn and a time to
dance. A time to throw stones and a time to gather stones; a time to
embrace and a time to shun embracing. A time to search and a time
to give up as lost; a time to keep and a time to throw away.
A time to tear apart and a time to sew together; a time to be silent
and a time to speak. A time to love and a time to hate; a time for
war and a time for peace ... He has made everything appropriate in
its time.
— *Ecclesiastes 3:1-8, 11a*

The Peace of God's Sovereign Control

Over the many years of many scholars trying to interpret God's word
a lot of ink, a lot of paper, a lot of energy and a lot of time has been used
(and mostly wasted) trying to find a coherent connection in these verses
of Ecclesiastes — even what some of the phrases mean. Perhaps it is
good from time to time, for scripture to be a bit illusive or even confusing
and difficult to figure out. Why? Maybe because life can be like that
at times, too. What is important for you and me to take away from
these verses, however, isn't difficult at all. It is simply this: God is in
control of everything, and not only is God IN control of everything, He is
sovereign OVER everything. We may not understand what is happening
at a particular time in our life, we may not even be able to see an end to
a problem. Doesn't matter. Even if we can't see it, God is still in control.
And ... having the faith and *patience* to trust in God's absolute sovereignty
over all these things is the key to real, deep, and lasting peace in your life.

And there are also many other things which Jesus did, which if they were written in detail, I suppose that even the world itself would not contain the books that would be written.
— *John 21:25*

The Agenda of Jesus

You may know what it is like to have an agenda so full that there seems to be no empty space to add anything else. When you read about the life and ministry of Jesus in the gospels, all that he did, how tired he got, how some days seemed like just one interruption after another, it is easy to see that Jesus's agenda was crammed full. And yet, John writes this right here. It is a real shame that this magnificent verse is so often neglected and skipped over, or treated like a "P.S." at the end of John's gospel. It deserves better attention. Can we give it some today?

Of course John is writing in hyperbole here, but it is to make an important point. A powerful point. All the preachers of all the world and all their sermons since the time of Christ have not been able to exhaust what is contained in the gospel accounts of the life of Jesus. And yet — John says here that all of that — all of what is written about the life of Jesus in the gospels, is but a mere "Post-it Note" when compared to the volume of all that Jesus actually did.

Spend a moment or two dwelling on that ... and on the fact that Jesus is still active today. The Lord Jesus Christ is amazing and wonderful, and it gets even better when He becomes your personal Savior — you are on His agenda.

...the God who girds me with strength and makes my way
blameless? He makes my feet like hinds' feet, and sets me upon my
high places.
— *Psalms 18:32,33*

Sure Footing

Anyone who has had their foot slip in a life-threatening, or dangerous situation and has had their life flash in front of their face, can appreciate the security and relief that a position of sure footing can bring. The ability of the magnificent animals in this picture to not just "make their way up," but actually run up a mountainside where there seems to be no place to put their feet is amazing to say the least. These verses in this victorious warrior's psalm of David captures the life-truth of this image for all God's children.

This old world and all its trials may seem like an insurmountable climb sometimes for us, with no place to even gain a foothold, or even a toehold — much less make our way to the top of Mount Difficulty. Much of the time — correct me if I am wrong here — the problem is that we try to pound our own crude "mountain-climbing weapons" out of the ground in our own strength. Go on, you can admit it ... I'm right, aren't I? We need to remember that we have a Heavenly Arms Supplier, who not only equips us for any battle in life, but also provides us a path up the slope that isn't just good — it is perfect, and — it has a non-slip surface. If you don't believe me, just check out the next three verses (34,35,36).

Our Commander-in-Chief is the King of Kings and the Lord of Lords. For the one who will trust in God, sure footing in all of life's battles, like the feet of the deer, is assured. But there is more than that. Certain victory awaits no matter how dark the day may seem. That is the meaning of "sets me on my high places." Sets me" — the certainty. "My high places" — the high ground always belongs to the victor. That means you too, my friend!

"Do not store up for yourselves treasures on earth, where moth and rust destroy, and where thieves break in and steal. But store up for yourselves treasures in heaven, where neither moth nor rust destroys, and where thieves do not break in or steal; for where your treasure is, there your heart will be also."
— *Matthew 6:19-21*

The Lord's IRA

It is just plain smart to have a savings account of some type. I don't know a single financial advisor who would argue against that. In this day and age, with economies — and governments — that come and go, if a person can "put a little back" each month, even if it is only a small amount, it all adds up and every little bit helps when retirement age arrives. IRAs, or Individual Retirement Accounts is one way many choose to save.

Jesus talks here about two kinds of savings: He talks about the wrong kind of treasure and He talks about the right kind of treasure. We have all seen the wrong kind, and the kind of people who are almost addicted to amassing it. They never have enough money, always wanting a newer or fancier car, expensive clothes or jewelry, which they make sure everyone sees. They want more and more earthly treasure, and that is where their heart is.

Jesus presents a "spiritual IRA" that beats all of that. You don't need any of those fancy things to be happy, or to have hope in this world. Jesus says to focus our hearts and lives on our eternity, not the car in our driveway or the clothes in our closets, all of which is merely temporary. If we do things the way the Lord says, when we retire for good from this earth, we will have a treasure waiting for us in heaven that is absolutely secure. In fact, it is protected by God Himself. Check it out, it is in 1st Peter 1:4,5. (Ok, ok, I can't resist. Here is what it says: "… an inheritance which is imperishable and undefiled and will not fade away, reserved in heaven for you, who are protected by the power of God through faith for a salvation ready to be revealed in the last time."). How's ***that*** for an IRA?

"You shall have no other gods before Me."
— *Exodus 20:3*

The Mother of all Commandments

Here it is. The mother of all commandments: commandment #1. I have long ago lost count of the conversations I have had with folks who have said to me, "I can't be a Christian. I can't keep all those commandments.", to which I have consistently replied, "You don't have to. Just keep the first one and all the others will take care of themselves." And that, dear friend, is the absolute truth.

So many people wonder why God doesn't seem close, or attentive, or powerful in their lives. These are the same people who normally have a long list of gods that they place in front of the one true, and living God. The Lord God Almighty. It doesn't have to be a statue of Buddha, or Mohammed, or Marduk or Baal. The devil steers us away from Commandment #1 in much more subtle ways. Some examples — for both the guys, and for the girls:

Guys — Pleasure as a god. How many times have we stayed home from church to watch sports on TV? As big a fan as I am, try praying to the Dallas Cowboys front office the next time you need something and see what happens. Fishermen, try bowing down to your top water jig the next time you need a miracle in your life and see what happens. So often we find ourselves caring more about how we feel, than giving God what He deserves.

Girls — Vanity as a god. How many of you have wasted money on a dress that you never wore again around your friends because you saw someone else with the same dress? Or even better, contrast how much time you spend on your personal appearance (make up, hair, nails, etc.) with how much time you spend in prayer. How much more do you care about what people think of your outward appearance than what God thinks of your spiritual appearance?

See how easily placing other things before God can happen? One of the simplest keys to a life of incredible hope and joy is keeping Commandment #1. Now, I chose the word "simple" on purpose. I didn't say "easy." It is simple to understand, it is NOT always easy to do. But is it worth it? Absolutely. Every single time.

> ... just as He chose us in Him before the foundation of the world,
> that we would be holy and blameless before Him. In love He
> predestined us to adoption as sons through Jesus Christ to Himself,
> according to the kind intention of His will ...
> — *Ephesians 1:4,5*

Premeditated Love

This is one of my all-time favorite passages of scripture. In truth, the whole chapter is nothing short of stunning. But let's have a look at three incomparably beautiful truths in just these two short verses:

1. Don't just skip over "before the foundation of the world" — that means that before Genesis 1:1, before God ever said "Let there be light!", He said, "I am going to love YOU — personally.
2. In God's own loving eyes, as Christians we — even with all our faults and sins — are holy and blameless. Because of Jesus, God sees only the end product.
3. "according to the good pleasure of His will" means it made God happy to do it. Of all the other things that might encourage you today and make you smile, this ought to sit right at the top of the list. There is no "maybe" to the things mentioned here. It is already a "done deal," and it made God happy to do it. Because He loves you.

I searched for a man among them who would build up the wall and
stand in the gap before Me for the land, so that I would not destroy
it; but I found no one.
— *Ezekiel 22:30*

Standing in the Gap

"Easier said than done" is an expression that is common to all of us. It
is true in this verse of the Bible as well. Easy to say, courageous in its
sound — not so easy to do. In God's search for someone to stand in
the gap between His judgment and a disobedient Israel, He found no
one. No one. Did it mean there were no righteous or good people in
Jerusalem? Of course there were. But still the fact remains that can't be
ignored — He found no one to stand in the gap.

Well, what about today? What about God's judgement on an America
that has legalized the murder of its own unborn children ... and with
each new day makes celebrities out of people who espouse a deviant,
homosexual lifestyle that God's word says is an abomination? And that's
not being "phobic" or judgmental — that's just stating a Biblical fact.

And — what about us when God says, "I need someone to stand in the
gap."? We say, "Oh, that's not me — God couldn't use me that way." No?
Take heart, my friend! God has been in the business of using unlikely people
for mighty purposes for a long, long time: Moses (a hidden baby of Hebrew
slaves), David (the "runt of the litter"), Isaiah (the man of unclean lips), Jesus's
disciples (cowards to a man when He needed them the most), Paul (the self-
proclaimed chief of all sinners). And the list could be much longer ...

You know, when you think about it gaps are not restricted to standing
between God and the judgment of a nation. There are all kinds of gaps:
a neighbor or friend who has lost a child to drugs or an accident (gap
between their conscience and guilt), an 80-year-old friend whose wife or
husband dies (gap between love and loneliness), a workmate goes through
a divorce because of infidelity (gap between trust and betrayal). And God
is still searching today for someone to stand in these gaps. These and
others. When He comes to you, will He find someone willing to stand
in the gap? If you want hope and encouragement in your own life, try
filling the gaps of hope and encouragement in someone else's life — and
watch what happens.

For in Him all the fullness of Deity dwells in bodily form, and in Him you have been made complete, and He is the head over all rule and authority;
— *Colossians 2:9,10*

Telling It Like It Is

In a couple of places in this collection of devotionals, I have used the same passage twice. This is one of those places, because these verses emphasize two things that are so good, you just can't leave one out. One devotional on these verses is "Who's In Charge." This one is "telling it like it is." So let's do that. Let's tell it like it is.

Mormonism says Jesus was less than God, Jehovah's Witnesses say that Jesus was less than God, Islam says that Jesus was less than God ... and the list goes on and on. The problem is, that is not what the Bible says. They are all wrong. All of them. For in Christ "ALL the fullness of Deity dwells in bodily form." God dressed Himself in skin and flesh and bone, came to Earth — and His name was Jesus. And it still is. Don't overlook the present tense of the verbs in these verses.

You can't become complete by performing a compilation of good deeds, chanting and clinking little cymbals together, sitting with your legs folded while humming, memorizing the teachings of a dead fat man or Confucius, or by deifying a mortal Arab, pedophilic prophet-wanna-be. You become complete, or perfect, only by the grace and love of Jesus Christ, the Lord God Himself who came to Earth and was with us for 33 years in bodily form. It is nothing you do. It is what He does IN you — if you give Him the chance.

According to some figures, there are over 8,700 recorded names of false gods. But, Zeus is not God, Artemis is not God, Baal was not God, nor Marduk. Confucius is not God, Muhammad is not God, Buddah is not God. Only Jesus is God — and He is the head over all rule and authority.

Our God IS God. And that's not being hard — that's just telling it like it is.

For in Him all the fullness of Deity dwells in bodily form, and in Him you have been made complete, and He is the head over all rule and authority;
— *Colossians 2:9,10*

Who's In Charge?

Jesus is, that's who!

First — No matter what person, religion or book tries to tell you that the Jesus you call Lord is actually less than the one and only Lord God Almighty, and that the Bible never explicitly says He is God, they are just flat wrong. Jesus was Lord BEFORE His birth (John 1:1), DURING His life on earth (John 1:14), and still is now, AFTER his resurrection (present verse).

Second — Note "dwells" (not, dwelled), present tense — Jesus IS the risen Lord, very much alive and well, and very much still God.

Third — The Jesus you call Lord is the CEO of absolutely everything. He outranks everyone and everything ... on earth, or in heaven. He reports to no one. All the power belongs to Him and His authority is unchallenged. On earth OR in heaven. He is King of **_all_** kings and Lord of **_all_** Lords.

Fourth — In this same Jesus, you are complete. No outside help needed. In the original language it means "crammed full." It means you need no other source of grace, no other source of salvation, no other source of power, no other source of forgiveness ... and it renders you perfect, righteous, holy and worthy in God's eyes — because in Christ, you are complete.

For Christ also died for sins once for all, the just for the unjust, so that
He might bring us to God, having been put to death in the flesh, but
made alive in the spirit ...
— *1ˢᵗ Peter 3:18*

The Just For The Unjust

I love this verse. I mean, I really love it. It absolutely bulges with powerful theology, hope and promise, but the reason I love it so very much is that small, second phrase — "the just for the unjust." The only person in the history of the world who never deserved to die because of sin, DID die because of it — but not because of His own sin: He died for MY sin, "the just for the unjust." I was unworthy to the core, and still am. He died for me anyway — the just for the unjust, because He loves even me. I have tears every time I read it or think about it.

If this devotional finds its way to someone who has never accepted Jesus as their Savior because you think whatever it is that you have done is so bad that Jesus couldn't possibly love you ... let me encourage you to think again. Your sin — regardless of what it is, will not exhaust the power of the blood Jesus shed on the cross, it will not drain the limits of God's grace, it will not strain the strength of Jesus's love ... "the just for the unjust" means you too.

"For whoever wishes to save his life will lose it, but whoever loses his life for My sake and the gospel's will save it. For what does it profit a man to gain the whole world, and forfeit his soul?
— *Mark 8:35,36*

Spiritual Economics 101

In our work-a-day world, the matter of trying to accumulate dollars and pennies consumes a vast amount of our life, our time and our energy, wouldn't you agree? It seems to be the law of economic survival in an increasingly competitive jungle. How about some hope and encouragement today for those of us whose bank balances look more like a pimple than Mount Everest?

Jesus gives a lesson here in spiritual economics that turns our social economic model on its head. No matter what happens in the arena of the world's economics, the driving passion of our life should not be our job, it should be Jesus. Spiritual economics isn't about dollars and pennies. It is about life and death. The kind that lasts forever.

Jesus teaches us here that on the day we leave this earth, what we have deposited in the bank will have a value for us of exactly $0.00, no matter what the bank statement says. In God's economy, success isn't measured by money, it is measured by faith. A person who has deposited their faith in Jesus may leave this world a pauper, but they will arrive in heaven as heirs with Christ. I love spiritual economics. How about you?

> Now in the first year of Cyrus king of Persia, in order to fulfill the word of the Lord by the mouth of Jeremiah, the Lord stirred up the spirit of Cyrus king of Persia, so that he sent a proclamation throughout all his kingdom, and also put it in writing ...
> — *Ezra 1:1*

With God = With Hope

Through this failure or that failure, this situation or that situation, hope can seem a million miles away at times. But, as God's children we need never feel that way. Why? Because as we see here and in many other places in the Bible, with God there is always hope.

Sometimes, an imposing power can make hope hard to see. Cyrus the Great was the greatest conqueror of all time. He was the first leader ever to officially be called "Great." He was the first leader to establish a true empire. He defeated the Medes. He defeated the Babylonians. An alliance between Babylonia, Egypt and Sparta failed to stop him. His empire was so strong that it survived for 200 years after his death.

Sometimes, a crushing defeat can make hope hard to see. Israel was a defeated nation and had been forcibly removed from their land 70 years before Cyrus issued this proclamation. Their storied past and relationship with God must have seemed like a fairytale to many. But there are some wonderful things about the power of God ...

God's power isn't limited by His children's lack of hope, nor their lack of strength, nor their lack of resources, nor their lack of resolve, nor their lack of faith. Neither is God's power limited by His children's enemies. Not their power, not their position, not their size, not their influence, not their wealth.

The Lord God is always in control. Just like here, with the proclamation of Cyrus that set Israel free to return to Jerusalem. Was it because of some initiative of Israel. No. Was it Cyrus's idea? No. It was God's initiative: the Lord stirred up the spirit of Cyrus the king of Persia. Cyrus's power was insignificant. The Lord was in control then, and the Lord is in control now. No matter how bad your situation might seem, no matter for how long, no matter the forces around you that may seem so powerful, the Lord is always in control. Always. With God, there is always hope.

I persecuted this Way to the death, binding and putting both men and women into prisons, as also the high priest and all the Council of the elders can testify. From them I also received letters to the brethren, and started off for Damascus in order to bring even those who were there to Jerusalem as prisoners to be punished. "But it happened that as I was on my way, approaching Damascus about noontime, a very bright light suddenly flashed from heaven all around me...
— *Acts 22:4-6*

What Happened?

What happened here in the book of Acts, is that the fiercest persecutor of the Christian faith got zapped by the love of Jesus. That's what happened. Maybe you have had one of those "what happened?" moments too, where something in life came at you out of nowhere and whacked you on the blindside. These verses describe how it happened to the apostle Paul. One minute, Paul had a frothing-at-the-mouth hate for Christians ... the next minute, Jesus put a "detour of love" in the middle of the Damascus Road and the worst persecutor of the Christian faith became its most passionate voice. Thirteen books of the New Testament of God's Holy Word were penned by this one man.

Jesus hasn't stopped changing the lives of persecutors. During the writing of this very devotional, I also read an account of a brutal Islamic terrorist who admitted, as did the apostle Paul, to enjoying persecuting — even killing — Christians. The last one he killed said to him, "I know you are going to kill me, but I want to give you my Bible." He began reading it and Jesus appeared to him in a dream — and he became a follower of Jesus Christ. True story. Now, I am pretty sure you don't know any brutal terrorists, but just about all of us know someone who is vocally loud and negative about Jesus and Christianity, right? It can be a workmate, schoolmate, neighbor, or even a friend. Sometimes it can be someone we care about deeply. Sometimes it can even be us, if Jesus isn't our Savior ... yet. The good news is this: Jesus still changes lives today. Jesus still knows where the Damascus Road is — and who is on it. And He loves them.

For I have come to have much joy and comfort in your love, because the hearts of the saints have been refreshed through you, brother.
— *Philemon 7*

The Clause That Refreshes

"The pause that refreshes" is a line so memorable that even though it was first used by Coca Cola in 1929, it is remembered and used in many ways still today. If there is a "clause that refreshes," surely it must be "love you!" It can brighten the darkest day. It is an all-natural facelift, and a soothing salve for the aching heart.

For Paul to have written this to Philemon, he must have said it — and showed it — as a habit of life, in many ways. Philemon was a joy and a comfort to one of the Lord's greatest servants and a font of refreshing encouragement to all God's children around him. Why? Because he was a gifted actor or entertainer, or speaker? No. A skilled psychologist? No. A wise pastor? No. Philemon was a joy and a comfort, and refreshed the hearts of those around him because as a habit of life, he lived out the clause that refreshes: "love you."

Want to do something really helpful and important to God? You too, can make a profound and uplifting difference in the lives of those around you. You don't have to know how to preach, teach or sing. Just give the love of God inside you to others. Who knows how many hearts could be uplifted and encouraged, just by you doing that one thing — by being the "clause that refreshes."

Then the Lord God called to the man, and said to him, "Where are
you?"
— *Genesis 3:9*

Come Out, Come Out Wherever You Are

Anyone who has ever played the game of hide and seek as a child knows
this little phrase well. It is interesting, to say the least, that even though
we stopped playing the game years ago as children, we still try playing it
as adults with the Lord God Almighty.

The very first man and woman tried it, too. Hide and seek is a very old
game with God. Adam and Eve tried hiding behind fig leaves after they
had sinned against God. How effective do you think **_that_** was? God's
question to them, "Where are you?" was certainly not because He didn't
already know where they were. Or what they had done.

We look at what Adam and Eve did and think, how pointless of them to
try that. But — don't we do exactly the same thing today when we try
to hide from God? No matter how good you think your hiding place is,
it is no more than a fig leaf between you and God. And God is saying,
"Come out, come out wherever you are … ," already knowing the whole
time where you are. And what you have done. There is no place you can
hide from God. You can run, but you can't hide. And trying to hide only
prevents you from experiencing something truly wonderful …

That "something wonderful" is this: There is no need to hide. Ever. God
knows who you are, what you have done, and all that you ever **_will_** do —
and He loves you anyway. How can you be sure? Well … He sent His
only Son, Jesus, to die in your place and pay the price for your sins. That's
pretty compelling proof — don't you think?

"There is a lad here who has five barley loaves and two fish, but
what are these for so many people?"
— John 6:9

The Master's Multiplication Table

5x0=0, 5x1=5, 5x2=10 ... and on and on we could go. As children we all
studied our multiplication tables, right? When it comes to Jesus though,
the "laws" of multiplication sort of go out the window. Case in point; the
scene that unfolds around this short, little verse. I can't resist telling it ...
here it is.

Jesus had a crowd of hungry people around Him. Not just a "hungry
handful." It was about 5,000 men, plus the women, plus the children. The
disciple Andrew took a quick inventory of the available food supply. The
result of that inventory is this little verse — and it reveals a beautifully
encouraging lesson about the Master's multiplication table. Jesus fed
them all and had food left over.

If you didn't know who He was and if you had been there, would you
have thought that Jesus could feed over 5,000 people with that tiny bit
of food? Be honest. 5 small loaves of bread and 2 fish does NOT equal
5,000 people fed, does it? But there is still more. There were 12 baskets
of food left over at the end, and it leaves us with one of the most beautiful
lessons in the Bible.

You may be facing what seems like an impossible situation with little to no resources to fix it. You may want to be a part of something like the young boy here, but feel like what you can contribute is insignificant. The beautiful encouragement this "dinner on the ground with Jesus" teaches us is this: how much you think you have — or don't have … isn't important. What Jesus can do with it, is. Never forget — there is no limit to what Jesus can do if you will put your 5 loaves and 2 fish in His hands.

Though the fig tree should not blossom and there be no fruit on the vines, though the yield of the olive should fail and the fields produce no food, though the flock should be cut off from the fold and there be no cattle in the stalls, yet I will exult in the Lord, I will rejoice in the God of my salvation.
— *Habakkuk 3:17,18*

The Poster Child for Bad Luck

Judging from just these two verses, Habakkuk could have been considered a good candidate for this poster child. You may have felt that way, too, at one time or another. I know I have. There have even been times I have said something like this to Claudia, "I can't even concentrate on the problem I am trying to solve because of the two or three other problems pushing and shoving from behind it, trying to take its place."

This magnificent declaration from Habakkuk teaches us the proper attitude we should have about our problems. Here the prophet lists six — count 'em, six — problems that, in Habakkuk's day would not have been mere irritations ... they would have been devastating. Habakkuk says that all of them — put together — would not even dent His joy in the Lord. As fruitless as a cat trying to scratch a stainless steel pole. Sort of makes me feel embarrassed at how frustrated I got earlier today when our clothes dryer stopped blowing hot air.

Habakkuk took the entire list of his problems and BURIED them behind the joy in his soul at the thought of the God who was the author of his salvation. We would be wise to follow his example, because having that one gift from God is more important than anything else in our lives.

Now on the last day, the great day of the feast, Jesus stood and cried out, saying, "If anyone is thirsty, let him come to Me and drink. He who believes in Me, as the Scripture said, 'From his innermost being will flow rivers of living water.' "
— *John 7:37,38*

Water Supply

Anyone who grew up on a farm like I did knows the critical importance of a good water supply. If you have cows and the lake goes dry, you have a serious problem. Same thing if you have a crop in the field and it doesn't rain. In the days of the Old West, a lack of water in the middle of nowhere could mean the difference between life and death. The reason drinking wine was so common in Jesus's day was that, more often than not, the water was contaminated with germs and disease.

The feast in which Jesus was participating in these verses, and which He used as a backdrop for this stunning proclamation, had a ritual in which a golden pitcher of water from the pool of Siloam was carried in a procession once a day for 7 days. Note well, the contrast that Jesus portrays. As opposed to a pitcher of water, Jesus was saying the REAL source of salvation, the real source of living water was Himself. And it is poured from His heart, not a ritual golden pitcher. And, it comes as a never-ending river gushing from the heart of Jesus ... as opposed to a couple of cups of water poured out on the ground.

Are you thirsty today my friend? Thirsty for someone to love you, thirsty for someone to care? Thirsty for a friend who will never leave you, never forsake you? Thirsty for hope in the middle of a desert that seems to have no end? Then come to the One who is just waiting for the chance to quench your thirst—in such abundance that it is like the flow of a mighty river.

The Lord lives, and blessed be my rock;
and exalted be the God of my salvation.
— *Psalms 18:46*

One of a Kind

We have heard this expression countless times in our lives. Its truth is presented more vividly than any other place, in the Lord God Almighty. There is a long, long list of superlatives to describe our Lord. "One of a kind" may not be one of the most majestic sounding, but it is for sure one of the best.

Budda is dead. Confucius is dead. Mohammed is dead. The Lord Jesus Christ lives!!! He lives victorious over death and the grave!!! He lives and He reigns — King of Kings and Lord of Lords forever and ever. No other god (with emphasis on the little "g"), real or imaginary can say that. They are either all dead or never existed in the first place. Our God, however, IS God ... unique, living, one of a kind, all-powerful, who still sustains the entire universe by the word of His power (Hebrews 1:3, Colossians 1:17).

AND — the King of Kings and Lord of Lords who lives forever is MY rock. Personal and individual. MY foundation ... that all the storms of hell itself cannot shake.

AND — the King of Kings and Lord of Lords who lives forever and who is my Rock has also given to me, my salvation ... personal, secure and eternal.

Do I exalt Him? You betcha!! Want to join me?

and hope does not disappoint, because the love of God has been
poured out within our hearts through the Holy Spirit who was given
to us.
— *Romans 5:5*

The Gift That Keeps On Giving

This is one of the most popular advertising phrases in history. Its first
commercial use can be traced all the way back to the 1920s when it was
used by the Victor Radio Company, and it has been used countless times
since. However, the idea was not original with Victor Radio. It was
God's original idea when he decided to love you and me. Love that
began before time (Ephesians 1:4), and still exists today. The incredible
promise in this verse we have before us exists because of that love — the
promise of hope that never fails. Nothing this world can provide comes
even close. In the original language it is even prettier ... "has been poured
out and continues to be poured out."

Where has His love been poured out? In our hearts. Isn't that
a lovely thought? And what's even better is that it is more than merely
a thought — it is the truth. And it just keeps getting better for everyone
who believes in Jesus. The One who puts that love in our hearts is none
other than the Holy Spirit, who was (pay attention here) **_given_** to us.
Us — you and me. Given. Salvation isn't the only thing we have that
is without cost because of God's love. The abiding presence of the Holy
Spirit of God is free, too. And He is with you right now. Right now.
The gift of God's love that just keeps on giving.

In the beginning God created the heavens and the earth. The earth
was formless and void, and darkness was over the surface of the
deep, and the Spirit of God was moving over the surface of the
waters. Then God said, "Let there be light"; and there was light.
— *Genesis 1:1-3*

Who Done It

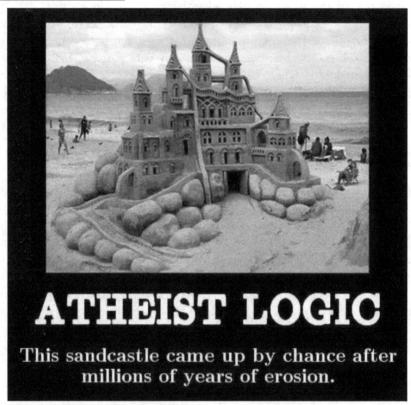

ATHEIST LOGIC

This sandcastle came up by chance after
millions of years of erosion.

This old expression for a murder mystery, could almost be applied to the
creation of the universe, couldn't it? Other than God, there were no eye-
witnesses to either affirm, or discredit the Biblical account. We are presented
here with what is known as a "mutually exclusive alternative" — a situation
that allows only one choice of two opposite possibilities. The choice about
whether or not God created the universe is a good example. He either
did — or He did not. I know of no other possible choice, do you?

Option "NO": Let's look at the logic of atheism, which chooses this option. Atheism believes that there was nothing — and then nothing happened to nothing — and then nothing magically exploded for no reason, creating everything — then a bunch of everything magically rearranged itself for no reason whatsoever into self-replicating bits — which then turned into dinosaurs. That logic is somewhere on the opposite side of brilliant, wouldn't you agree?

Option "YES": God did it — and He did it exactly as the Bible records it in the book of Genesis. All around us is visible evidence of intelligent design and incredible power behind the creation of our infinite universe, plus mind-boggling complexity in life even at the simplest microscopic levels.

Which one makes more sense to you? I, unapologetically, choose option #2.

Who done it? God done it! The evidence all around us is overwhelming to the honest, and open mind. I choose to believe that the Lord God Almighty really exists. That He really created everything, just like it says in the Bible, and the only thing more incredible than the beautiful universe God created around us, is the fact that He really loves you and me.

"Whoever receives this child in My name receives Me, and whoever receives Me receives Him who sent Me; for the one who is least among all of you, this is the one who is great."
— *Luke 9:48*

The Domino Effect

Don't believe everything the world tells you about what it means to be great. Don't believe me? Ask the kings who lost their kingdoms and were paraded like animals in front of their conquered people. Ask the CEOs whose companies went bankrupt. Ask great military commanders like Douglas MacArthur who were relieved of their command. Ask "powerful" pastors of megachurches, or mega-ministries, who had to resign in disgrace.

Jesus gives the formula for true greatness right here — in just two sentences. I call it "the domino effect." The first domino is not who you know, how much money you have or what position you have attained — it is humility. Jesus taught it by valuing the dignity and importance of a little child. Far from insignificant, it is the domino that leads to a true relationship with Jesus. A true relationship with Jesus is the domino that establishes forever, a relationship with our Father who is in heaven.

The world, at its best, offers a "greatness" that is fleeting. Jesus offers a greatness that is forever. Want to talk wealth? How about an eternal inheritance that lasts forever. Want to talk position? How about a place at the table of the Lord God Almighty that is forever. It is available to the least of all ... who is willing to just tip over that first domino.

"But go, tell His disciples and Peter,
'He is going ahead of you to Galilee; there you will see Him, just as
He told you.'"
— *Mark 16:7*

Singled Out

Being singled out for an achievement or an award carries a nice feeling with it. If it has ever happened to you, you know that to be true. However, being singled out — or even just feeling singled out — for a fault or a mistake is quite a different story. If it has ever happened to you, you know this to be true as well. It can be embarrassing, or hurtful in all sorts of ways, can't it? In this beautiful little sentence, recorded only in the gospel of Mark, Jesus provided a rare exception to the rule of being humiliated or hurt when someone was singled out for something negative that they had done. Peter, who denied Jesus three times when He needed him the most before the crucifixion is the example.

Through an angel, Jesus gave this beautiful message to the woman at the empty tomb, to deliver to His disciples. Try to imagine the abyss of sadness and humiliation that was Peter's, denying the Lord three times after boldly asserting he would never do such a thing. And yet, with just two words ... "and Peter" ... Jesus extends a tender, loving, accepting, forgiving reach to erase the shame felt by the one who had denied Him. By singling Peter out with just those two words, Jesus let Peter know that He still loved him, in spite of what he had just done. That he was still a disciple, in spite of what he had just done. That Jesus was still going to do what He said He would do, in spite of what he had just done. That is how much Jesus loved Peter.

And that is how much Jesus loves you, too, my friend. If you feel (or have ever felt) excluded by a group of "friends," or family, or even members of your church for something you have done wrong, and it has left you feeling embarrassed, or ashamed, or ... singled out — know this: The way Jesus singles you out is to let you know that, different from all the others, He never stops loving you, He doesn't remove you from HIS group, and He never changes His promises to you.

But after hearing of Him, a woman whose little daughter had an unclean spirit immediately came and fell at His feet. Now the woman was a Gentile, of the Syrophoenician race. And she kept asking Him to cast the demon out of her daughter. And He was saying to her, "Let the children be satisfied first, for it is not good to take the children's bread and throw it to the dogs." But she answered and *said to Him, "Yes, Lord, but even the dogs under the table feed on the children's crumbs." And He said to her, "Because of this answer go; the demon has gone out of your daughter."
— *Mark 7:25-29*

Jesus, A Mother, And The Crumbs

It is important to know at the very beginning, that Jesus was not being hard with this woman as it might appear on the surface. In fact, it was quite the opposite. First things first, though. As we enter Mother's Day weekend, look at this mother. Our relationship with Jesus would improve instantly if we could be more like her. Look at her **knowledge of Jesus**. She knew Jesus well enough to know that when He was available, "immediately" was the best time to go to Him. Look at her **position** in her audience with Jesus. "Falling at His feet" meant that she didn't treat Jesus like some old lantern on a shelf that she dusted off and used when the lights went out. Hers was the approach of humility in front of One much greater than herself. Look at her **determination**. She "kept asking Him." Look at her **passion**. When — on the surface — it would seem that Jesus rejected her, she appealed to Him yet again, this time not just to His power, but to His limitless love, "Yes, Lord, but even the dogs under the table feed on the children's crumbs." And mark this next fact well — in all the Bible, there were only two people who "contended" with God and won. Jacob (who wrestled with Him all night and God blessed him and gave him the name "Israel") — and this mother.

Now look at Jesus ... once again very tired from crowds and constant ministry. Did Jesus send the woman away because of this? No. Jews referred to Gentiles as dogs. Did He send her away because of this? No. A mother came to Him, pleading, because of a demon in her daughter, and He healed her — sight unseen. On the surface, what Jesus said first to the woman would seem harsh to us. But He said what He said,

I personally believe, with a twinkle in His eye and I will tell you why. First of all, in reminding her that His mission was first to the Jews, Jesus did not insult the woman. He would never do such a thing to someone who came to Him for help. The word here for "dog" isn't the common word. It is the word for "little puppy." Sort of like the beloved family pet. Second, you are looking here at the same Jesus who verbally and intellectually scalded alive the religious leaders of His day who presumed to banter theology with Him. Do you think for one minute that this woman's response would have really been a test for Jesus? Of course not. What this mother did was reveal a profound depth of faith in Jesus's power and love — just the crumbs of it would be sufficient to heal her daughter. And Jesus, as He always does, rewarded that faith.

Picture in your mind the following scene: A mother bakes some fresh and delicious cookies. As she puts them in the cookie jar, she shakes her finger at her young son and says, "Now don't you forget young man — stay out of this cookie jar, these are for later when our company arrives." After what seems like an eternity to the little boy, his mother leaves the kitchen. He heads straight for the cookie jar, dragging a chair behind him. With his hand inside the jar, grandpa catches the little boy and with a twinkle in his eye, and a very transparent false admonition says, "Young man, you know those cookies are for later when the company arrives." And the little boy says, "but, grandpa ... they are soooo good, and there are so many — mom will never miss just one." And grandpa smiles and responds, "Aw ... I suppose you are right. Go ahead. In fact, I bet she won't even miss two. I'll have one with ya!"

Did it bother Jesus that this mother was putting her hand in the cookie jar that Jesus said was for the Jews? Not one bit. And — that's the same Jesus who loves you and answers your prayers too. He will never ever say to you, "My love is for someone else."

> Your adornment must not be merely external — braiding the hair, and wearing gold jewelry, or putting on dresses; but let it be the hidden person of the heart, with the imperishable quality of a gentle and quiet spirit, which is precious in the sight of God.
> — *1ˢᵗ Peter 3:3,4*

I Found My Mother in the Bible

… and … my bet is that many who read this could say the same thing about their own mothers when they read these two verses from the little letter of 1ˢᵗ Peter. I know for sure many of my friends could say it, because I knew their mothers. All of us grew up together. As I pen these words of gratitude to God today for my mother on Mother's Day, I can't help but be reminded of just how thankful I should be, because not all children are so fortunate. Is she perfect? Of course not, but she's darn close.

So many people interpret the first part of this text wrong, thinking that women have to look plain and can't "dress up." Hogwash. Peter is merely drawing a line between ostentatious ("look at me"), prideful beauty, and where the focus of real beauty is — the person inside the heart. It is the perfect picture of my mother, and maybe yours too. She can look snappy and well-dressed with the best, but the beauty of my mother that is so profound and has blessed so many people over the years, is the beauty that resides permanently … in her heart.

I have had the blessing of seeing that beauty many, many times, and in many forms, but perhaps never so fair as the focus of the beauty Peter mentions here. Her gentle and peaceful spirit when I have come to her hurt, or confused, or defeated, or without a place to lay my head — even as a grown man. Doesn't matter what other focus she may have, or what other mood she is in, the inner beauty of her heart is still as beautiful as ever and shows itself instantly, when it comes to caring for her "baby boy," which she still calls me, even though I was born in 1953.

The loveliness of her heart is very precious in the sight of God. It is precious in my sight too.

My mom. I told you she was a snappy dresser!

> "He who is without sin among you,
> let him be the first to throw a stone at her."
> — *John 8:7*

The Opinion That Really Matters

There is no meter in the world that can measure the depth or the power of the hope and encouragement in the words of Jesus between John 8:3-11. The scene is a woman caught red-handed in adultery being dragged into the street by the "religious elite" with the penalty of being stoned to death staring her in the face. Trying to set a trap for Jesus, they asked Him what should be done. The words in John 8:7 record His response.

I know what it feels like to be publicly accused ... even by "well-meaning, church folks," and I am betting that there may be one or two who read this who also knows how that feels. The temptation is to feel angry, or defeated or ashamed. The reality is, the only opinion about your life that really matters is Jesus's opinion. And Jesus believes our sins are forgivable. All of them.

Something else really fascinating is recorded here, too. Jesus writes something in the sand. It is the only time in all of scripture that He writes something. The Lord Jesus Christ, the Son of God could have written a library during His time on earth. He didn't. That tells me that whatever it was that Jesus wrote here, must have been really something ... here — in the middle of defending an adulterous woman who was being humiliated by the "religious elite." Jesus said, "He who is without sin among you, let him be the first to throw a stone at her." Those words, and whatever it was that He wrote in the sand after that, caused every single one of the "religious elite" accusing her, to turn around and leave. Jesus's opinion is the only opinion that really matters.

The rest of the story: Jesus asks, "Woman, where are they? Did no one condemn you?" She said, "No one, Lord." And Jesus said, "I do not condemn you either. Go. From now on sin no more." Friend, if you have ever been accused of something — justified, or unjustified — don't lose one minute of sleep over it. Let Jesus handle your accusers, He is very good at it. What they think doesn't matter anyway. The only opinion that really matters is Jesus's opinion, and Jesus believes all your sins can be forgiven. All of them. Did I say that already? All you have to do is ask Him.

For I delight in loyalty rather than sacrifice, and in the knowledge of
God rather than burnt offerings.
— *Hosea 6:6*

Ritual or Relationship — What's It Gonna Be?

This little verse from the prophet, Hosea, is like a "golden key" if you
are interested in unlocking a deep and joyful relationship with God. It
is so important to God that in various and beautiful ways, it is repeated
over and over in the Bible: 1st Samuel 15:22; Psalms 40:6-8; 51:16,17;
Amos 6:21-24. Especially beautiful is Micah 6:6-8. Matthew 9:13 has
the words of Jesus Himself. Take the time to look them up, it's more
than worth it.

The key is the difference between mere ritual, and a real relationship with
God. This world has no shortage of people who are very good at the
former and absolutely miserable at the latter. God wants hearts that burn
for intimacy with Him, that have compassion for those who are dying
without Jesus, that have genuine love for each other, that bring confession
from deep in the soul and are willing to kneel in contrition. Without
these things, God couldn't care less about our "burnt offering church
services" full of stand now, sit now, sing here, pray here, 3-points-and-a-
poem sermons. I know, because I've been there.

If your *church* is like that, you can help change it. If your *life* is like that,
you **_must_** change it, if your true desire is a close and joyful relationship
with God. Try it, you'll like it, trust me.

And He is the radiance of His glory and the exact representation of His nature, and upholds all things by the word of His power. When He had made purification of sins, He sat down at the right hand of the Majesty on high ...
— *Hebrews 1:3*

Meet Jesus Christ

It seems almost impossible that over 20 years has passed since the movie "Meet Joe Black" was made (1998). Brad Pitt starred as the Grim Reaper, or, the Death Angel. Well, meet the exact opposite today — meet Jesus Christ. This is one of the mightiest verses in all the Bible that speaks of just who Jesus is, and what He has done in the lives of all God's children who have trusted Him as Savior. Let's look, phrase by phrase, at this incomparably beautiful verse together, shall we?

1. — **He is the radiance of His glory** — this means that everything that combines to produce the glory of God shines out of the person of Jesus.

2. — **the exact representation of His person** — picture here, if you will, a die and the coin that it cuts. When you see the coin, you are also seeing the exact form of the die that cut it. Taken together, this phrase and the one before it mean that when you are looking at Jesus, you are unmistakably looking at God Himself.

3. — **upholds all things by the word of His power** — when you look up at the night sky and see all those beautiful stars shining, it is because Jesus said "Let there be light." ... and He has never rescinded that command. Their light continues today, as does everything else in the universe — upheld by, and because of, the word of His power.

4. — **when He had purged our sins** — Everyone knows what "purged" means, right? Cleaned out, removed, swept away. And here it is important to note that it is past tense. Do we still sin today? Of course we do, and it can cost us dearly ... but the eternal penalty of it — Jesus has already paid for it and erased it.

5. — **sat down at the right hand of the Majesty on high** — "sat down" means that the work of purging our sins is finished — and will stay finished. And "at the right hand of the Majesty on high" means the place of power, position and authority.

Of all the choices a person has today of where they could place their faith and hope, the best choice — always — is the person of the Lord Jesus Christ. If you have never met Him before, today would be a good day to do it.

In the year of King Uzziah's death I saw the Lord sitting on a throne,
lofty and exalted, with the train of His robe filling the temple.
Seraphim stood above Him, each having six wings: with two he
covered his face, and with two he covered his feet, and with two he
flew.
— *Isaiah 6:1,2*

What A Real Angel Looks Like

Have you ever wondered what angels really look like? I have, many
a time. And I bet you have, too. We get at least a glimpse of one kind
of angel in this breath-taking and majestic vision of Isaiah. One day
we will know, but for now we can only imagine what it must be like to
actually be standing in the presence of the Lord where these angels exist.

For all we don't know about angels, one thing I believe we can safely
assume is that they don't have the appearance of cuddly, chubby little
babies with stubby little wings like we see so often in paintings. In
addition to the incredibly majestic seraphim described here, God placed
a Cherubim with a flaming sword to guard the tree of life in the Garden
of Eden. Remember?

Another thing I believe we can safely say is that they can be very powerful.
Just two angels completely destroyed the cities of Sodom and Gomorrah.
The archangel, Michael defeated lucifer and a third of the angelic host all
by himself. And ... just a single angel destroyed the entire Assyrian army
(185,000 men) overnight.

So, where's the hope and encouragement for you and me in all this? Don't
forget — these angelic beings right here? God Himself created them, and
commands them. The same God who created you. And loves you.

"But seek first His kingdom and His righteousness, and all these
things will be added to you."
— *Matthew 6:33*

First Things First

Ever get your priorities out of order? I know I have to raise MY hand
on that one. More than once. Or twice. We all get caught up in the
"necessities" of life — how will I eat, how will I pay the bills, how will
I replace the worn out clothes in the closet, how will I provide for my
family? Jesus has the solution right here before your very eyes: get your
priorities straight.

In this passage from Matthew, Jesus was teaching His disciples about
that very thing. And what He taught them was, "seek first the kingdom
of God and His righteousness" ... and don't worry about the future,
because you don't need to. It doesn't mean not to continue to work
hard. Doesn't mean not to continue to plan wisely. Doesn't mean not to
continue to prepare diligently for the future (all actions which the Bible
repeatedly commends). — But — as God's children what we need to
always remember is this: the ultimate success of our work, our plans, our
preparation, is driven by how well we "seek first the kingdom of God and
His righteousness." THAT should always be priority #1. THEN, "all
these things will be added unto you." It is a promise — straight from
Jesus.

And He has said to me, "My grace is sufficient for you, for power is perfected in weakness." Most gladly, therefore, I will rather boast about my weaknesses, so that the power of Christ may dwell in me.
— *2ⁿᵈ Corinthians 12:9*

The Security Blanket

I love this verse like Charlie Brown's friend, Linus Van Pelt, loves his security blanket.

Reason #1 — "He said." In the original language the verb tense means what follows is "a settled fact, never to change."

Reason #2 — I don't have to be ashamed of being weak. As it is used here, "weak" is NOT the same as being afraid or being a coward. In fact, the weaker I am, the more evident and powerful is Christ's strength in my life.

Reason #3 — the picture of the resting of Christ's power on my life. A.T. Robertson beautifully describes the word "rest" here in his Word Pictures: "to fix a tent upon, here upon Paul himself by a bold metaphor, as if the Shechinah glory of the Lord was overshadowing him — the power of the Lord Jesus." Talk about a security blanket!

And what was true for Paul is true for you and me, too.

"I am the Light of the world; he who follows Me will not walk in the
darkness, but will have the Light of life."
— *John 8:12*

Hey! Watch Where You are Going!

Ever had those words shouted at you before? I have. More than once.
I needed someone to shout them to me one night when I walked outside
our house in the dark, turned the corner (or so I thought) and ran smack
into the concrete corner of our house. I hit it so hard that I saw a big
flash of light inside my head — not just a few of those tiny little blue
sparks. My wife, Claudia, still laughs about it to this day. Probably
because there was a light switch right beside the door that I could have
flipped on and the whole thing would have been avoided. I could write
a book on "Dumb Things Not To Do."

With the destination of our very souls hanging in the balance, I wonder
how many times God has wanted to shout the same thing to us? "Hey!
Watch where you are going!" — with the Light Switch right beside us
the whole time. The darkness of an eternity separated from God is too
terrible for words. Jesus tells us here that He is the Light Switch that lets
us avoid that path. In Him there is no darkness at all. The best news is
that the light of life in Jesus is for the whole world — no matter who you
are or what you have done — and that Light is as close as a whispered
prayer.

Then I heard the voice of the Lord, saying, "Whom shall I send, and
who will go for Us?" Then I said, "Here am I. Send me!"
— *Isaiah 6:8*

Pick Me! Pick Me!

When I was just a boy in grade school, we used to play various sports
games during recess and P.E. I was never even close to being one of the
better players, but it was exhilarating just to be in the game.

The worst part of it all however, was the "picking process." It was
excruciating for those of us in the "mediocre to inept" category, standing
there while the two team leaders for the day took turns picking their
players. Close friends got picked first whether they could play good or
not, then the better players ... then my group. You would always start out
hoping to get picked early, a sign of status and popularity — then that
would give way to "just please don't let me be last."

This vision of Isaiah (vs. 1-8) is one of the most majestic in all the Bible
and yet I think, "Here is one of the greatest prophets of the Bible who
knew the anxiety of "the picking process." The breathtaking vision of
God on His throne, surrounded and worshiped by the 6-winged Seraphim
angels, drove Isaiah to the realization of his own unworthiness. But the
best part was after he was cleansed and his sins were forgiven — this
verse right here — when God asked the question, "Whom shall I send,
and who will go for Us?"

There was Isaiah, standing there twitching, wanting to be picked. His
hands start to wriggle at his side, then he can't stand it any longer. Arms
go up in the air, hands waving, jumping up and down, "Over here!! Over
here, Lord!! Look over here!! Here I am, Lord!! Oh please, please pick
me ... pick me!!!"

When you become one of God's forgiven children, God Himself picks
you as a part of His team and asks, "Can I send you? Will you go for
Me?" Wouldn't it be wonderful if we all responded the same way Isaiah
did?

For this reason also, God highly exalted Him, and bestowed on Him the name which is above every name, so that at the name of Jesus every knee will bow, of those who are in heaven and on earth and under the earth, and that every tongue will confess that Jesus Christ is Lord, to the glory of God the Father.
— *Philippians 2:9-11*

Truth be Told

Sometimes it isn't so easy to be a Christian, is it? Even in places where we are free to worship as we want. We seem to find ourselves in an ever-decreasing minority while the world around us grows ever more evil. Because of that, if you are a believer in Jesus, you may be one of those who finds your life of faith a challenge. You may have to go to a workplace every day where you are belittled or made fun of because of your faith. When your family gets together, you may be the only person who likes to pray before a meal, or who likes to give Jesus His rightful place during Christmas, amidst the frenzy of everyone tearing open presents on Christmas Day. You may have a neighbor who purposely tries to destroy your peace because they know you are a Christian.

... But ...

Truth be told, one day, none of that will matter because one day the truth WILL be told. By everyone. Truth be told (no matter who doesn't believe it), Jesus is exactly who the Bible says He is — King of Kings and Lord of Lords, the Alpha and Omega, the Beginning and the End. And truth be told, one day every single person — whether they believed it or not when they had the chance, whether they want to or not ... will bow to their knees and confess with their own tongue, the truth that you and I already know — Jesus Christ is Lord.

One thing I have asked from the Lord, that I shall seek: that I may dwell in the house of the Lord all the days of my life, to behold the beauty of the Lord and to meditate in His temple.
— *Psalms 27:4*

Longing For Home

We all have desires, don't we? Some of them are very strong. Sometimes it even seems that our desires control us instead of us controlling them. We are a society that hates to wait for anything — especially when it comes to something we deeply desire. The credit card debt in the United States is stark testimony to that. I would venture to say that one of the strongest desires of people is longing for home. I know exactly how strong that desire is. I have lived in Brazil for many years now, but longing for Texas never leaves my heart.

In Psalm 27:4, King David gives expression to the passionate desire that burns in the hearts of all true Christians. Oh, we all ask Him for things from time to time; we desire this thing or that — but here, in verse 4, is the banner that waves high over all of it. Longing for home in heaven. We can't rush this desire though, no sir. This one is all God's timing. We can't put it on a credit card. Our "gotta have it now" frenzy is powerless here. All we can do is thirst for it, and dream of it. Until God says it is time.

I have had friends and family precious and loved beyond words (as I am sure you have, too), for whom God has said it was time: my grandparents, my brother-in-law Mike Jones, aunts and uncles, Mac and Lynda Sticker, my first pastor, Millard Bennett, and many others. For all of them, the beauty of this verse is no longer a dream or a wish. Safe and sound and at home in heaven, and beholding the beauty of the Lord has become real for them — and eternal. And one day when God says it is time, we will see that beauty, too. It is our inheritance as children of God. We won't have to long for home any more.

You are from God, little children, and have overcome them; because
greater is He who is in you than he who is in the world.
— *1ˢᵗ John 4:4*

You Are A Winner

The devil starts working on us early, doesn't he? Trying to convince
us that we are weak, that we are inferior, that we are losers. In school
year after year I had friends who were elected most beautiful, or most
handsome. Not me. I had others who were voted most popular. Not
me. My grades were nowhere near one of my best friend's valedictorian
level. Was I mentally inferior? I watched while other friends became
popular sports athletes. Allergies and resulting breathing problems kept
me from being a part of that group. Was I physically inferior? Today,
the world is full of much better preachers and theologians than me. Am
I vocationally inferior?

The devil uses all sorts of things in our lives, doesn't he? Never resting
in his goal to convince us that we are not good enough, not strong
enough, that we are defeated before we even begin to fight. And it
is a lie. Maybe he whispers in your ear today that you can't beat an
addiction, or that after falling down in life you can't make your family
proud of you again, or after losing a girlfriend or boyfriend you are not
good enough for someone to want you, or love you again. He has many
arrows in his arsenal that he throws at us to try to make us feel defeated
and unworthy. All lies. How can you know that?

It is a lie because if you are a Christian, "greater is He who is in you
than he who is in the world." Not some of the time. *All* of the time.
You are a blood-bought child of God, indwelled by the Holy Spirit of
God. Not some of the time. *All* of the time. And He has the power to
kick the devil like the dog he is. Not some of the time. *All* of the time.
To paraphrase something I read the other day: "The devil whispers to
the child of God, "You cannot withstand the storm." The child of God
whispers to the devil, "**I AM** the storm."

The King of Kings and Lord of Lords is your heavenly Father — and He
is with you all the time. You are the devil's worst nightmare. Make no
mistake about it — you are a winner.

Make for yourself an ark of gopher wood …
Thus Noah did; according to all that God had commanded him, so
he did.
— *Genesis 6:14a, 22*

Attempting Great Things For God

In the "library of well-worn phrases," the church of today certainly has its share. One of those phrases has to be: "attempt great things FOR God, expect great things FROM God." It is invigorating and encouraging, and there are some wonderful churches that actually do it. The only problem is — not many individuals actually do it. Let's be honest, if we were to build a boat for God today that reflected the size of our faith, most of us would end up with something like a canoe … or a matchbox, instead of an ark. I'm right, aren't I?

Noah built a boat that was a football field and a half in length and taller than a 4-story building. And it was even wider than it was tall. You can read all about it between verses 14 to 22. He did it because God told him to do it — with only his sons for help, in the middle of the desert, and up until that point the Bible makes no mention of rain at all, much less a flood. Can you imagine the cat-calling and ridicule he must have had to endure from all those around him? And yet, Noah did everything God commanded, exactly the way He said to do it.

Is God going to ask you to build an ark? Probably not. But then, He didn't ask anyone else to build another one either. However, if you were willing to do "all that God commands" the way Noah was, who knows what great things God might want to accomplish through you. I already know what you are thinking: "There was only one Noah." And, that would be true — but — consider this:

… there is only one you, as well.

But about midnight Paul and Silas were praying and singing hymns
of praise to God, and the prisoners were listening to them;
— *Acts 16:25*

This Little Light of Mine

I love this old song. Normally it is relegated to being sung only by children's groups in church, and that is such a shame because even with its simple melody and words, it has a convicting message for adults. There have been various "versions" of it over the years, but they all say, essentially, the same thing: Don't hide your witness for Christ — no matter what.

Often times we think we could never be like the great characters of the Bible, but this is one area that we can. The "midnight" of Paul and Silas here can be lots of things besides just an hour on the clock, can't it? It can be the middle of a crushing trial in your life, or the inexorable approach of something bad — like knowing you are going to be laid off work.

Joni Eareckson Tada is one of the best examples of this verse I have ever seen. She has received numerous awards and honorary degrees, recorded songs, has visited over 47 countries and written more than 50 books. All from the confines of a wheelchair — her prison since 1967, when, as a perfectly healthy 17-year-old girl, a diving accident paralyzed her and changed her life forever. Her attitude when asked about it — "If by my being in this chair, I have more opportunities to share the love of Jesus ... then I am glad I am in it." That is praying and singing hymns to God in prison at midnight.

You can do it too. Just like Joni, just like Paul and Silas. There are lots of prisoners out there who need to know the love of Jesus. They could be listening to you, just like these prisoners were listening to Paul and Silas. Perhaps hearing your prayer, or your song in the middle of their "midnight" — or yours — is the "little light" the Lord will use to change their lives.

Sitting down, He called the twelve and said to them, "If anyone wants to be first, he shall be last of all and servant of all."
— *Mark 9:35*

The Pecking Order

This was a famous phrase around our house growing up. Funny and famous. Well, I guess it was funny depending on where you were in the pecking order. One example: Whenever we had a family gathering, there was never room enough at the "main table" for everyone. When it was time to eat, the older adults got the "main table" and the young kids got a card table. Even younger kids got TV trays. Everyone always looked forward to "moving up" in the pecking order as they got older, and never hesitated to tell the ones finally younger than them, when they complained, "That's just your position in the pecking order."

Jesus tells us that as Christians we have a "pecking order," too. His very own hand-picked disciples argued about which of them was the greatest and who would sit on His left side and right side in the kingdom of heaven. Or in other words, who got to sit at the "main table" and who got the "card table." Jesus dropped the hammer on their pride right here, and turned their own ideas of the pecking order upside down: whoever wanted to be first would be last of all and servant of all. As always, Jesus is our best example, telling them in the next chapter (10:45) as they continued to argue about the pecking order, that He did not come to be served, but to serve, and to give His life a ransom for many.

Jesus's instructions are never hard to understand — and they are always important. What a difference it would make in our lives if we would dedicate ourselves to what Jesus tells us here in Mark 9:35. At least three things would happen almost immediately:

1. It would stop a LOT of bickering in church.
2. People who don't know Jesus and who don't go to church would find themselves wanting to go instead of making fun of it — because they would be seeing it the way God intended it to be.
3. In our quest for hope and encouragement from God's word, Jesus is telling us here a sure way to secure a very high pecking order position on God's list. The list that counts.

Now may our Lord Jesus Christ Himself and God our Father, who has loved us and given us eternal comfort and good hope by grace, comfort and strengthen your hearts in every good work and word.
— *2ⁿᵈ Thessalonians 2:16,17*

Personal Attention

Let me see if I can strike some kindred nerves here:

1. You call a place trying to get some urgent and important information. Instead of getting a person who can give you some personal help, you get a recording — Press '1' if ... press '2' if ... press '3' if ... press '4' if ... all the way to about '10.' Of course, none of the options are your problem so you just wait for a real person. Instead, the list simply starts over again ... Press '1' if ...
2. You give up on the phone and go to the office. Instead of being able to leave your name, you have to take a number to wait in line. You are number 59. After what seems like an eternity, an intercom voice comes on and says, "Now serving number 7."
3. After waiting forever, you actually get in front of a live person — who can neither spell nor pronounce your name correctly, and who cares nothing and knows nothing about what you need. They give you the name of the person who (supposedly) does. They are not there that day — sound familiar? In this day and age, wouldn't a little personal attention be nice?

Well, read these verses again and pay close attention to the word "Himself." This is a wonderful passage from the Bible about hope and encouragement, and comfort, and it comes with the personal attention of the Lord Jesus Christ Himself — to you. Not from a friend, not from a teacher, not from a book. From the Lord. Himself. Personal attention to your need for hope, and encouragement, and comfort and strength. And not in just a few things ... in every good work and word throughout your life.

> For my father and my mother have forsaken me, but the Lord will
> take me up.
> — *Psalms 27:10*

Wanted

Many of us today know the blessing of being part of a family, and the feeling of being surrounded by that family, both in times of joy and in times of trouble. Feeling the joy of being loved and wanted by our family is something that money just can't buy.

This devotional today is for another group. It is for those who don't know that feeling. Those who may have never been a part of a family Thanksgiving, or family Christmas for a long, long time. Those who feel that their only two companions today are rejection and loneliness. Abandoned by friends, rejected by family, with only the pillow of loneliness on which to rest your head. For this group; know today that you are not alone, you are not unloved and you are not unwanted.

If you will but let Him into your life, there is another Father, who wants to be your heavenly Father, around whose table you are always welcome ... who will take you in, even when everyone else has thrown you out. A Father who has loved you since before the world began and who loves you still today, who had His eye on you even when you were still in your mother's womb, and who had a plan written for every day of your entire life — before you were even born.

Take heart today, my friend. You are not alone. The One who loves you more than anyone else ever has ... has never stopped wanting to be your heavenly Father. Not for a day, not for an hour, not for a minute, not for a second. You are welcome and you are wanted all the time. Once you are family, you are family forever. You are His child.

But may it never be that I would boast, except in the cross of our Lord Jesus Christ, through which the world has been crucified to me, and I to the world.
— *Galatians 6:14*

Keeping The Main Thing The Main Thing

Some of the most wonderful people I have ever met in my life, I met in church. With a smile I say that some of the most "challenging" individuals I have met ... have also been in church. I'm sure you have met one or two of the latter examples as well. You know the type. They wear their religiosity like a diamond necklace around their neck. Nose so high in the air that you wonder how they don't get nosebleed. Yes?

The apostle Paul, who wrote this letter to the Galatians had every right to be that irritating kind of person. He had a religious pedigree as long as your arm. You can find the list in Philippians 3: 3-6, check it out. Instead of boasting in his own accomplishments and position, however, Paul offers this head-bowed, humble, yet emphatic declaration: "Far be it from me that I should ever glory, except in the cross of our Lord Jesus Christ." This came from the lips of one of the most fierce and ruthless persecutors in the history of the early church before he became a believer in Jesus.

A real encounter with Jesus does that to a person. It reorganizes your priorities. Your list of what to take pride in. When to take a stand ... and when to take a knee.

But whatever things were gain to me, those things I have counted
as loss for the sake of Christ. More than that, I count all things
to be loss in view of the surpassing value of knowing Christ Jesus
my Lord, for whom I have suffered the loss of all things, and count
them but rubbish so that I may gain Christ, and may be found in
Him, not having a righteousness of my own derived from the Law,
but that which is through faith in Christ, the righteousness which
comes from God on the basis of faith,
— *Philippians 3:7-9*

Keeping The Main Thing The Main Thing, part 2

Remember that religious pedigree I mentioned in the devotional from
Galatians 6:14? Here's that very pedigree (from verses 4 — 6, just before
you get to our text today): Circumcised on the eighth day, of the stock
of Israel, of the tribe of Benjamin, a Hebrew of the Hebrews: concerning
the law, a Pharisee; concerning zeal, persecuting the church; concerning
the righteousness which is in the law, blameless. That's 7 sheepskins
hanging on Paul's wall. And just so you will have an idea of the impact
of the last one about "blameless as to the law" — it means he kept over
600 laws of the Torah ... perfectly.

What you read in the verses here starting with verse 7, is Paul's own
response to his "religious pedigree." Did Paul strut around with his chest
all puffed out because of all this? Nope. Quite the contrary. After his
smackdown with the risen Lord Jesus Christ on the road to Damascus (to
bring Christians back in chains), he took all those sheepskins off his wall,
wadded them up, and threw them in the trash. He didn't even put them
in a drawer somewhere to save them as keepsakes. Then ... he turned his
face to the horizon, and the change Jesus wrought in his life — and he
never looked back.

Our joy, our hope, our encouragement will NEVER come from our
"religious pedigree." It comes from our own "quest for Christ," and the
fullness of understanding just what He has done in our lives.

Therefore the Lord Himself will give you a sign: Behold, a virgin
will be with child and bear a son, and she will call His name
Immanuel.
— *Isaiah 7:14*

Jesus is the Real Deal

This is a well-known verse that is popularly used around Christmastime.
But, wait a minute. Isn't it still a long time before Christmas? Yep. It
was a long time before Christmas when these words were first written,
too. About 700 YEARS before. Note the author, Isaiah, the Old
testament prophet. Nope, these words were not original with the angel of
the Christmas story with which we are so familiar — the angel who came
to comfort Joseph about the birth of Jesus.

....The angel quoted Isaiah, and Isaiah got them from God.

It might surprise you to learn that this verse in Isaiah is not unique. There
are other places in the Old Testament that announce the birth of Jesus,
even pinpointing the town, Bethlehem. But here — Isaiah uses words
that indicate Jesus, specifically, with no chance for exceptions — "The
virgin shall conceive ..." Never before, never since, has that happened.
By sheer definition of the word, a virgin cannot become pregnant. The
only exception in all of history is the birth of Jesus Christ.

Other babies have been born with the name, Jesus. Other babies have
been born in Bethlehem. Other babies have been born at Christmas. But
there is only one Jesus Christ.

Tell me, what are the chances ... let's suppose that Joseph and Mary try
to cover up her out of wedlock pregnancy by concocting the wild story
that their son is the long-awaited Messiah. Then by sheer coincidence
he grows up and fits all the Old Testament prophecies written hundreds
of years before right down to the ground, claims to be God in the flesh,
teaches like no one ever taught before, performs miracle after miracle,
rises from the dead, escapes the tomb with Roman guards watching it,
and changes the face of the entire religious world. Permanently. The real
truth is — Jesus Christ is exactly who the Bible says He is.

For the word of God is living and active and sharper than any two-edged sword, and piercing as far as the division of soul and spirit, of both joints and marrow, and able to judge the thoughts and intentions of the heart.

— *Hebrews 4:12*

"He's Got A Knife"

I admit it. I am a big fan of good movies and I use them regularly to illustrate great and eternal truths from the Bible. This is another one of those times.

An all-time favorite movie of mine is Crocodile Dundee. A favorite scene of many people in that movie is where Mick and Sue are approached by several young men at night on a street in New York. One of the young men produces a knife and demands Mick's wallet. Sue says, "Mick, give him your wallet." Mick says with a smile, "What for?" Sue says, "He's got a knife!" Mick grins again and says, "That's not a knife." Then, from a sheath under his jacket he produces a Bowie knife over a foot long, puts it under the young man's nose, grins and says, "THAT'S a knife!" It didn't take the would be thieves long to leave after that.

There are many situations in life today in which this ol' world would like to make us fearful or nervous and say, "He's got a knife." Perhaps a boss or group of workers trying to intimidate a Christian employee, or a peer group putting pressure on a young Christian teenager to ignore their faith ... or, perhaps it is someone threatening to end a relationship because of your faith, and the world says, "He's got a knife."

The most effective knife in the world is described in this verse of the letter to the Hebrews. It is the word of God. Alive. Powerful. It re-defines the concept of "sharp as a razor." It can do far more than separate a set of ribs from a backbone — it can separate the soul from the spirit. It can filet out and lay bare, the thoughts and intents of the heart. It doesn't matter — not even a little bit — what the world tries to pull on you to make you think it has a knife. You pull out God's word, smile ... stick it under the nose of the world and say, "THIS is a knife!"

...,"If you continue in My word, then you are truly disciples of Mine; and you will know the truth, and the truth will make you free."
— *John 8:31,32*

To Tell the Truth

One of the longest running game shows in the history of television is "To Tell the Truth." Three people claim to be the same person. Two are lying, only one is telling the truth. A panel, through a series of questions tries to guess which one.

In a world where many "religions" claim to be telling the truth, our Lord Jesus Christ does something way more profound. He told these people in the gospel of John, and He tells us today that He is not only telling the truth — He IS the truth — in chapter 14, verse 6 of this same book. Believers in Jesus don't just know a set of facts to be true, they know a Person who IS truth itself. And that Person sets them free. Free from the guilt, bondage, burden and penalty of sin. The key? Only this — abide in His word. It will lead you to the faith that creates an eternal relationship with the Lord Jesus Christ, by believing in who He is and what He has done for you. But you must abide there, dear friend. Abide. That is more than a glancing look.

You know, a dictionary is full of truth, too. If you feel crushed by life and by sin, try abiding in one and see how quickly it sets you free. Jesus is different. A lot different. Give Him a chance in your life. Abide in His word, know the truth and let Him set you free.

(Memorial Day 2021) … the Lord Jesus in the night in which
He was betrayed took bread; and when He had given thanks, He
broke it and said, "This is My body, which is for you; do this in
remembrance of Me."
— *1ˢᵗ Corinthians 11:23,24*

Memorial Day

The weekend of Memorial Day is a very famous weekend in the history
of America. They are the days we set aside to give honor and thanks and
remembrance to all the brave men and women in our armed forces who
have given their lives on battlefields all around the world — the ultimate
sacrifice — to preserve and protect the precious freedom that is so special
and unique to America. This weekend is not about "just another holiday
from work," or an excuse to have a backyard party and barbecue. It is
about the sacrifice of real lives of real soldiers … for the precious gift of
freedom.

Jesus created a very special "Memorial Day" too. It is recorded in the
gospels and here, in the Apostle Paul's first letter to the Corinthians.
Today it is known as "The Last Supper," or, "The Lord's Supper," and
sadly, many times, the memorial of it that we observe in church is treated
almost as an afterthought, with almost no emotion at all attached to it.
I have often wondered what attitudes we would have, if we knew that
a particular supper we were eating was going to be the very last one _we_
would ever eat. My bet is that the significance needle would go way up.

The encouragement we have because of Jesus's "do this in remembrance of Me," is almost too wonderful for words, and when we "do" the Lord's Supper in church, our attitude should reflect our gratitude. We talk about being "soldiers of the cross," but the truth is the real Soldier of the cross is Jesus Christ. He was the one who bled there. It was His body that was broken there. He was the one who died there. He was the one who gave the ultimate sacrifice there ... for our precious gift of freedom. Freedom from the penalty and weight of our own sin, freedom from death and the grave ... and the joy of knowing that heaven is a place we call "home."

Then you will call upon Me and come and pray to Me, and I will listen to you. You will seek Me and find Me when you search for Me with all your heart.
— *Jeremiah 29:12,13*

With All Your Heart

"With all my heart" is a phrase we often use, but rarely mean, except in the most serious or darkest of times. When Jeremiah wrote these words from God, it was the darkest of times for the nation of Israel. It had been destroyed, and to add insult to defeat, many were taken captive to Babylon, the capital city of their conquerors.

The words in these two verses are so powerful and beautiful, however, even in the middle of this very dark time. One reason is because God is letting Israel know that this time wouldn't last forever, and that He was going to restore their future and their hope. And, even though these events happened over 2,500 years ago, the truth of Jeremiah's words reach all the way to you and me today.

I know what it is like to go through the darkest of times and I bet some who are reading this do too. In these verses, God promises to hear, and to listen to us — and be "findable." So, how do you reconcile heart-wrenching sadness and disappointment with the promise of God in these words? I can only tell you how I was able to find the answer from the dark time in my own personal life, and that the key to understanding for me was in the words "with all your heart."

"With all your heart" doesn't mean with all your mind or knowledge. It doesn't mean with all your strength or passion. It is more than sincerity. I believe "with all your heart" happens when you give absolutely everything you are (the good with the bad) to God, and arrive at that place where you truly feel the presence of God beside you, just like He said He would be. It is the place where, even though your prayers haven't been answered in the way you had hoped, you feel an indescribable peace, and a hope because God fills your heart with His own assurance that he has something better for you than your problems. For me it was when He told me, "You don't need to cry any more. You are still here because I have more for you do to … and because I love you."

"Or what man is there among you who, when his son asks for a loaf, will give him a stone? Or if he asks for a fish, he will not give him a snake, will he? If you then, being evil, know how to give good gifts to your children, how much more will your Father who is in heaven give what is good to those who ask Him!"
— *Matthew 7:9-11*

Knowing What To Give Someone

How many times do you suppose all of us have wondered about that at one time or another? Someone we truly care about has a birthday, or anniversary and we want to do our best to make sure our gift will be special to them. It isn't always easy to know what might be the best thing to give.

There is one person though, who always knows the best thing to give someone. That person is our Heavenly Father. Jesus teaches here about how God, who is also our Heavenly Father, knows how to give us — and will always give us — good things, if we will just give Him the chance. Our part is to ask (see verses 7 and 8).

Sometimes we may not understand what God gives us, sometimes we may not even agree with what God gives us, but — that doesn't mean it isn't good. Sometimes a challenge is best for us, instead of the chest full of diamonds we ask for. Sometimes without realizing it, we can ask for something dangerous, so God gives us something less. Sort of like a 7-year-old who asks his father for a Corvette and his father gives him a bicycle instead.

Our Heavenly Father hears and answers our prayers, but He will never, ever, give us what is not good for us. *We* may choose from time to time something that isn't good for us, but God never does that. He always knows the best thing to give us, and always gives good things to those who ask.

In Him, you also, after listening to the message of truth, the gospel
of your salvation-having also believed, you were sealed in Him
with the Holy Spirit of promise, who is given as a pledge of our
inheritance, with a view to the redemption of God's own possession,
to the praise of His glory.
— *Ephesians 1:13,14*

The Guarantee

When you purchase something, one of the things you are always careful to
look for — especially if the item is expensive — is the guarantee that comes
with it. Let's say you found a TV and home entertainment system you just
fell in love with. Cost: $8,000.00. Guarantee: 2 days. Will you buy it
just because you love it, with a guarantee of just 2 days? I doubt it. The
salesman offers it for $6,000.00 with the same guarantee. Will you buy it
now? I doubt it.

For the one who may be giving a careful look at Jesus today, here is a deal
to really fall in love with. The offer, the item, the guarantee and the
Guarantor mentioned here in Ephesians is nothing less than exhilarating
(not to mention life-changing):

• The item: the gospel of Christ.
• The offer: salvation and eternal life through faith in Him.
• The guarantee: the Holy Spirit Himself — sealed, iron clad, irrevocable,
  immutable, unconditional, eternal.
• The Guarantor: the Lord Jesus Christ ("in Him"). Your destiny with
  eternity in heaven will not change.

Cost for you and me: $0.00

Delight yourself in the Lord;
and He will give you the desires of your heart.
— *Psalms 37:4*

I Will Grant You Three Wishes

How many times have we all heard that little phrase at the beginning of a joke about finding a genie in a bottle? Incredibly, there are some in the "ministry by the miracle business" today who look at what our God does for us just about like that. The real truth of how God works, and the desires of our hearts is much, much better. For real hope and encouragement that lasts, it just doesn't get any better than this verse in the Psalms right here.

First, and very important — which desires are mentioned here? Desires of the flesh? That "I just can't live without it" craving? Nope. It is much better than that. It is the desires of your heart that God will give to you. It is those deep places of your soul ... where things reside that money could never hope to buy or fix; where the roots of real peace and joy grow deep and firm. That is where this promise lives.

Second, and very important as well is the key to God's promise here — "Delight yourself in the Lord." It is more than just enjoying reading the Bible, for example, or even these devotionals. "In the Lord" means that His ways, His will, and His heart are the abiding passions of your life. And "delight" — oh boy — in the language of the Old Testament this means "a delicate, or soft luxuriousness." Imagine being cold and lying down on top of the most comfortable, warm blanket or cover you can remember in your whole life (for me it is one of those really thick, goose down comforters). Now wrap yourself in it. That is the Hebrew idea of "delight."

Snuggle up and get all comfy inside that "delight," and God will give you a lot more than three wishes.

And the wolf will dwell with the lamb, and the leopard will lie down with the young goat, and the calf and the young lion and the fatling together; and a little boy will lead them.
— *Isaiah 11:6*

Peace

From the speaking of it with two fingers held up in a "V" in the "hippie generation" of the early '70s, to its use with the word "accord" attached by various governments of countries to signify an agreement that ends conflict, the word "peace" is a universally familiar concept. Familiar concept — unfamiliar reality. It exists only in varying degrees of imperfection, regardless of whether one refers to it in a worldwide sense — or a personal sense.

On the night of Jesus's birth which we celebrate every year, the angel proclaimed, "... and on earth, peace toward men of good will." It was the announcement of the ages of the hope and opportunity for peace. Real peace. The Christmas story, when Jesus first came, was the beginning of that kind of peace.

This beloved and familiar passage from Isaiah before us here — is actually the END of the story. This is the peace Jesus will bring with Him when

He comes the **_second_** time. And it was written about 700 YEARS before the night of Jesus's birth. God has had His plan in place for a looooong, long time. A plan that includes peace for the entire world, a plan that includes peace even for the entire animal kingdom — and a plan that includes peace for you, too. Perfect peace. But, the best news is that you don't have to wait for Jesus to come back to have that kind of peace — you can have it right now, just for trusting in Jesus today. Have a look in Isaiah 26:3.

Jesus said to them, "Truly, truly, I say to you, before Abraham was
born, I Am."
— *John 8:58*

The Master Planner

"You've got to get up pretty early in the morning to get the best of
_____." (You fill in the blank.) That's a time-
honored phrase we are all familiar with, right? It means it is nigh on to
impossible to be better at something than the person named at the end of
the phrase, or to outsmart, out-plan, or surprise that person. It is a great
phrase to illustrate the perfect, planning mind of God. "You've got to get
up pretty early in the morning to find God without His plan in place."
In fact, it is impossible.

Jesus was saying as much here in this short sentence, to some Jews who
were questioning Him. Short, yet words that reach from eternity to
eternity. If you think God's plan to love you and give you a way to
heaven didn't start until Christmas day, think again, my friend. Jesus
existed before Abraham — AND Adam and Eve. He was there in the
beginning with God before Eve even bit the apple. In fact, it was Jesus
Himself (because Jesus is absolutely God) who spoke everything into
existence (John 1:1-3,14).

There are two magnificent points of hope and encouragement for us today
in these few words from Jesus Himself:

1. Jesus is MUCH more than just a good man or a prophet. He claimed
   with His own lips to be the living and reigning Lord God Almighty.
   And that is exactly who He is.
2. God has loved you for a loooooong, LONG, long time. In fact, you
   can't get up early enough in the morning to find a time that He didn't.

All Scripture is inspired by God and profitable for teaching, for
reproof, for correction, for training in righteousness; so that the man
of God may be adequate, equipped for every good work.
— *2nd Timothy 3:16,17*

There's Just Something Missing

Something missing ... maybe, but not in these two majestic verses of
God's Word. We hear this little phrase in all sorts of areas of life, don't
we? Someone tasting a new recipe decides, "It's good, but there's just
something missing." A detective trying to solve a case puts together
a line of evidence, but before he can solve the puzzle, he sees that "there's
just something missing." A design that *almost* works perfectly, but "there's
just something missing." An absent ingredient that prevents something
from being quite right. It can happen in our lives too, can't it?

If you are feeling today that "there's just something missing" in your life,
may I recommend God's Word? No matter where you may have searched
before for that "something missing" in your life, nothing can match how
God's Word can put the missing pieces into your personal puzzle.

First of all, it is from God Himself. No other book can claim that. The
Bible stands alone. Second, look at what it does for you: if you need
wisdom it is God's own teaching, if you need to be disciplined just a bit
(as we all do from time to time), it comes from our Father in heaven
who loves us. If the path of your life has gone off course, God's Word
provides perfect mid-course correction. To be a better person, to be
a better reflection of the Lord, to better follow the teaching of Jesus, to
better demonstrate that you are a son or daughter of God ... it is all right
there in God's Word. And it provides much more than just an "improved
you." Note carefully the fullness of the word "adequate" in the original
language of the Bible — it means "perfected, complete, able to face all
that is demanded in life." And that remains true even though all of us
will still make mistakes. God's Word will see to it that you are completely
equipped to follow and succeed in the path God has created for you.

A person, a life, a human journey complete in every respect — because it
is lived under the eye and love of God. Nothing missing.

'Ah Lord God! Behold, You have made the heavens and the earth by Your great power and by Your outstretched arm! Nothing is too difficult for You ...
— *Jeremiah 32:17*

I Can Handle It

PickensPhotos

There are few things — if any — more breathtaking than gazing up into a clear night sky with no lights from civilization to dim the profound depth of space, and seeing all those stars like diamonds on black velvet. And what we see with our eyes, or even the most powerful telescopes — is only a tiny fraction of that breathtaking sky. And God made it all by His power.

That is the same God who loves you. Deeply. And you can rest assured that whatever you are going through ... there is nothing too difficult for Him. Anything you bring to God in prayer, His response will always be "I can handle it."

... having canceled out the certificate of debt consisting of decrees against us, which was hostile to us; and He has taken it out of the way, having nailed it to the cross.
— *Colossians 2:14*

Debt Free

It is hard to appreciate the exhilarating beauty of those two words unless you have had the experience of drowning in credit card debt like I have. Or some other type of crushing financial debt. You spent what you didn't have and now you can't pay for it because you still don't have it. Not only that, the interest on the debt is so high that your payment never even dents the balance you owe. And you suffocate in debt. Sound familiar?

The law that man was required to follow in order to meet God's moral standards was exactly like that. God's moral standards demand perfection. You can never hope to meet those standards because none of us are perfect. We all make mistakes, we all sin. Moral debt. And the balance grows daily because that's the way we sin. Daily.

What Jesus did changed all that. Permanently. Nowhere in the Bible is it more powerfully described than in Paul's words here. They place a magnificent finality on what Christ accomplished on the cross for you and for me. On the cross Jesus removes a debt you could never hope to pay DOWN, and replaces it with a grace you could never hope to pay FOR. Because it is free. Your sin debt died forever on that cross. Forever. Perfection is no longer needed — just forgiveness, and it is yours for the asking.

> ... And His song will be with me in the night ...
> — *Psalms 42:8b*

The Night Watchman

Have you ever felt the cold, breath-sapping chill of fear in the middle of a nightmare? It happens — even to adults. When it happened to us as children, who doesn't remember the overwhelming sense of security and safety of being held in our mother's arms, or grandmother's arms, singing soft words of comfort to us? It is one of the best feelings in the world.

As adults we no longer have those arms and song to reassure us in the middle of the night — but, still we are not alone. We have something even better. The Night Watchman who created the heavens is never far away from you. As adults, our "nights" do not depend on the sun being absent from the sky. Our cold chill of fear in the night can take many forms: lost job, lost relationship, lost hope, lost health, lost confidence, rejection by those who you love ... fear that tomorrow may be even worse ...

Never fear, the Night Watchman is on duty, faithfully and forever — to hold you and comfort you with His song in the night — all you have to do is open the door and let Him in the room with you.

Therefore if anyone is in Christ, he is a new creature; the old things
passed away; behold, new things have come.
— *2 Corinthians 5:17*

A New Beginning

I will confess, I have had that wish in my own life more times than
I would like to admit. A chance to erase old mistakes, things I wish
I hadn't said ... or done. You may even know what that feels like, too.

For me, one of the best expressions of a new beginning is a new-born
baby. Have you ever held one in your arms? It is one of life's supreme
pleasures. Especially if it is YOUR baby — or grandbaby. You are
looking at, and holding in your arms, a brand new life. A brand new
human being. It always makes me think, "God hasn't given up on the
human race just yet."

A new-born baby is a perfect picture of what this incomparably beautiful verse is all about. When you accept Jesus as your Lord and Savior, God doesn't just "melt you down," pour you into a Christian mold and then make someone new out of the old material. No. He BREAKS your old mold, throws AWAY all the old you, and creates a completely new you. This time a child of God ... and that is a fact that will never change. It is spiritual genetics. It is why Jesus said to Nicodemus, "You must be born again."

And just like a parent who loves holding that new-born baby in their arms, God loves doing the same thing with you. And, He will do it for your whole life, if you will let Him.

(Oh! — and just in case anyone is wondering, the picture is me with my brand new, and VERY handsome grandson, Knox Nathan Adkins)

"I am the rose of Sharon, the lily of the valleys."
"Like a lily among the thorns, so is my darling among the maidens."
— *Song of Solomon 2:1,2*

It's All a Matter of Perspective

Any good photographer will tell you that. Perspective can transform an average photograph into a great one. A different perspective can introduce a whole new attitude or appearance about anything — or anyone.

That is what these two preciously beautiful verses are all about. One can "theologize" about the Song of Solomon until the cows come home, but at the end of the day, it is simply a beautiful letter between a man and a woman deeply in love.

With hushed humility, the woman begins here by saying, "There is nothing special about me. I am as ordinary as the most common of flowers, the lily, that grows everywhere in the Sharon Valley." How very different is the perspective of the man who responds, "Compared to all the others, you are like a single, beautiful flower in the middle of a sea of thorns." That is the special perspective that true love brings.

In the day-by-day temptation to think of yourself as just one more drop of water in the "Sea of the Common," you might be surprised at those around you who see you from a completely different perspective. A beautiful rose in the middle of a sea of thorns. One of those admirers is the Lord of heaven and earth — whose perspective of love finds you very special and beautiful. So much so, in fact, that He was willing to die for you to prove it.

It doesn't get much more special than that.

"No one, after lighting a lamp, puts it away in a cellar nor under a basket, but on the lampstand, so that those who enter may see the light."
— *Luke 11:33*

Light Source

I have never known anyone who enjoyed feeling useless, have you? "Oh hot diggity, I'm useless, I can hardly contain my joy!" In truth, it is a horrible feeling, isn't it? Also true: as a Christian, we need never feel like that. Regardless of whether you feel useful to anyone else or not, you are useful to God. That's some pretty good company.

When you accepted Jesus into your life, God did some wonderful things. One of those things was that He put the light of Christ inside you. He lit your lamp ... then He put you, on a lampstand, with a purpose: to shine the light of Christ to others. Through your personal testimony God gives you the honor — and joy — of showing another person how their own life can be changed forever, too. That's a pretty good purpose.

As long as you are alive, you have a purpose — and a privilege. God never takes us off the lampstand. Never. Sometimes though, we take ourselves off it — don't we? We extinguish the light in our secret place of sin, we hide it under our basket of anger, selfishness, envy — the basket of a bad witness. The good news is that God never "blows out our lamp" just because we haven't done the right thing with it. Ask God to forgive those sins, put yourself back in God's hands, and He will put you back on the lampstand where He put you in the first place. Because God wants you to shine.

... and all of you, clothe yourselves with humility toward one another,
for God is opposed to the proud, but gives grace to the humble.
— *1ˢᵗ Peter 5:5*

Your Key to God's Grace

A number of years ago a gifted songwriter from East Texas, Gene
Thomas, wrote an amazingly beautiful song called "The Weed." It was
a conversation between a weed and a bee. The weed admitted to the bee
its lack of beauty, but then said, "... but if by my growing wild, I make
flowers seem more mild, then I guess it's all worthwhile; my being here."
Wouldn't it be a beautiful world if we could all adopt the same kind of
selfless humility of that weed?

From the words he wrote here it would appear that the impulsive, volatile
Peter had finally learned this lesson, and one can't help but wonder
(because the word for "clothe" here is actually "gird") if he had in his
mind one of the greatest scenes of humility in all the Bible — the scene
of Jesus washing the feet of the disciples when it should have been one of
the disciples doing the washing.

The word "opposed" here was used to describe the action of an army
setting itself in battle formation against an enemy. Want God's grace
instead? This verse gives you the simple key. All you have to do is pick
it up and use it.

It is a trustworthy statement: For if we died with Him, we will also
live with Him;
— *2ⁿᵈ Timothy 2:11*

A Ticket Home

A few years ago, a group of my lifelong friends bought tickets for Claudia
and me to do something we could not do for ourselves — go home to
Texas. We just didn't have the money. After years of not being able to
see family and home, because of the love and sacrifice of those friends,
we were able to do it. And the great majority of those friends, I had not
seen for over 40 years ... since we graduated from high school. They are
true friends in every sense of the word, and NO words can describe how
much what they did meant to me.

Our final stop in eternity — heaven — is much the same, isn't it? It is
only because of the love and sacrifice of Jesus that one day we will go to
heaven. We could never get there on our own. It is because of Him that
we have a ticket home. This little verse in 2ⁿᵈ Timothy is but one of many
in the Bible that gives us a beautiful promise: If we give our life to Jesus
on this earth, He will give us His life in heaven. No ifs, ands, or buts.

— But — Living with Jesus!! Wow!! Have you ever spent much time
wondering what that is going to be like? Would you like to spend a few
minutes together on an imaginary trip? Now, to be sure, I have never been
to heaven ... but there is nothing wrong with taking a little "imaginary
journey" there. Especially if we use the Bible itself for transportation.
Shall we go to heaven together for a few minutes?

The first thing you're gonna LOVE when you get there, is your new
body **(Philippians 3:20, 21 — For our citizenship is in heaven, from
which also we eagerly wait for a Savior, the Lord Jesus Christ; who will
transform the body of our humble state into conformity with the body
of His glory, by the exertion of the power that He has even to subject
all things to Himself.)** No more aches, no more pains, no more disease,
missing limbs are back in place. Your body will be perfect because we
will be just like Jesus **(1 John 3:2 — Beloved, now we are children of
God, and it has not appeared as yet what we will be. We know that when
He appears, we will be like Him, because we will see Him just as He**

is.) And then my friend ... before you have had much of a chance to truly enjoy the rush of having a new and perfect body on the outside, comes the even greater rush of being perfect on the inside. For the first time ever, you feel that the weight of your sin is gone — because you have become holy and blameless **(Ephesians 1:4 — just as He chose us in Him before the foundation of the world, that we would be holy and blameless before Him.).** You have also become something else: a real citizen of heaven. Not a visitor, not a tourist. A citizen **(Philippians 3:20 — For our citizenship is in heaven, from which also we eagerly wait for a Savior, the Lord Jesus Christ;).**

Then the reality and the beauty of heaven begins to sink in. It is as beautiful as a bride adorned for her husband **(Revelation 21:2 — And I saw the holy city, new Jerusalem, coming down out of heaven from God, made ready as a bride adorned for her husband.).** You stand there — and stare — at the entrance gate to heaven. It is as tall as a city wall ... and it is one solid pearl — and there are 12 of those gates **(Revelation 21:21 — And the twelve gates were twelve pearls; each one of the gates was a single pearl. And the street of the city was pure gold, like transparent glass.).** As that gate is opened, before you stretches the splendor of heaven, shining as bright as day even without any sun, because the glory of God lights it **(Revelation 21:23 — And the city has no need of the sun or of the moon to shine on it, for the glory of God has illumined it, and its lamp is the Lamb.)** and then suddenly you are on those streets you have heard about for so long — those streets of pure gold, and you and Jesus start out together, walking on them. As you begin to walk, you hear the mighty chorus of heaven's choir. So mighty with its praise of God that it shakes heaven itself like thunder ...

(Revelation 19:6 — Then I heard something like the voice of a great multitude and like the sound of many waters and like the sound of mighty peals of thunder, saying, "Hallelujah! For the Lord our God, the Almighty, reigns.)

You turn onto another street, still feeling that pure gold beneath your feet, and Jesus says, "There are some people here I'd like for you to meet." You look up as an old man with hands like leather takes your hand and shakes it. "Proud to make your acquaintance." he says, "My name is Noah." Standing next to him to greet you, is Abraham. Next to him saying "Pleased to meet you" is the man who God used to part the Red Sea ... not Charlton Heston, but the real Moses. The man who held the original 10 commandments in his hands, shakes YOUR hand. Walking on a little further King David, and then the mighty prophet Isaiah extend to you their welcome, too.

Then, with some extra love and tenderness Jesus stops by a man and his wife and says, "I'd like you to meet my mom and dad for 33 years — Joseph and Mary." And the earthly parents of Jesus embrace you and say, "It's so nice to have you here." A little further down the street, is John the Baptist and the original disciples of Jesus. Then the man who wrote thirteen books of the New Testament walks up and gives you a strong bear hug. The apostle Paul himself.

There are others down the street, but Jesus takes a turn onto another street as He says to you, "This is the street of your family and friends." And you look to see loved ones and family that passed away long ago. They all turn to greet you. Just then, Jesus stops by another large and immaculately beautiful house, but different from all the others, there seems to be no one there … and you ask Jesus, "Who lives here?"

Then — as you turn and look into the eyes that have loved you for an eternity, Jesus smiles and says –

"You do. Welcome home."

While I was fainting away, I remembered the Lord, and my prayer
came to You, into Your holy temple.
— *Jonah 2:7*

Anywhere, Anytime

These two words have been used countless times when issuing a challenge.
Apollo Creed said it at the beginning of the movie "Rocky II" wanting to
goad Rocky into a rematch. However, here in the story of Jonah, it has
a completely different purpose. I so love this little verse. How comforting.
How encouraging. These words from Jonah assure us that no matter what
our station in life, our prayers can reach the heart of God.

When we feel like we have reached the end of our rope ... there is God
with a firm grip on the end of that rope. When life has thrown us
overboard like what happened to Jonah, when it seems that everyone else
has turned their backs, when our love has been thrown back at us with
a laugh, when it seems that all the best of our plans have failed and hope
is a distant memory, there is God — waiting to see if we will call home.

Even if we have been disobedient in our Christian walk like Jonah, and
we wait until there is nowhere else to turn, there is God — ready and
reachable — even if our prayer seems more like a desperate plea than
a prayer. This plea of Jonah, prayed from the belly of a great fish reached
God with no problem at all. And so will yours.

No matter where you are in life, cry out to the One who knows you best
and loves you most — and there God will be — putting His ear to your
lips and His hands around your heart.

Jesus said to her, "I am the resurrection and the life; he who believes in Me will live even if he dies, and everyone who lives and believes in Me will never die ..."
— *John 11:25,26a*

Hope Is Alive And Well

Power, authority, hope and encouragement — all merge together in Jesus.

Don't you just love the way Jesus speaks? Such power — such authority! And when He is talking to Christians, this power and authority seems always to pulse and surge with a deep sense of eternal hope and peace.

Jesus doesn't simply know ABOUT resurrection from the grave — He IS the resurrection.

Jesus doesn't simply teach a path to life — He IS the life.

He tells it like it is — straightforward, to the point and honest. No wavering, no stuttering, no exceptions. Powerful ... and gushing with hope.

Friend, if Jesus is your Lord and Savior and you are going through a hard time, a sad time, even a time that seems to be trying to tear your will to go on right out of your chest — take heart, it is not the end. If you feel like you are drowning in the problems of life, take heart — our Lifeguard walks on water. Even death is not the end.

Jesus is Lord over everything. Everything.

For we do not have a high priest who cannot sympathize with our weaknesses, but One who has been tempted in all things as we are, yet without sin. Therefore let us draw near with confidence to the throne of grace, so that we may receive mercy and find grace to help in time of need.
— Hebrews 4:15,16

No One Knows How I Feel

If you tell me you have never said that — or thought it — you will have to forgive me for having a hard time believing you. We've all been there, haven't we? A teenager whose parents won't let them date the person they want, a parent who has lost a child, a business owner who worked his heart out only to lose the business anyway, a person down and out who needs a single friend and can't find one. The list could go on and on …

If you are thinking today, "no one knows how I feel," I'd like for you to know this: Jesus knows. And cares. Jesus knows agony so intense that it caused Him to sweat drops of blood in the Garden of Gethsemane. Loneliness, abandonment? When Jesus needed His disciples the most, every one of them forsook Him and ran away. He lived a sinless life, only to die a sinner's death. And His Father watched it happen. Jesus knows very well, my friend, how you feel. You can take great comfort in that.

And that sinner's death He died — He died for you, in your place — and gave you a place to go in your times of need, and those times when you think no one knows how you feel. That place is a throne full of grace and mercy and understanding, where Jesus will show you more love than you could ever imagine.

God is our refuge and strength, a very present help in trouble.
Therefore we will not fear, though the earth should change and though
the mountains slip into the heart of the sea; though its waters roar
and foam, though the mountains quake at its swelling pride.
— *Psalms 46:1-3*

Don't Sweat the Big Stuff

Don't sweat the small stuff. OR the big stuff. No fear.

You are standing in California and the ground begins to shake, and it's not just a ground tremor or earthquake this time. It shakes more and more violently until the entire Sierra Nevada mountain range begins to fall, slide to the west and then is consumed by a raging Pacific Ocean. Welcome to the calamity of verses 2 and 3 of this psalm. Could YOU remain calm and unafraid? I confess, it would be a challenge for me.

Life can seem like the storm in these verses sometimes too, right? But even in the strongest storms of life, there is a cure for fear and a source of calm repose. The good news is in verse 1. The good news is what God is in our lives. God is not a temporary comfort zone. He is, right now, our eternal refuge that never changes. Added to that, He is — right now — our strength that never fades. Added to that, He is — right now — all the help we will ever need. No matter the trouble. And God is not "out there" somewhere. He is WITH you ... all the time. Present and ready. No matter what.

> ... and Joseph awoke from his sleep and did as the angel of the Lord
> commanded him, and took Mary as his wife.
> — *Matthew 1:24*

Sometimes Being a Dad ... Isn't Easy

Father's Day is a day when many of us have the opportunity to honor and give thanks for our dads or granddads who sacrificed a lot to raise us the way they did. My grandfather, who raised me was one of the best men I ever knew. I wish I could reflect better, the raising that he gave me.

However, for many of us who are fathers, the road has been a difficult one. Unashamedly, this devotional today is aimed at giving this group some hope and encouragement. That's why this verse about Joseph is the text.

Here was a good man, who was asked to endure some monumental challenges. Not the least of which was to be the stepfather to the Son of God ...

1. He was asked to do something unheard of in those days: marry a woman who by all outward appearances had already been unfaithful to him. And ... she asked him to believe that the child was from the Holy Spirit. Would you have believed her story? Imagine what it must have been like for Joseph in public, before it was known who Jesus really was. And with Joseph knowing the truth the whole time.
2. He raised Jesus as his own, knowing the entire time that he would be little more than just a figure in the background to who Jesus was.
3. He left his business, his family and his country — in the middle of the night — to take the baby Jesus and his mother to a place where they would be safe.
4. He fulfilled his responsibility in the shadow of a woman who would be venerated for generations to come as the mother of the Messiah.
5. After enduring all of these things in virtual obscurity, he passed from this life without so much as a footnote in scripture about his death or funeral. The Old Testament records the death of every single king of ancient Israel, even the lousy ones. Not one word is offered in remembrance of the death of the man who raised Jesus as his own son.

Nope. Sometimes being a dad isn't easy, but look how God used Joseph. And, if you are a father in a difficult situation, He can use you too. And you know something else?... Joseph may not have had a headline written about him in the Bible, but I bet Jesus had a pretty nice place waiting for him in heaven. I bet the same is true for any dad who loves the Lord and has done his best, even in the middle of difficult circumstances.

"Ask, and it will be given to you; seek, and you will find; knock, and it will be opened to you. For everyone who asks receives, and he who seeks finds, and to him who knocks it will be opened."
— *Matthew 7:7,8*

The 1-2-3 Prayer Strategy of Jesus

There are some exciting things here. Really exciting.

Exciting thing #1 — "No Exceptions" is an expression that normally has a negative connotation ... for example, "No Shirt, No Shoes, No Service — No Exceptions. Prayer is different. Wonderfully different. Positively different. Note well the word "everyone." Jesus just gave an iron clad, no loopholes promise to God's children. That means you, too. No exceptions.

Exciting thing #2 — What is taught about these verses (and rightly so) is persistence in prayer. The truth of this is vivid in the original language: "ask and keep on asking, seek and keep on seeking, knock and keep on knocking." But Jesus wasn't teaching mindless repetition, He meant a habitual lifestyle. It is a lifestyle that brings with it an intimate communion with God. But ... the beauty and the power of these verses get even sweeter. Care to go there with me?

Exciting thing #3 — Don't miss the fact that there are THREE actions here: ask, seek, and knock — and THREE results: receive, find, door opened. The 1-2-3 prayer strategy of Jesus. I don't think that was an accident, or that Jesus was just trying to be wordy. My personal belief is that there is a profound beauty waiting for us in these words. Stay with me now ...

What about when we don't get what we want? What about when it seems that God is silent? What then? Well, it doesn't mean that God hasn't answered our prayer. Sometimes the answer is "no," or "wait." But that doesn't comfort us much when our heart is hurting — does it? THAT is where "seek" and "knock" and their results can comfort our lives. I believe Jesus may be teaching a path to a spiritual depth that can let us see inside God's "no" in our lives. Seeking means that you are looking for something, right? If we do it like Jesus says here, I believe it will lead us to "finding" the reason behind what God did with our prayer. But there is even more ...

There is the last step. Knocking. It gets us past just knowing the reason. When you knock on a door it usually means you want to see, or meet with someone, right? This is where I believe we can touch the heart and mind of God — where God Himself opens the door and lets us understand.

I have been crucified with Christ; and it is no longer I who live, but Christ lives in me; and the life which I now live in the flesh I live by faith in the Son of God, who loved me and gave Himself up for me.

— *Galatians 2:20*

The Hokey Pokey

The other day some friends and I were laughing about this funny little song. Everyone knows it: "You put your right foot in, you put your right foot out ..." and on it goes with various parts of your body. It is a fun, whimsical, group participation song for children.

Too often, however, as adults we are still "doing the Hokey Pokey" — with our commitment to the Son of God. We put a little part of ourselves in ... usually when we have a crisis, or need something, then we take it back out again when the crisis passes. And we do it over and over, just like children when they "do the Hokey Pokey." We put a little part of ourselves in for a couple of hours on Sunday, then we take it back out the other six days of the week. We put our wallet in for God to fix when we have a money crisis, then we take back control of it when the problem passes. And on it goes ...

Aren't you glad Jesus never does that to us? Our salvation wasn't something He dangled like bait, only to yank it away again. He never puts just a part of Himself into your life only to take it back out again. When Jesus comes into your life, He comes to stay. He never leaves. He is committed. Because He loves you ... enough to die for you. Jesus doesn't do the Hokey Pokey with your eternity. He deserves the same from us. No more Hokey Pokey. The shout of commitment by Paul here in this verse should be our shout, too. Let this be your pledge to God and watch what happens to the joy and excitement meter of your life.

But someone may well say, "You have faith and I have works; show
me your faith without the works, and I will show you my faith by
my works." You believe that God is one. You do well; the demons
also believe, and shudder.
— *James 2:18,19*

Where The Rubber Meets The Road

Am I writing to anyone today who has ever felt the "fervor" of their
Christian walk slipping away? In church the hymns don't stir you like
they once did, the sermons seem to all fall a little flat. You see others
excited, but for you it all just seems like more of the same old thing.
Ring any bells? May I offer a suggestion? The problem might just be
that you have separated your "faith" from your "works" for too long. Ask
yourself this question: When was the last time I really, truly, honestly
did something significant for God — something I really had to work at
and make sacrifices to accomplish? I have never met a happy, excited
Christian who was not sacrificially involved in serving the Lord in one
way or another.

James says that faith can't even truly exist without works — that it is
a "both/and" relationship, not an "either/or" option. Today we might
would paraphrase what James is saying with "talk is cheap." But he goes
even further. He boldly says that this is where the rubber meets the road
in a relationship with Christ — that works are the fruit of genuine faith
and that the absence of works is proof that faith isn't even real. That even
the demons believe — and tremble. In other words, knowledge does
not equal relationship, and a relationship with Christ by its very nature,
produces service.

Does watching a cooking show make you a chef? No. Does putting
on a uniform and watching a football game make you a football player?
No. Does standing beside a track holding a baton make you a relay
sprinter? No. James is saying that neither does sitting in church make
you a Christian. Suggestion here. If you are looking for some excitement
in your Christian walk, blow the rust out of your tank, file the carbon off
your spark plugs, get busy for God and watch your excitement meter roar
to life again.

The steadfast of mind You will keep in perfect peace, because he
trusts in You.
— *Isaiah 26:3*

Roadmap to Perfect Peace

Here is another free lesson on how to achieve peace from the best self-help book ever written. And not just any sort of peace — perfect peace.

The question is, will we follow the instructions? We can't blame God for not having peace in our lives if we refuse to do what He says to do in order to achieve that peace. That's sort of like having a map, but staying lost because you refuse to follow the turns to get to where you want to go. Who on earth would do that, right? But, we do it spiritually every day. Here's the map to peace that works:

Our part — keep our minds/thoughts FIXED on God. That happens through trusting God. Trusting God happens through spending time WITH God, quality time, through prayer, reading God's Word and doing what it says. A mind fixed on God — steadfast — doesn't happen by accident.

God's part — perfect peace for your life.

Want to give it a try? It worked for the apostle Paul. You can read all about it in Philippians, chapter 4, beginning at about verse 4 and going on through verse 13.

Be anxious for nothing, but in everything by prayer and supplication with thanksgiving let your requests be made known to God, and the peace of God, which surpasses all comprehension, will guard your hearts and your minds in Christ Jesus.
— *Philippians 4:6,7*

The Worry Pill

For whatever type of anxiety that exists, God's word has a 100% cure rate. How comforting is THAT to know? It provides another cure here. What worry, or collection of worries are we to allow to grind on our life? None. Which ones exist outside the boundary of God's power? None.

Our part is to pray. That is the pill that kills, as far as worry is concerned. It is, however, prayer with an attitude — the attitude of thanksgiving. Not thanksgiving for whatever the situation may be — thanksgiving for God's grace that is available and sufficient, no. matter. what.

Do that, and God sends to guard your heart and mind, a soldier whose power is so great that you can never even hope to understand it. A soldier whose name is "peace" — and Jesus is his commander.

I will ransom them from the power of the grave; I will redeem them
from death: O death, I will be thy plagues; O grave, I will be thy
destruction: repentance shall be hid from mine eyes.
— *Hosea 13:14 (KJV)*

My Mind is Made Up

There are two legitimate, yet opposing ways to interpret this verse.
Option #1 is God's powerful judgement on Israel. Option #2 is the exact
opposite — God's powerful salvation. I choose option #2, my mind is
made up. Those who choose option #1 do so because of the context
around it, and they adjust the construction of the language to fit their
view. Many Bible translations reflect that view. Option #2, however
(in my opinion), is the interpretation that is more true to the original
text, even though it may look out of place at first glance because it is
surrounded by judgement. The more literal interpretation of the original
language in this instance is reflected in the King James Version of the
Bible, and it is the translation I have used here. It is also the view the
New Testament writers used, like Paul in 1st Corinthians 15:55.

Please forgive my descent into interpretation that is a bit detailed, I don't
normally do it ... but it was really important for us this time. Important,
not just to be true to what the Bible is really trying to say, but because *it
is why this verse gives you and me such astounding hope and encouragement
today instead of judgement*.

In the verse just before this one (verse 13), God details how Israel is
unwise in its approach to judgement. God wants to spare Israel and bless
Israel, but Israel, by its own actions won't allow it. This attitude is as
ridiculous as a child that refuses to come out when it is time to be born.
Here is why I believe verse 14 interpreted as salvation is NOT out of
place: I believe it is God saying what He *WANTS* to do for Israel, and
what He *WILL* do for Israel, *IF ISRAEL WOULD JUST ALLOW IT.*

And it is what He *DID* do in the New Testament through the Lord Jesus
Christ. Here is the prophecy and the promise of your salvation at its very
finest, 700 years before the world's first Christmas. Death cannot touch
us and the grave cannot hold us. God destroys them both. Resurrection
to eternal life is your destiny. And the very last phrase — "repentance

shall be hidden from My eyes" — is God's seal on top of it all. It appears that God is saying that He won't see the repentance of His people, but that isn't what He is saying at all. God is saying here that He will never even glance at the idea of changing His mind about your salvation. His mind is made up. It is a done deal.

"We must work the works of Him who sent Me as long as it is day;
night is coming when no one can work."
— *John 9:4*

Make Hay While the Sun Shines

Ask anyone like me who grew up on a farm what that means, and they can tell you. You don't waste time when there is important work to be done. If you waste good weather when the harvest is ready, you can lose all the winter feed for your cattle.

There is a harvest much more important than a harvest of grain. It is the harvest the Son of God died for. The harvest of the souls of men — and it is urgent. In Jesus's language, He said, "Night is coming — rapidly — when no man can work." And His words to His disciples in this verse carry the same urgency for His disciples today: We MUST do the work now — not should do it — MUST do it, while it is still day. And wasting time in THAT harvest is much more tragic than losing winter feed.

Here's a word for a Christian brother or sister today who may be going through a tough time: Maybe your emotional gas tank is on "empty." Maybe you have lost all hope ... or think you have, and you feel no sense of purpose in your life. I can show you one. Remind yourself that you are part of the Lord's harvest that is already safe. Someone cared enough about you to not leave you in the field for the storm — or the night. ... Now it is your turn. That neighbor, or friend, or workmate, or family member who you know needs Jesus, but you have put off and put off telling them about the beautiful eternity they can have with Christ ... now is the time. Put them in this picture on the horizon, with the night — and that storm — closing in.

You have a God-appointed purpose. A noble purpose, important — and urgent.

I pray that the eyes of your heart may be enlightened, so that you
will know what is the hope of His calling, what are the riches of
the glory of His inheritance in the saints, and what is the surpassing
greatness of His power toward us who believe. These are in
accordance with the working of the strength of His might ...
— *Ephesians 1:18,19*

Heaven's Treasure Chest

Paul jumps into that treasure feet first here, in his prayer for the
Ephesians. He prayed for God to "open the eyes of their hearts" so they
could understand it and see the riches inside it. At least some of them.
Here he mentioned three of its precious jewels:

1. — the hope of His calling. "Hope" in the New Testament is not
    "wishing expectantly" for something, as we think of it in modern
    English. In the New Testament it is the confident joy of certainty
    in the results of God's actions. Here it is the certainty of eternal life
    because God Himself opened the door — to you — personally.
2. — the riches of the glory of His inheritance in the saints.
    Commentators will argue about this until Jesus returns. I believe it
    to be the aggregate glory of the new heaven, the new earth, the new
    Jerusalem, the presence of God in the midst of it all, and our ability to
    witness all of it because as children of God, heaven is our home. We
    are joint heirs of it with Christ.
3. — the exceeding greatness of His power toward us who believe. The
    God who created, and maintains, the entire universe with the word of
    His power, focuses that same power on the lives of His children. All
    the treasure of all His children is well-protected.

The deliverers will ascend Mount Zion to judge the mountain of
Esau, and the kingdom will be the Lord's.
— *Obadiah 21*

A Day Of Reckonin'

From the smallest book in the entire Old Testament comes one of the
greatest words of encouragement. Using just 21 verses, it didn't take
Obadiah long to communicate the vision God had put in his mind's
eye — and his brief prophecy reaches across more than 2,500 years to
deliver an exciting promise for us today.

Obadiah's prophecy was a blistering proclamation of the complete
destruction of what was thought to be indestructible: the land and capital
city of Edom. It happened though, just like Obadiah said it would.
And it is still desolate today. Enduring testimony of the anger of God
unleashed against the enemy of His children.

It is just possible that you might know how Israel felt in Obadiah's day ...

Edom was blood kin, descendants from the same line through Esau, yet
they rejoiced in the problems Israel faced and even aided the enemies of
the children of God. If you are one of God's children and know what
it feels like to face ridicule in the midst of your problems, maybe even
from friends or family, this great promise of victory from Obadiah shouts
across the years to your heart today. Why? Because this verse looks
forward not just to Edom, but to God's final crushing of the enemies of
His children through the work of Christ. The trials of God's children
may endure for a season, but the judgement of God's enemies will endure
for eternity. And the kingdom that is established, make no mistake about
it ... will be the Lord's.

Take heart, child of God, there is a day of reckonin' coming. The smile of
your enemy will one day be erased. It is God's promise. And, if you are
not yet one of God's children, you can be ...

"For God so loved the world that He gave His only begotten Son,
that whoever believes in Him shall not perish, but have eternal life. "
John 3:16

"Whoever causes one of these little ones who believe in Me to stumble, it would be better for him if, with a heavy millstone hung around his neck, he had been cast into the sea."
— *Mark 9:42*

Jesus Loves The Little Children

… all the children of the world. Red and yellow, black or white, they are precious in His sight, Jesus loves the little children of the world. And we adults had better love them too, if we know what is good for us. To mistreat one, or even mislead one — for ANY reason — exacts a swift, and terminal reaction from God.

Jesus never prohibits correcting a child when they misbehave, but — as parents, or aunts, or uncles, or older siblings, or friends, or neighbors of people who have children, our responsibility toward the most innocent life on earth is awesome, and Jesus pulls no punches here as to the consequences of failing in that responsibility. He doesn't demand perfection, but His instruction is explicit and direct.

In my way of thinking, this creates a chilling scenario of the eternal fate reserved for the monsters of our society who abuse or mistreat their own children, or anyone else's children for that matter. And we haven't even addressed the horror of murdering children through abortion before they even have a chance to draw their first breath. It will be terrifying one day, for those who commit these kinds of crimes against God's little children.

And … how much more wonderful is it anyway, when we love children the way Jesus does? To know you have helped one of them learn how much Jesus loves them, to know you have protected them from harm, or taught them something that will help them as they grow up. Playing with them and letting them feel loved and important. I could go on and on. And tell me if you can, of a greater blessing or joy, if you have known the feeling of having a child look up at you and smile, or hug you, or give you a kiss on the cheek because of something you have done for them. If you don't have any adults in your life to love on and hug on (or even if you do), find a way to get involved with a group of children in your church. Loving and being a friend to children is just about the most precious feeling in the world.

Whatever you do, do your work heartily, as for the Lord rather than for men, knowing that from the Lord you will receive the reward of the inheritance. It is the Lord Christ whom you serve.
— *Colossians 3:23,24*

Remember Who Signs Your Check

If you have ever had a dead-end or frustrating job with a difficult boss, hearing this little phrase can become a repetitive, and irritating experience. When circumstances make it nigh on to impossible to "take it with a smile," take heart — it might encourage you to know that Paul was writing to slaves, or bond-servants here. They were well-acquainted with the expression, "dead-end job."

Paul makes no distinction as to the task he mentions here ("whatever"). That means what follows is still a command, even if it proves to be difficult. The attitude: "heartily." Be honest. That's the really hard part, isn't it? "Heartily" literally means "from the soul." We can grit our teeth and do almost anything, but swallowing our anger and doing it with a real smile from the heart? Go on — tell me how easy that is. It isn't. But that doesn't change the command. And — the reward is more than worth it. Much more.

Slaves had little hope in life, no social position, and no standing in the family they served. Paul encourages them here — and us — by reminding them that the way they perform their responsibilities is determined not by the lord of the house, but by the Lord of Hosts. That changes everything. Our citizenship is in heaven. Our position is sons of the living God. Our recompense is the inheritance we share as sons — not slaves — with Jesus.

It doesn't matter where we work. It matters Who we serve — and we serve the King of Kings and Lord of Lords!

Cease *striving* and know that I am God.
— *Psalms 46:10a*

Short and to the Point

Very short, very powerful, very important. Would that more of us preachers could preach that way. It doesn't even fit our tried and true cookie cutter "formula" of three points and a poem. There are just two points, and no poem, and being just one half of one sentence, it is still one of the greatest keys to comfort in the entire Bible.

"Cease striving," or, "Be still," as many Bible versions say. How often are we really and truly "still?" We are bombarded daily with literally thousands of bits of information competing for our attention and many times our lives seem like ping pong balls caught in a tornado. It is difficult — nigh on to impossible — to do the second part of this one-phrase sermon, "know that I am God" ... or "let God be God," in our lives when our lives so much of the time seem to proceed at a frenetic pace. First, we have to learn to "be still."

However, "still" here (or cease striving) doesn't mean an absence of action. The Bible is replete with commands for Christians to never dissolve into apathy or non-action. Jesus, as always, is our best example. He was the epitome of what it meant to be a "revolutionary" for God. But He also knew how to "be still." And He knew who God was — all the time.

To cease striving, we have to learn to relax and let the Lord have all our mind, all our will, and all our heart. To let all our anxieties be dissolved by our faith in who God is, and what He can do in our lives. A daily "quiet time" that is just for you and the Lord is a wonderful way to do that. A daily time to pray. A daily time to read God's word. Leave the tornado behind for a while and be still. Truly still. And bathe yourself in the peace that comes when you see who God is, and know that He is in control — of everything.

"In My Father's house are many dwelling places; if it were not so, I would have told you; for I go to prepare a place for you. If I go and prepare a place for you, I will come again and receive you to Myself, that where I am, there you may be also."
— *John 14:2,3*

Condo In The Sky

If these two verses don't fill your tank with hope and encouragement, you ain't breathin'. There can be no other explanation.

Ladies, imagine if you could fill your closet with clothes, each piece handmade personally for you by Christian Dior himself. What would that be worth? Men — same thing. A car handmade (not assembly line) especially for you by Enzo Ferrari himself. That would be worth a pretty penny too. How about a home hand built by Frank Lloyd Wright himself?

Jesus is a pretty famous designer, too. He created a universe that is one of a kind. It is no accident also, that Jesus was a carpenter on this earth. He still is. Only now He is building houses in heaven. If He is your Lord and Savior, one of those houses is for you. Want to try to put a price on a "dwelling place" in heaven, hand made for you by Jesus Himself?

Everything Jesus does, He does in abundance. The place He is building for you is certainly no exception. Carpenter — Jesus. Location — heaven. Talk about a room with a view!!! ... and ...

The company you will keep there ain't bad either!

"For even the Son of Man did not come to be served, but to serve,
and to give His life a ransom for many."
— *Mark 10:45*

Independence Day

July 4th ... the day Americans celebrate the winning of their independence. We are proud, and we should be — there is no other nation on earth like the United States. America has never known a despot, a sovereign or a dictator. Again and again when asked, those from other countries always say that the most beautiful word in our language is "freedom."

That brings up an important point: winning independence is one thing — keeping it is quite another, and on the day we celebrate winning our independence, we also honor our military — without equal in the world — men and women who have served with honor and courage, many giving the ultimate sacrifice, to keep us the greatest nation on earth.

Sometimes our military is referred to simply as "the service." Jesus was well-acquainted with the concept and is the best example of it in all eternity. And not only did He "not come to be served, but to serve," He too gave the ultimate sacrifice — "His life a ransom for many." With that sacrifice Jesus defeated death, He defeated the devil, He gave us freedom forever from the penalty of our own sin ... and created an Independence Day like none other the world has ever known.

Five times I received from the Jews thirty-nine lashes. Three times I was
beaten with rods, once I was stoned, three times I was shipwrecked,
a night and a day I have spent in the deep. I have been on frequent
journeys, in dangers from rivers, dangers from robbers, dangers from my
countrymen, dangers from the Gentiles, dangers in the city, dangers in
the wilderness, dangers on the sea, dangers among false brethren; I have
been in labor and hardship, through many sleepless nights, in hunger and
thirst, often without food, in cold and exposure. Apart from such external
things, there is the daily pressure on me of concern for all the churches.
— *2 Corinthians 11:24-28*

Just How Real Is A Real Encounter With The Lord Jesus Christ?

Saul of Tarsus, later renamed Paul by Jesus, was one of the fiercest
persecutors of the early Christian church in its entire history. The evidence
is undisputed, being both recorded by early historians and affirmed by his
own confession. He assisted in the death of the first Christian martyr,
Stephen (Acts 7:57-8:1). He ravaged the early church, dragging both
men and women off to prison in chains (Acts 8:3). He caused their
deaths (Acts 26:10,11).

Just how real is a real encounter with the Lord Jesus Christ? Well, that
same man is the man who wrote the words of this text in 2nd Corinthians.
The very same man. On a dusty road to Damascus intending to drag yet
more Christian men and women off to prison in chains, he had a real
encounter with the Lord Jesus Christ (Acts 26:12-20) — and he was
never the same again.

The fiercest persecutor of the early church became its most courageous
champion. Never doubting, never turning back, never backing away from
his faith in Christ to avoid whatever hardship, torture or persecution that
came his way. Before his encounter with Christ, he had religious glory,
fame and success at his fingertips, if he would just stay a Jew. But, he
turned his back on it all and said, "I too, saw Him!"

You can't say he was crazy or deluded, because his education at the feet
of Gamaliel and his writings prove his intelligence. 25 percent of the

New Testament comes from the pen of this one man. Through three missionary journeys from Jerusalem to Rome, all on foot, he set aflame a trail of Christianity that no government or power of hell has ever been able to extinguish.

Now, to be sure, the apostle Paul was one of a kind ... but, so are you. You are the only "you" that exists in all the earth. God may have a different plan for you, but a real encounter with the Lord Jesus Christ will always be the same: The spiritual DNA of a real encounter with the Lord Jesus Christ is measured by devotion. If you have had the encounter, you also have the devotion — and its light never goes out.

He gives strength to the weary, and to him who lacks might He
increases power.
— *Isaiah 40:29*

You've Lost That Helpless Feeling

Ok, I admit it, the title I chose here is a shameless alteration of the song "You've Lost That Lovin' Feeling," made famous by the Righteous Brothers (and the movie "Top Gun"). It's just that it is such a good description for what Isaiah wrote right here.

Has there ever been a time in your life when you have felt helpless? You want to do something, but feel powerless to change what is happening. I know it has happened to me WAY more than once or twice. If you let it, it can lead you all the way down into the dark street of despair. I've walked around those cold and lonely corners in the dark, and I bet I am not alone.

The good news is — no — the GREAT news is, that is doesn't have to be that way. There is more than one way to define power and might and our great God is in charge of both — power AND might. He is the same God who has promised that He will never leave us or forsake us (Hebrews 13:5). You are never EVER alone ... and if you are interested in losing that helpless feeling, the God who could play marbles with the planets if He wanted to is always available – always – to lend you His power when you feel weak, and His strength when your own fails.

Therefore humble yourselves under the mighty hand of God, that He
may exalt you at the proper time, casting all your anxiety on Him,
because He cares for you.
— 1ˢᵗ Peter 5:6,7

Well-placed Humility

This is one of my all-time favorite verses for times of worry or despair ...

Sometimes the two things God asks us to do here are difficult because we tend to be proud and self-sufficient, but the results are more than worth the effort.

First, humble ourselves — pride is out. That's the difficult part. Place ourselves where? Under the mighty hand of God — that's the comforting and secure part. This isn't God's smashing hand of judgment, it is His hand of protection, strong enough to keep you from all harm. Do this, and your time will come — that's the promise part.

Second, let go of your worries. How much of it? ALL of it. This is not the naïve negligence of responsibilities, but the placing of all the worry about them on the strong shoulders of God.

Why do you have this privilege? Because God loves you.

Then God said, "Let Us make man in Our image, according to Our likeness; and let them rule over the fish of the sea and over the birds of the sky and over the cattle and over all the earth, and over every creeping thing that creeps on the earth."
— *Genesis 1:26*

A Little Anthropology Is Good For Ya!

(Don't stop reading just because of the title ... there's some really good stuff here.)

And — the title is true especially when the subject is Christian anthropology. I have heard over the years, any number of attempts, usually from the book of Genesis, to "separate and elevate man from the animals." Here are some of the more interesting attempts I have come across:

1. God made man superior to the animals because man has dominion over them (here in this verse). The biggest problem with this theology is that a lot of ANIMALS have dominion over other animals too. Besides that, try slapping a silverback gorilla on the jaw and see how much dominion you have.
2. Some say that man is uniquely different from the animals because God personally blessed man (Genesis 1:28). The biggest problem with this is that God blessed the animals, too (Genesis 1:21,22).
3. Another theory is that God breathed the breath of life into man and he became a living soul (Genesis 2:7). The biggest problem with that is that animals are called souls too in the original language (Genesis 2:19), and it is the exact same word that is used with the creation of man, "nephesh," translated "soul."
4. One more good one states that we are different from the animals because God personally formed man from the dust of the ground (Genesis 2:7). The biggest problem with this is that God made the animals the same way (Genesis 2:19).

The real reason man is unique from the animals — and the reason you are unique in all the universe, and uniquely separate from all the rest of creation is found right at the beginning of this verse: "And God said let Us make man in Our image, according to Our likeness ..." That is not said of any other created thing in the universe. The only thing God made like Himself was man. You are created after the image of the living God. No other animal is. We messed up that image with sin, but God has taken care of that too, when Jesus died for each of us on that old rugged cross a long time ago, to pay for our sin.

And — if you have trusted the Lord Jesus Christ as your personal Savior, that original image is ready and waiting for you to reclaim it ... the day you see Jesus face to face.

"Therefore everyone who hears these words of Mine and acts on them, may be compared to a wise man who built his house on the rock. And the rain fell, and the floods came, and the winds blew and slammed against that house; and yet it did not fall, for it had been founded on the rock.
— *Matthew 7:24,25*

Spiritual Structural Engineering 101

Everyone in the "Tornado Belt" from Texas to Oklahoma to Kansas, and everyone who lives in coastal areas where hurricane season causes annual nervous sweat can tell you: it doesn't matter how pretty your house is, if it folds up and blows away during a storm.

Jesus teaches that the same is true in life. Even as a Christian ... an obedient Christian, life is not stress-free, it is not problem-free, it is not storm-free. Rains come, floods come, winds blow and beat against the house of your life. You can obey everything Jesus says, and still the storms will come. What is so wonderful about being a follower of Jesus, though, is that when we have faith in Him, when we do things His way, our house never folds up and blows away when the storms come. Why? Because our life is built on a foundation called Christ the Solid Rock, a foundation that the worst tornado from hell itself can't dent. It is the lesson we learn here, in Jesus's Spiritual Structural Engineering 101 class.

For by grace you have been saved through faith; and that not of yourselves, it is the gift of God; not as a result of works, so that no one may boast. For we are His workmanship, created in Christ Jesus for good works, which God prepared beforehand so that we would walk in them.
— Ephesians 2:8-10

When Your Best Seems Not Good Enough

For the person who has reached the point where your best never seems good enough, these 3 verses from Paul's letter to the Ephesians are some of the most beautiful and encouraging words in all the Bible. There are many ways for this "never good enough" disappointment to attack us, aren't there?

Not good enough at your job — you try your best at work, only to be passed by for promotion again and again ... or, even worse, in spite of being good at your job, you still lose it. Not good enough at being a husband or wife — nothing you do seems to satisfy or bring joy to the one you are married to. Not good enough at being a parent — despite your best efforts, your children make wrong and ungodly choices in life. Not good enough at being a Christian — you are largely ignored at church, your faults seem to always outweigh your faith, and you feel like you are a disappointment to God no matter how hard you try. Am I getting warm? If I am, these three beautiful verses are for you.

First of all, there is the beauty of your salvation. It is an act of grace by the Almighty God. It is real. It is certain. It, along with your faith are God's personal gifts to you because He loves you — and NO one has the right to question it, doubt it or try to make you feel like you don't have it ... no matter how they might gossip. And the salvation you have by the grace of God is good enough to carry you all the way to eternity in heaven and into God's presence. Also: no matter how inadequate you may feel as an employee, parent, Christian or anything else, know this — YOU and everything about you is the workmanship of God Himself. You are a handcrafted original, formed by the hand, and heart, and will of God.

And — you are a handcrafted original with a purpose. A good purpose full of good works. Good works placed in the plan for your life by Jehovah God who loves you. And ... as long as you do your best to walk in that plan, you never — ever—have to worry whether or not your best is good enough. In the eyes of your Heavenly Father, it is. Always. Because you have been created in the image of Christ.

"By this all men will know that you are My disciples, if you have
love for one another."
— *John 13:35*

Witnessing For Jesus 101

You know all those "canned approach," sales pitch type programs for
winning the world to Christ where you memorize about a hundred
scriptures and page after page of "do this, say this, then this …"?

You can forget all that.

Jesus gave the most successful "program" ever for evangelizing the world
a long, long time ago. And He did it in a single sentence. It is all that is
necessary, still today. All we need to do — is do what He said.

Other than the raw power of the Holy Spirit, your personal testimony
is your mightiest sword. When you show Christian love, you take that
sword out of its sheath and stick it right up the devil's nose.

But as for me, I shall sing of Your strength; yes, I shall joyfully
sing of Your lovingkindness in the morning, for You have been my
stronghold and a refuge in the day of my distress.
— *Psalms 59:16*

Battle Hymns

Not talking about the famous hymn that starts off, "Mine eyes have
seen the glory ..." These are battle hymns that sooner or later, all God's
children write. Sometimes there is a big misconception among non-
Christians, and even some of the more charismatic "Christian" groups
that the Christian life is all peachy keen, one success after another, and
daily roses with no thorns. Then, if something bad happens it's your fault
because you are not "right" with God. Wrong!! Countless places in the
Bible reveal that there are "days of trouble," even for Christians.

Many of our personal "battle hymns" that are born in those days, may
never even be heard by another person because most of the time they
don't get sung in church. Some may never even leave our hearts. They
are, nonetheless, powerful and beautiful because they are inspired by the
power and care of Almighty God in our lives. Power and care in our
day of trouble. Power and care that has sustained us and protected us in
battle.

Real Christians who really practice their faith know from personal
experience that days of trouble will come. They also know that the truth
of God's care in this verse is one of the most powerful and wonderful
blessings we can know. Blessings that create battle hymns in our hearts.

Therefore there is now no condemnation for those who are in Christ Jesus ... who do not walk according to the flesh but according to the Spirit.
— *Romans 8:1,4b*

Free to Go

For anyone who has ever stood before a judge accused of a crime you didn't commit, the phrase "the accused is free to go" has a fragrance too wonderful to describe. Someone reading this may even know that smell themselves. One thing we are all guilty of, however, is sin. Are sins a problem? You bet. We can even suffer because of another person's sins, like if a thief decides to rob me. And we most certainly suffer because of our own sins. Are we condemned for them? Nope. Not if Jesus is your Lord and Savior. We may suffer because of them, but the difference between suffering for sins and being condemned for them is enormous — and eternal.

The scene is heaven's courtroom. You stand before God. Guilty as charged. It is a date with justice we will all keep one day. The penalty is not life in prison, it is death. As God opens His mouth to pronounce your sentence someone speaks up — "Your Honor, before You pronounce sentence I'd like to say a word on behalf of the accused." It is your Lawyer, the Lord Jesus Christ. Never forget, you have an Advocate with the Father (1st John 2:1).

Jesus continues to speak — "Your Honor ... You know, I know, everyone here knows that my client is guilty. The evidence against him is obvious and overwhelming. I am not here to contest his guilt. I am here to contest his sentence. Then, Jesus opens His shirt and shows the gaping tear in His side. He rolls up His sleeves and shows the holes in His wrists. Then Jesus says, "Your Honor, I have already paid the penalty for His crimes Myself." Then God puts aside His gavel and says, "The accused is free to go." That, dear friend, is what "therefore there is now no condemnation" means.

> ...and I will put enmity between you and the woman, and between your seed and her seed; He shall bruise you on the head, and you shall bruise him on the heel."
> — *Genesis 3:15*

Beat at the Buzzer

A little twist on the familiar basketball phrase "buzzer beater," which means a shot made in the last second of the game. The result is an exhilarating win for the team making the shot, and a crushing disappointment for the losing team. Here we have the same thing, except here in Genesis 3:15 it happens at the ***beginning*** buzzer, instead of at the end.

Allow me to explain. This is really good — and, it is one of the few times that language study and theology is actually very, VERY exciting. Trust me. Here is God — at the very beginning of human existence — pronouncing the ultimate defeat of satan. Victory at the end of time revealed from the very dawn of time. It doesn't look like that on the surface, but it is. The human author, Moses, could not have seen it, but having the New Testament, you and I can. It can only be seen looking back from the cross of Christ. There is no other explanation for Moses's words here. If you want to dazzle and amaze your friends with a fancy "theologian's" word, you can tell them that this verse is the "proto evangelium," or, in English, the first mention of the gospel.

God announces the conflict between Jesus and the devil. The Bible uses VERY interesting language here. In a world where men ruled, here is a battle involving a woman. Not only that, this is the ONLY time in the entire Bible that the "seed" of someone is attributed to a woman. In all other instances the "seed" always comes from the man. There is only one instance in all eternity where a birth occurred that didn't involve the seed of a man. The birth of Jesus Christ.

God announces the outcome. The Bible uses VERY interesting language again. God's words in the language of the Old Testament describe two types of wounds: one that is an injury, "shall bruise His heel" — and a wound that is lethal, "shall bruise your head." This describes the crucifixion and final victory of Christ perfectly — and what will ultimately happen to satan as well. Jesus died on the cross, but He didn't stay dead, did He? He rose on the third day ... the "bruise on the heel." You have to go all the way to the book of John's Revelation to see the end of the story, the "bruise on the head." Check it out — it's in Revelation 20:10 — "And the devil who deceived them was thrown into the lake of fire and brimstone, where the beast and the false prophet are also; and they will be tormented day and night forever and ever."

I have often wished I could have been there after the devil thought he had, in the end, won the fight — to see the look on his evil face, staring at that empty tomb. The proof of God's power — and His love — for us. A love He announced in the shadow of the very first sin.

Therefore He is able also to save forever those who draw near to God through Him, since He always lives to make intercession for them.

— Hebrews 7:25

What Have You Done For Me Lately?

Let's be honest. In those times of our lives when we were down and defeated, at the end of our rope and the end of our hope, haven't we been guilty of wondering sometimes if Jesus even remembers that we are alive? Well, He does.

In this beautiful verse from the letter to the Hebrews, we learn that Jesus never loses anyone who puts their trust in Him as Savior and Lord. He doesn't get you just part of the way to heaven and then forget who you are. The power of His forgiveness doesn't limp off the playing field of life at halftime to leave you once again drowning in unforgiven sin. Anyone, meaning you too, who trusts in Jesus, He brings all the way to heaven and into eternity. No exceptions.

And — if you are ever tempted to wonder what Jesus has done for you lately, here you have the answer: His work in eternity this very minute, and without ceasing … is to pray — for you.

Yet those who wait for the Lord will gain new strength; they will mount up with wings like eagles, they will run and not get tired, they will walk and not become weary.
— *Isaiah 40:31*

Wait

"Wait" is probably one of the most unpopular words ever. No one likes to wait, or to be told to wait in this day and age of "hurry, hurry, hurry," and instant gratification. Sometimes, however, it is infinitely more wise to wait than to rush on ahead. Running a red light instead of waiting for it to turn green is a good example — especially when you didn't see the policeman hidden around the corner.

If we are going to be honest with each other today, we would have to admit that many times the same is true of our walk with the Lord isn't it? As we begin our look into Godly "waiting," may I be so bold as to offer a sort of "expanded" translation (from the Hebrew) of this very famous verse?

"But those who exercise patient, expectant, faith in the Lord shall have new, powerful strength springing forth, they shall take off with wings as eagles, they shall run with vigor and never grow weary, they shall march forward and never tire in the journey."

Instead of exercising that discipline, however, our tendency is to run ahead of the Lord's plan for our lives, isn't it? We don't take the time we need to really pray and talk to God, we rush ahead of both His wisdom without asking for it, and His timing without waiting for it ... and on top of that, many times we lack the faith to really trust either. It is sort of like children "playing house" and believing they can run a household without needing to ask their parents a single thing about how to do it.

No one is saying that Godly waiting is easy because it, just like a good physical "get fit" plan, requires discipline and effort and practice. But is it worth it? You decide. Do the little exercise I am so fond of — re-read this verse at least 10 times ... slower each time, so what God is trying to say to you through it can really sink in ... wait for it. Let the Holy Spirit fill your heart as only He can do.

"If you abide in Me, and My words abide in you, ask whatever you
wish, and it will be done for you."
— *John 15:7*

Real Prayer. Real Results.

Can we talk for a minute about authentic, successful prayer?…

If there was such a thing as a "Success-O-Meter" for prayer, where would
the needle point with your prayers on the scale? Wouldn't it be great if
for all of us it pointed without fail at 100%? Well … we may not ever be
able to peg the needle on 100%, but we can for sure move it up the scale.

Prayer is our greatest, and most powerful privilege from God. It works.
Period. Unfortunately, there are many who intentionally mis-teach
others about prayer. I have seen it many times on some (not all) big TV
evangelist's ministries. The purpose almost always is to generate more
money. They will point to the last half of this verse to teach a sort of
"free for all" theology about prayer — and that is tragic. God takes
prayer seriously … and so should we.

Do you know, for example, that there are at least 15 things you can do
that will cause God to not attend your prayer at all? (If you want to
know what they are, let me know and I will send you the list.) However,
the two things Jesus tells us to do in the first part of this verse will erase
all 15. And they are essential for authentic, successful prayer. Not always
easy, but always worth the effort. Just look at the results.

Jesus makes this astounding promise about answered prayer because doing
these two things puts God's will and your will side by side, His wisdom
and your understanding side by side, His heart and your heart side by
side.

THEN you can peg the meter.

"I am the door; if anyone enters through Me, he will be saved, and will go in and out and find pasture."
— *John 10:9*

Doors to Nowhere

PickensPhotos

Thanks to my good friend and brother in Christ, Danny Pickens, for this evocative picture of these two old doors. If you were to "open" them, where would you go? Can we agree on nowhere? Even with them wide open, you're still staring straight into the ground. Doors to nowhere.

Life offers lots of doors like that, doesn't it? Haven't we all tried to go through a few of them? A relationship you knew wasn't right, but you tried it anyway. Trying to be someone you are not. Looking at the world through the bottom of a bottle ... all doors that lead to nowhere. And there are many more.

There is one door that is always the right choice. Always. A door with a destination and a purpose on the other side. Always. That door is the

Lord Jesus Christ. Lost and alone? Jesus is the door to being saved (John 14:6). Feeling desperate with no hope? Jesus is the door to green pastures (Psalm 23). Life full of stress? Jesus is the door to peace (John 14:27). Ready to give up? Parched and burned out? Jesus is the door to rivers of living water (John 7:37,38).

Want to really go somewhere in this life — and AFTER this life? Then open the door that will always lead you to the right place. Jesus said, "I am the door." And when you enter through Him, the sky — quite literally — is the limit. In fact, you will meet Him there someday (1st Thess. 4:17).

Fire shall be kept burning continually
on the altar; it is not to go out.
— *Leviticus 6:13*

Eternal Flame

If we are going to be honest today, most of us would have to admit at least a deficiency with our worship of the Lord. Sometimes it can even go "missing in action." It may have been there once — but what happened to it? Let me pull out a list: busy lifestyle — like a job that consumes our week, raising kids, keeping house, week end chores that we can't do any other time, family or friends that merely grin at our mention of God. Sound familiar? If searching for your worship time of the Lord is like looking for a needle in a haystack, there is an old solution that still works.

Here it is. In an Old Testament book that is close to 99% about the law, there is snuggled this beautiful little verse — an instruction even for us today about what our worship should be like. For Israel it was a physical fire on a physical altar. Its purpose was visible, perpetual, public evidence of Israel's worship of the Lord God that all could see and that never went out. An eternal flame.

It is the same instruction for us today. Worship isn't — and was never supposed to be — just a few hours in church each week, or a month, or a year. Our worship of the Lord should be a fire, not a tiny flicker. A fire that never goes out, and that no one can put out. An eternal flame that all can see anytime they look. That's what "on the altar" means for us today. Visible to all. All the time.

And to be fair to God, why shouldn't it be that way? God's love for us never stops. Why should our worship stop ... right?

Hear my cry, O God; give heed to my prayer. From the end of the earth I call to You when my heart is faint; lead me to the Rock that is higher than I.
— *Psalms 61:1,2*

When Hurt Crushes Your Heart

I know what it feels like to have my heart twisted into something unrecognizable, crushed, then discarded like yesterday's trash. A heart so crushed that it hurt to even take a breath. A hurt that bled out through tears every day for two solid years. A heart overwhelmed, just like David here in this psalm.

I am so grateful for our wonderful God who hears our prayers, and who is stronger than all our hurt, aren't you? Look with me at this beautiful psalm where we learn:

Even a king can cry out in despair ...

Even a king can cry out from a place that seems without hope ...

Even a king's heart can be overwhelmed ...

And we learn from it all that our Almighty God is a rock to which we can go in the middle of the darkest despair. On which we can rest. In which we can trust. A foundation that nothing can shake and is higher than ourselves and all our problems. And it is ours for the asking.

> Brethren, I do not regard myself as having laid hold of it yet; but one thing I do: forgetting what lies behind and reaching forward to what lies ahead, I press on toward the goal for the prize of the upward call of God in Christ Jesus.
> — *Philippians 3:13,14*

Spiritual Alzheimer's

As we all know, Alzheimer's is a terrible disease. One of its characteristic symptoms is the way it slowly, inexorably wipes a person's memory away. There is a sort of "spiritual Alzheimer's" however, that can actually improve your life and wipe the dust off of faded hope and joy and focus in your Christian life.

If you can't say anything else about the devil, he is at least predictable. He uses the same tactics over and over again — because they continue to be successful. "Spiritual Alzheimer's" is the cure for two of those tactics:
1. guilt FROM the past.
2. boastful pride IN the past.

Both of these rob us of our Christian hope and joy and focus, and neither belong in a Christian's life. Paul's cure — self-inflicted, spiritual Alzheimer's: wipe from the memory ALL those things which are behind — both sides of the ledger — the positive and the negative ... those memories that either beat us up, or puff us up. Then, and only then, can Christian hope and joy and focus rise to the position they deserve.

Put yourself in Paul's painting here. Imagine that one thing, or one person, or one goal you are more passionate about that anything else on earth. Imagine it is waiting for you as a prize at the end of a racetrack you are standing on. For Paul it was the call of God on his life. Imagine that you are wearing several heavy coats and carrying several large and heavy bags as you begin to run. To run faster and faster and win the prize you so long for, one by one you shed each coat and drop each bag ... as you strain with all your might, reaching out for that goal.

That is the picture Paul paints here. Want to be in it? Want to lift Christian joy and hope and focus to the position it deserves in your life? Try a little spiritual Alzheimer's.

Though He slay me, I will hope in Him…
— Job 13:15

Every Day Above Ground is a Good Day

The character Tony Montana (Al Pacino) in the movie, "Scarface," made this phrase popular. The man from the Bible named Job might have begged to differ. He was a man tested like none other in all of Biblical history. He was so severely tested that an entire book of the Bible is devoted to a personal testimony that bears his name.

Job was a righteous man who God allowed to be tested by the devil himself. Piece by piece, Job's life fell apart. He lost everything — all his possessions, all his children were killed, and in the end even his health was taken away. He was covered with boils and was so weak that dogs came up to lick his wounds and he could do nothing to stop it.

Job's response to it all is this astounding proclamation of faith: "Though he slay me, I will hope in Him." Or, "yet will I trust Him," or, "I wait for Him." Regardless of which translation you choose, it is a shout of defiant faith, stronger than steel that refused to bend under the weight of life's circumstances. It is one of my favorite places in all the Bible.

Then … just in case you don't know "the rest of the story," the devil lost the challenge (as usual) and in the end God restored everything to Job — and He restored all of it two times over. Even his children. When it seems that all is lost and the only option left untried is to give up, remember this tried and tested man from the Bible named Job, to whom the devil gave every reason to turn his back on God. He didn't. Because Job knew that no matter what life brings to the game, every day above ground is a good day to trust the Lord God Almighty.

When the Pharisees saw this, they said to His disciples, "Why is your Teacher eating with the tax collectors and sinners?" But when Jesus heard this, He said, "It is not those who are healthy who need a physician, but those who are sick. But go and learn what this means: 'I desire compassion, and not sacrifice,' for I did not come to call the righteous, but sinners."
— *Matthew 9:11-13*

The Right Stuff

That's the title of one of the all-time great movies, made "way back" in 1983, about the first astronauts of the American space program, and what special men they were. You may not be astronaut material, but it might surprise you to learn that you are still "the right stuff" ... at least in Jesus's eyes. His words here prove it.

Once again, the scribes and Pharisees were indignant with His disciples and asked why Jesus was eating with tax collectors and sinners. These words were His response — and — if you think Jesus couldn't mount a stinging response to hypocrisy, flavored with a hint of sarcasm, pay close attention. He tells them that healthy people don't need a doctor, sick people do, then he uses a phrase that rabbis of the day used with their students: "go and learn what this means," as if Jesus was teaching the self-proclaimed experts of the law like they were His own beginning students. He also called attention to their self-righteous opinions of themselves.

The scribes and Pharisees were obviously not "the right stuff" — but you are. The right stuff group from God's perspective are those who want and need Jesus, and for whom Jesus came. Those who are hurting, those who are suffering, those who are weak spiritually and struggle with sin ... are all candidates for this group. If that is you, welcome to "the right stuff" group. It is not the proud and self-righteous with whom Jesus wishes to dine and spend time, it is you and me — those who need His healing, and cleansing, and forgiving power — and with whom He wishes to spend time. See how special you are? Your part is just letting Him in the door.

> The Spirit Himself testifies with our spirit that we are children
> of God, and if children, heirs also, heirs of God and fellow heirs
> with Christ, if indeed we suffer with Him so that we may also be
> glorified with Him.
> — *Romans 8:16,17*

Family Resemblance

We have all known people who were just the "spitting image" of their mom or dad. One look at them and there is no doubt who their mother or father is. You may be one of those people. If you are a Christian, you are definitely one of those people. These verses in Romans tell us as much.

The Holy Spirit has an unmistakable appearance, it is called "fruit" (love, joy, peace, forbearance, kindness, goodness, faithfulness, gentleness and self-control ... Galatians 5:22,23). He is also described in various other ways throughout God's word. When we are children of God, we have that same appearance — the Spirit Himself testifies with our spirit. Not the same perfection, of course, but the same "family resemblance." And it marks us identifiably as children of God.

But better still is what we have because we ARE children of God. We don't need a reading of the inheritance from our Father because we already know what it is. The Bible says that Jesus is the heir of all things. Heaven included. And we are joint heirs with Christ. That means that we don't just simply GO to heaven when we die (which would be wonderful enough), but, — we own it. It is ours. Right now. How's that for a little hope and encouragement?

"I came that they may have life,
and have it abundantly."
— *John 10:10b*

Hope Unleashed

But for want of space, we could fill a book the size of "War and Peace" with the hope and encouragement contained in just this one sentence from Jesus. Let's look at all we can, however, in this little bit of space. At the outset, let this be underlined: <u>It does NOT justify the "gospel of prosperity" vomited out like a sweet, but poison theological honey by some "gospel" TV personalities onto a gullible and grasping audience</u>. ... This verse is much, MUCH better than that.

First of all, the life Jesus is talking about here is life in Him — eternal life (see John 10:28). He said here that He came to give it. That means BEFORE He came, that kind of life didn't exist — not anywhere, not in any thing, not in anyone. And, apart from Jesus that kind of life STILL doesn't exist. ("I am the way, the truth, AND the life. No man comes to the father, but by Me." John 14:6).

Second, that fabulous phrase: "may have it abundantly." The words Jesus used meant to "have it and keep on having it." It is like an artesian spring that just keeps on gushing. But we can't stop there. Let's take that magnificent word "abundantly," turn it like a diamond in the light of the Bible and see what reflects. Shall we have a look? ...

When we have Jesus as our life, that means we have a treasure chest of other things too. In Matthew 28:20 He promises that He is with us all the time. There is never a moment, never a second, never a cloudy day, never a lonely night that He is not there. The abundance here comes from having a real grasp of just Who is with you all the time. It's time to "lock and load" —

get ready ...

Since Jesus is God, it means that the "Great I AM" is with you all the time: When you are lonely, I AM your Companion. When you are desperate, I AM your Peace. When you are despairing, I AM your Hope. When you are afraid, I AM your Comfort. When you are weak, I AM your Strength. When you are swallowed by the night, I AM your Light. And we could go on and on ...

The One who forgives your sins, the One who gives you eternal life, the One who spoke the universe into existence, the One who defeated the devil on the cross, the One who defeated death at the resurrection, the One who can still the storm with a single word, the Alpha and Omega, on whose thigh is written "King of Kings and Lord of Lords" — it is He, who is with you all the time.

How's THAT for some abundance?

looking for and hastening the coming of the day of God, because of which the heavens will be destroyed by burning, and the elements will melt with intense heat! But according to His promise we are looking for new heavens and a new earth, in which righteousness dwells.

— *2nd Peter 3:12,13*

The Real Global Warming

It is almost impossible these days, to turn on the television without having some doom and gloom prediction about supposed "global warming" shoved into our living room. There is, however, a very real "global warming." The apostle Peter tells us about it right here, and the earth's historical, fluctuating, warming and cooling patterns look sort of like spitting against a hurricane when placed beside the "global warming" of the Lord.

There has never been anything like it before, and there never will be again. It is what is known as "the day of the Lord." For those who have chosen to live their lives without Jesus as their Savior, it will come as a sudden catastrophe from which there will be no escape. Just two verses earlier, Peter says it will come "as a thief in the night."

However, Peter gives us a beautiful "but" that reveals the hope and encouragement that all God's children have: "But ... according to His promise ..." For every single one of us who have trusted Jesus Christ as our Savior, the "day of the Lord" isn't a catastrophic end — it is a new beginning too beautiful for words. It is where the eternity in which God has always dwelled, becomes the eternity in which we all will dwell, too. All the heavens will be new, the earth will be new — and righteousness will be an eternal fragrance in the air.

You whom I have taken from the ends of the earth, and called from its remotest parts and said to you, 'You are My servant, I have chosen you and not rejected you.
— *Isaiah 41:9*

In The Middle Of Nowhere

Ever felt like you were there — the middle of nowhere? I know I have. There are lots of ways to feel like that. From being completely lost on a trip, which I have certainly done ... to being from a town too small to even make it on a map, to feeling lost in life because of bad decisions or even circumstances beyond our control that have left you feeling heartbroken perhaps ... and not knowing which direction to take. The farthest corners — the ends of the earth. I've been there, have you?

This verse of beautiful encouragement is hand-tailored for the person who finds himself or herself in any of those, or other groups — and in the middle of life going on all around you, you feel like you are in the middle of nowhere. This verse was God's beautiful promise to His very own chosen people in the Old Testament, whose city had been destroyed, whose temple had been razed to the ground, and who had been ripped by force from their homeland and scattered to the ends of the earth. The middle of nowhere.

Take heart, dear friend. God's promise to His children has not changed — from the time of His chosen ones in the Old Testament for whom Isaiah wrote this originally, right up to the moment you read these words today. The promise is for you, too. You are chosen, too. Did you notice how many times the word "you" appears in this single verse? Five. From the "ends of the earth" to what may seem like the end of dreams ... to every "you" who feels they are in the middle of nowhere ... God's promise reaches out to your heart today: I have called you, I have chosen you, and I will not cast you aside.

And this is love,
that we walk according to His commandments.
This is the commandment, just as you have heard from the
beginning, that you should walk in it.
— *2ⁿᵈ John 1:6*

Love is....

How many definitions of love, do you suppose, have ever been written that begin with the words "Love is ...?" I have no idea, but my guess is, a bunch.

In our relationship with Jesus, real love is not hard to define, nor is it complicated to understand. The apostle John captures its meaning here in one short sentence. Once so renowned for his explosiveness that he along with his brother James were called the "sons of thunder," John is one more living testimony to the transforming power of the love that Jesus lived and taught.

What are the keys to it? Well, they may not sound very romantic, but there are two: Key #1, knowledge — Key #2, obedience. To walk according to the commandments of Jesus, you first have to know them. Then after you know them, you have to actually do them. Not just read about them, not just think about them. Do them. It isn't just an idea, it is a commandment. And not just an "every now and then" commandment, or a "when you feel like it" commandment. "Walk" means a habitual lifestyle.

Are you tired of the daily path you walk being full of weeds and rocks? Want to see your life turn into a garden? Cultivate the kind of love John just described here and watch what blooms.

For our citizenship is in heaven, from which also we eagerly wait for
a Savior, the Lord Jesus Christ;
— *Philippians 3:20*

A Place To Call Home

There is something that feels really good about being able to call a place
"home." For many of us, the house we call "home" has family that loves
us — our home town where we grew up has friends who love us — our
home state has many places we have visited and know very well. Each
of these places we call "home" has its own unique way of giving us a very
special feeling — the feeling of belonging.

Some folks, however, are not so fortunate. Some folks don't have a home,
some don't have a family, some have moved so many times that calling
one place their "home town" would be difficult and they don't know what
having life-long friends feels like. I have had friends whose parents were
in the military and know exactly what that feels like. Maybe you know
the feeling too, and it's not so easy to feel that sense of belonging, or
maybe you know what it feels like to be shut out of a family circle or
other groups. There are all sorts of ways a person can be made to feel that
they don't belong. And it can be very lonely and hurtful.

There is one place that anyone can call home, where everyone will feel
that beautiful sense of belonging. It will never go away and no one can
take it from you. It is a place called heaven. In fact, if you believe in
Jesus and have trusted Him as your Savior, your citizenship is already
there, no waiting — it is already your home, you already belong. And
one day Jesus will come from there, get you, and take you back with Him.

There was no day like that before it or after it, when the Lord
listened to the voice of a man; for the Lord fought for Israel.
— *Joshua 10:14*

No Problem (part 1)

This verse describes a day unique in the entire history of the earth. No day
like it before or since. Joshua was in a pitched battle with the Amorites
and he prayed a one-sentence prayer — and God granted it: (vs.12,13)
"O sun stand still at Gibeon, and o moon in the valley of Aijalon." So the
sun stood still, and the moon stopped until the nation avenged themselves
on their enemies.

From this scene in the history of God's people, we learn several really
encouraging things:

1. Our prayers don't need to be long to reach the power of God.
2. Our prayers don't need to be full of "religious language" to reach the
   power of God.
3. A short prayer doesn't mean a "small" prayer. Just look at what Joshua
   asked for. It was an enormous request.
4. Perhaps best of all — if, some day you need to ask God for something
   really enormous, you don't have to feel nervous or afraid to ask,
   because ...

The size of your prayer is no problem for God.

Then it happened that night that the angel of the Lord went out and struck 185,000 in the camp of the Assyrians; and when men rose early in the morning, behold, all of them were dead.

— *2nd Kings 19:35*

No Problem (part 2)

This verse of scripture recounts one of the most astounding displays of God's power in all the Bible. Sennacherib, king of the mighty Assyrian Empire had destroyed nation after nation and now had Jerusalem and Judah in his sights. Militarily, Judah didn't stand a chance against the might of the Assyrian army, and that army was camped right outside Jerusalem. It is hard to imagine a bigger problem than the inevitable destruction of your entire nation. They didn't have a prayer.

Well, actually, a prayer is what they DID have. The king of Judah, Hezekiah, prayed to God and asked that He deliver them from the hand of Sennacherib. This verse records God's answer to that prayer: 185,000 soldiers of the Assyrian army dead — overnight. The work of a single angel of the Lord.

From this scene in the history of God's people we learn several really encouraging things:

1. God hears your prayer, even when your enemy seems overwhelming.
2. With God on your side, hope never dies, even when your enemy seems overwhelming.
3. Perhaps best of all — if, some day you need to pray for God's help with a problem so bad that it appears that there is not a single chance for hope, you don't have to feel nervous or afraid to ask, because …

The size of your problem is no problem for God.

Looking at him, Jesus felt a love for him and said to him, "One thing you lack: go and sell all you possess and give it to the poor, and you will have treasure in heaven; and come, follow Me."
— Mark 10:21

The Offer

Question: How many limousines, or mansions, or influential friends, or piles of money do you see in this picture? I count a total of ... none. But — there is something of infinitely greater value than all these things in this powerful and emotional photograph. It is the empty cross. Not a cross with Jesus still dying on it. An empty cross.

As this photograph dramatically communicates, it doesn't matter how many possessions you have, none of it will go with you past this life. Or, you may feel today that your life is already as lonely as this picture — no high-paying job that gives financial security, not many friends, not many possessions. That doesn't matter either. All that matters is what you will do with the offer contained in that empty cross — the offer Jesus gave to the rich man in this wonderful verse of scripture. Because He gives the same offer to you: "Put aside all the other things in your life that are not important, because you will have priceless treasure in heaven. Come — follow Me."

No one is excluded. The offer is for anyone who will take it. Ask the Lord Jesus Christ to be the Savior of your life, and whatever you may feel is your cross to bear in this life...one day you will leave that cross behind as surely as Jesus left His behind. And the words "follow Me" will mean that you will follow Him in victory off that cross ... from this life and into eternal life in heaven — where He has prepared a place, personally, just for you.

My soul, wait in silence for God only,
for my hope is from Him.
— *Psalms 62:5*

Mind Your Maker

Ok, a little play on words, I admit it. A little different take on the old phrase "mind your manners." If we are honest, sometimes manners can be a bit frustrating, can't they? "Turn the other cheek" (one that has given me a hard time through the years), all the way to "don't take the last piece of chicken" even if you feel like you are starving to death. What on earth does all that have to do with this Psalm? Well ... how fortunate that you have asked.

Before anything else, after you read this verse get your Bible and read all the way through verse 8. You will be glad you did — trust me.

Now — here in one sentence is another treasure from the best self-help book in the world. Easy, easy, easy steps to real hope and encouragement. There is only one fly in the ointment: we don't like to take them. Let's have a look at what they are:

1. wait — we don't like to do that.
2. in silence — we don't like to do that either.
3. for God only — we don't like to do that either. Normally, folks come to God as sort of a "last resort," not the ONLY resort.

Try the following: wait, just like it says here ... don't get all bent up and in a hurry. And do it in silence — that's patient waiting without doubting or complaining to God. And wait with the crosshairs of your faith fixed on God and God alone. Will you like it? Will it be easy? Maybe not. But — consider this: hope that is sent personally from the Lord God Almighty is probably more than worth the wait.

For by one offering He has perfected
for all time those who are sanctified.
— *Hebrews 10:14*

The Mistake Circle

Ever feel trapped in that circle? The one of mistakes. Old habits and old personalities die a hard death sometimes — in fact, many times, and we find ourselves making the same old mistakes over and over again. Then we let the devil beat us up about it — but we don't have to ...

Of course, no one is ever going to be able to live a perfect life and never make a mistake. The good news, for anyone who knows Jesus as their Savior and Lord, is that you don't have to try to be perfect. You don't have to be perfect because you have the perfect solution for your mistakes — the offering Christ gave for you on the cross — His own life. What you need to remember is that His offering **_for_** your sins, and His forgiveness **_of_** your sins has already sealed you as perfect in God's eyes. Does that mean we will be perfect here on this earth? Of course not — that will never happen. But, the perspective of God is not earthly. It is heavenly and eternal. And in God's eyes, you already look like His Son. Don't miss the past tense in the verse — "has perfected for all time."

We all should try our best, all the time — but we will all make mistakes because all of us are "a work in progress" in this life. But there is another life. One the devil can't even touch. So the next time the old devil tries to beat you up over mistakes, remind him that he is just wasting his time because you are already perfect in the eyes of the only One whose opinion matters.

'Do not fear, for I am with you; do not anxiously look about you, for
I am your God. I will strengthen you, surely I will help you, surely
I will uphold you with My righteous right hand.'
— Isaiah 41:10

A Hand Up

Year after year at Southwestern Seminary in Ft. Worth, they dedicate one
chapel service per semester to favorite hymns. Even with all the new
stuff that comes out, year after year one of the winners, because of the
richness of its words straight from scripture is "How Firm a Foundation,"
first published in 1787. It is one of the greatest hymns ever written —
and it is anonymous. It majestically sings back to God His own words of
mighty protection and serenely beautiful peace.

The third stanza of this beautiful hymn uses this tremendous verse from
Isaiah almost verbatim. These words from our Lord here of His promised
presence provide unshakeable comfort and powerful assurance, no matter
what you may be going through in life. In the chapter just before this
one (40:12), Isaiah tells us that God measured the waters of the earth
in the palm of His hand. That's the same powerful hand that is in this
verse — the same hand that holds you up.

But He gives a greater grace. Therefore it says, "God is opposed to
the proud, but gives grace to the humble."
— *James 4:6*

The Instruction Manual for Grace

Have you ever noticed how things (especially electronic things) seem to
have become increasingly and frustratingly more and more complicated
with the passing of time?

Time was — a LONG time ago — when you bought a new TV you
brought it home, hooked up the antenna, plugged it in, turned in on and
you were in business. The TV we just acquired the other day to replace the
one that died has an instruction book of 42 PAGES and a remote control
that looks like the console of a 747 jetliner. I can't even understand a lot
of the technical language of the instructions. It makes me feel sort of like
a monkey in front of a spaceship.

Aren't you glad the important things of God never change? And are
simple to understand? God's marvelous grace is one of those things.
Inexhaustible and easy to acquire. If you want to feel it putting joy in
your heart, meaning in your life and wind beneath your wings ... here is
the instruction manual. In a single sentence.

Therefore I am well content with weaknesses,
with insults, with distresses, with persecutions,
with difficulties, for Christ's sake;
for when I am weak, then I am strong.
— *2nd Corinthians 12:10*

When the Going Gets Tough

We have an expression in America: "When the going gets tough, the tough get going." But, I like much better something I saw from a friend the other day — "The same boiling water that softens the potato hardens the egg." It's not about the circumstances that determine an outcome ... it's what you're made of.

The apostle Paul knew all about tough circumstances. If you want the partial list, it is in 2nd Corinthians 11:24-27. In the middle of all that "boiling water," he says here that he is well content. Just how beautiful is that contentment? Well, it is the exact same word God used when His voice came from heaven at Jesus's baptism and He said, "This is my Son, in Whom I am well-pleased."

This is the same Son — the Lord Jesus Christ — who changed Paul's life forever in the middle of a dusty road on the way to Damascus. From that day forward, Paul's own weakness meant nothing to him. He could even rejoice in his weaknesses, because his strength was no longer determined by his circumstances, the "boiling water" of life. His strength was determined by what he was made of, by the man he had become — because of the love and forgiveness and indwelling presence and power of the Son of God. Pointing back to that for the rest of his life was all that mattered to Paul.

That same Son of God — the Lord Jesus Christ — loves you exactly the same way. And indwells you ... exactly the same way. No matter how hot the "boiling water" of life gets, it can roll off you like water off a duck's back — because it's not about the circumstances. It's what you are made of, tough guy.

> ... You shall be holy, for I the Lord your God am holy.
> — *Leviticus 19:2*

You Have Got To Be Kidding

Can God really be serious here? I mean, we already know the Bible says that no one is righteous — not even one person — and that the best of our "righteousness" is like filthy rags in the sight of God. And yet, there it is: You shall be holy for I am holy. And it isn't even a promise. In the original Old Testament Hebrew language it is a command. A command. How can God demand something of us that we already know is impossible? Where is the encouragement in such a demanding task?

Well, first of all, only God is holy. We can never be the "same holy" as God. But — God doesn't ask for that. What God commands in this verse is for our lifestyle to reflect His holiness. Not just try to reflect it — actually do it. Not perfection ... a reflection. Our best attempt at a mirror image. It will never be exactly like God, but it should be our best effort.

Where is the encouragement in such a demanding task, you ask? Well ... the encouragement isn't in the command. It is in God's belief that you can do it — or He wouldn't ask.

"My sheep hear My voice, and I know them, and they follow Me;
and I give eternal life to them, and they will never perish; and no
one will snatch them out of My hand."
— *John 10:27,28*

Here Are The Facts

"Here are the facts" has been a favorite phrase of lawyers and politicians
since forever. When they begin a sentence with these words, many times
what follows is anything BUT the facts, or a "curved version" of various
items held forth as "facts." However, when Jesus says something it is
always a fact. It is always true. The words are sometimes a parable,
sometimes loving and soft, ... and sometimes hard. But they are always
true. Always facts. John 10:27,28 is not an exception.

It is interesting to me how some writers can go on and on and on about
a subject which Jesus captures simply in just a sentence or two. He does it
again here. Volumes and volumes of material have been written over the
years, sometimes entire books, on "authentic Christianity." Jesus captures its
essence in just one sentence. Here are the facts:

If you are a true believer in Jesus, these two verses illuminate SIX —
count 'em — six, immutable and beautiful facts. Two are your actions
(pay attention), and four are Jesus's actions. Keep in mind, these are not
commands. Jesus is stating facts ... facts for the authentic Christian that
already exist. Not facts that might happen, or should happen, or will
happen — facts that already exist and will not change. Here they are:

1. You absolutely pay attention to what He says.
2. You are obedient to what He says.
3. He knows personally, all about you.
4. He gives you eternal life in heaven.
5. Your body may die, but YOU never will.
6. Not anything — person, event, circumstance of life or anything else
   can remove you from your relationship with Jesus. It is His promise.

Those are the facts.

"It will come about after this that I will pour out My Spirit on all
mankind ...
And it will come about that whoever calls on the name of the Lord
will be delivered;"
— *Joel 2:28a,32a*

A Peek Behind Door #3

One of the most popular games shows of all time is called Let's make
a Deal. It has been around for more than 50 years. Contestants are
asked to choose between a series of "deals," ultimately leading to an "all
or nothing" choice between what they already have, and what is hidden
behind one of three doors. You might win a dream car or vacation —
or — you might get a live chicken in a cage. It all depends on which
door you pick.

God has been saying "Let's make a deal" to each one of us for much
longer than 50 years. And, we don't even have to guess about how to
be a winner in the deal. Almost 3,000 years ago, recorded here in the
little book of Joel, God gives us a peek behind "door #3." God let it be
known way back in the Old Testament that there was "a new day coming."
Everything in the Bible from Matthew to the Revelation is devoted to
that new day. It is not hidden behind a door. It is not "maybe." Notice
the phrase "it will happen." No doubt. It will happen — the presence,
power, spirit, gifts and fruit of the Holy Spirit available for everyone. It
will happen — anyone who calls on the name of Jehovah will be saved.

The birth of Christ started it. The resurrection of Christ authenticated it,
Pentecost propelled it, God promised it. If you are like most of the rest of
us, you have made some bad choices in your life. It doesn't matter. Ever
since the first sin in Genesis to the end of John's Revelation, the Bible
is the story of God cleaning up the mistakes of His creation's rebellion.
He can clean up yours too if you will accept His offer. It is the deal of
a lifetime.

You can choose the right Door, right now. Jesus. God has already shown
you the eternal life behind it.

Therefore, having been justified by faith, we have peace with God
through our Lord Jesus Christ, **2** through whom also we have
obtained our introduction by faith into this grace in which we
stand; and we exult in hope of the glory of God. **3** And not only
this, but we also exult in our tribulations, knowing that tribulation
brings about perseverance; **4** and perseverance, proven character; and
proven character, hope; **5** and hope does not disappoint, because
the love of God has been poured out within our hearts through the
Holy Spirit who was given to us.
— *Romans 5:1-5*

Beating The Rat Race

It would be hard to deny that for many today, their pace of life could be
placed on a scale somewhere between "frenetic" and "impossible." The
daily grind at work trying to get ahead, raising children with Christian
values in an increasingly hedonistic world, keeping up with the Joneses,
demands eating away at the little "free time" that exists," trying to stay
one step ahead of the debt monster .... We call it "the rat race." These
few verses of scripture show us how to beat it.

The first step in beating the rat race is a right relationship with the Lord
Jesus Christ, and it is right there in **verse 1**. That step is taken through
faith in Him as your personal Savior. When He becomes Savior in your
life, He forgives all your sins, He also justifies you (makes right) before
God, and prepares a place for you in heaven. His position as Lord is a bit
different.

Jesus is already Lord over everything and everyone — in truth, no one
"makes" Jesus Lord over anything. It is unfortunate that this idea and this
phrase is used so repeatedly in the church, because it is dead wrong —
100% of the time. No one ... no one ever ... "makes" Jesus Lord over
anything. He is already Lord over all creation, and Lord ***over everyone's
eternity*** — Christian or not — but, what beats the rat race is *submitting*
to Him as Lord over your life. In the area of your own free will to
determine the course of your life, He will not intrude. He enters only if
He is invited. Be smart. Make the right choice — it is what brings the
peace with God mentioned in this verse. It is the antithesis of the rat
race. And having that peace, is how you beat that rat race.

Now for the rest of our text here. Are you ready?

Verse 2 — adds rejoicing to the peace.

Verse 3 — (being justified and having hope in the living God) we are able to rejoice in our trials and tests in life (refer to our list in the first paragraph), knowing that these things lead to perseverance;

Verse 4 — and perseverance leads to proven character; and proven character, hope;

Verse 5 — and hope does not disappoint, because the love of God has been poured out within our hearts through the Holy Spirit who was given to us! Peace WITH God means that you have the peace OF God as well. And as Philippians 4:7 tells us, that is the peace that passes all understanding — and it will guard your heart and mind. No more rat race.

If you are on the rat race highway, take the exit marked "peace with God." Trust me, you will never want to get back on that highway again.

"I will open rivers on the bare heights and springs in the midst of the valleys; I will make the wilderness a pool of water and the dry land fountains of water.
— *Isaiah 41:18*

Out of Gas

Have you ever been on a trip and you run out of gas in the middle of nowhere? I have. Or how about this — you passed the last gas station a long way back, supremely confident that you had plenty of gas to make it to the next gas station. Then, as the low-fuel warning light comes on, you spend the next half-hour or so in a frantic cold sweat, praying and hoping desperately to see a gas station around each corner. Been there? Done that? Even though running out of gas is silly with all the gas stations that exist today, we still let that happen, don't we?

Sometimes we treat our lives just like we treat our cars, don't we? Pushing the limits. Trying to run forever on empty. Most of us at one time or another have been there, haven't we? There, in life's "middle of nowhere" — those desolate places and valleys where we can feel so alone and empty — and our heart just runs out of gas.

God tells us through Isaiah here, that we need never reach that point. God is telling us here that no matter how desolate we feel, no matter how deep and dark the valley, no matter how parched and endless the desert, if we will just come to Him we can keep our tank full — gushing rivers and fountains, clear and cool pools of water, artesian springs — God's spiritual gas stations of hope and encouragement — and they are right there, around every corner, even in the middle of nowhere. — Fill 'er up, please. —

"… I tell you, there is joy in the presence of the angels of God over one sinner who repents."
— *Luke 15:10*

Joy Party

Everyone knows what a pity party is. What we have here is a joy party. I have tried many, many times in my years of ministry to imagine what heaven is like. I'm pretty sure you probably have too, am I right? The authors of the Bible … even Jesus Himself (like here in this verse) give us tantalizing glimpses.

For the incredible vision of joy contained in this verse to open fully in your mind and heart, let it sink in just how many angels there are in the presence of God: in Revelation 5:11, John says "myriads of myriads and thousands of thousands." It is another way of saying, "WAY too many to count or imagine." The united voice of all these angels, he describes in Revelation 19:6 as many waters and mighty peals of thunder, saying "Hallelujah! For the Lord our God, the Almighty reigns."

Now — Jesus says here that there is joy in the presence of this same enormous group whenever a sinner repents — just one. Imagine the size of THAT joy. Now imagine how many people who are repenting of their sins at any given time around the world. Add THAT to the equation. Let the vision of that amount of joy sink in for a bit. But there is something even more beautiful you can think about here, from the words of Jesus Himself.

Have you ever repented? Asked for forgiveness of your own sin and really meant it? If you have, you — personally — have been responsible for creating joy in heaven. How's THAT for a little encouragement today?

"Thus says the Lord, the God of Israel, 'It was I who brought you
up from Egypt and brought you out from the house of slavery.
I delivered you from the hands of the Egyptians and from the hands
of all your oppressors, and dispossessed them before you and gave
you their land, and I said to you, "I am the Lord your God; you
shall not fear the gods of the Amorites in whose land you live. But
you have not obeyed Me."
— Judges 6:8-10

You Gotta Dance With The One That Brung Ya

This was a favorite expression of University of Texas head football coach, Darrell Royal. In the world of sports, it means sticking with the players and plays that result in wins. This lesson is true along life's road as well — perhaps never more powerfully demonstrated than right here in the book of Judges.

"Deliverance disdained" is an apt description of these verses and of how Israel responded to God's grace in freeing them from 400 years of bondage, vanquishing their enemies in front of their eyes, and giving them the promised land free of charge. We look today at what God did for Israel, how quickly they turned their backs on the Lord, and wonder in stunned amazement at how they could do that. But — do we really have the right to do that?

As Christians, has God not delivered us as well? And from an enemy much more powerful and wicked than Egypt? Do we not have a promised land free of charge waiting for us as well? An eternal, heavenly home much better than Canaan? Do we not succumb to the "gods of the Amorites" all around us today? All those things in our lives that we put ahead of God ... like everyone else does. And we leave the God who saved us, neglected and unheeded in the shadows of our lives ...

If hope seems to elude you today, if you feel discouraged or defeated, there remains a sure cure. Hope and encouragement is just around the corner. All you need to do is get off the dance floor with the "gods of the Amorites" and dance with the One that brung ya — brung ya out of sin and death — and into eternal love, eternal forgiveness, and eternal life.

I have fought the good fight, I have finished the course, I have kept the
faith; in the future there is laid up for me the crown of righteousness,
which the Lord, the righteous Judge, will award to me on the day; and
not only to me, but also to all who have loved His appearing.
— *2nd Timothy 4:7,8*

Ladies And Gentlemen, Place Your Bets

This verse captures the belief on which I have bet my entire life and future.
Nothing I have ever experienced in life has ever been able to disprove
anything I have ever read in the beautiful, magnificent and powerful word
of God we call the Bible. Over the years I have had some interesting
conversations with some atheist and agnostic friends who find it foolish
that I bet my life on the idea of a loving God and eternal life in heaven
for those who believe in Jesus. Aside from the unmistakable presence of
the Lord Jesus Christ in my heart and personally watching His power in
action on countless occasions, I have always told my unbelieving friends
the following: "If, in the end, I am wrong, I have lost nothing for having
lived a life that knows peace in the middle of any storm, faith that is
stronger than any problem, and principles by which to live my life that are
set out in the Bible, the best self-help book ever written. IF, on the other
hand, YOU are wrong ... you have lost a great deal.

...He cried out with a loud voice, "Lazarus, come forth." The man
who had died came forth, bound hand and foot with wrappings,
and his face was wrapped around with a cloth. Jesus said to them,
"Unbind him, and let him go."
— *John 11:43,44*

Lost Cause

I would love to have been able to see this in person. The lost cause to
beat all lost causes. Lazarus was the brother of Martha and Mary, and
a friend whom Jesus loved. When he fell ill, the sisters implored Jesus to
come and heal him. Jesus delayed in coming. On purpose. When Jesus
finally did get there, Lazarus had already been dead 4 days. Jesus told the
people to remove the stone in front of the tomb. The sisters told him that
it would smell terribly because their brother had been dead for 4 days.
There was no doubt — Lazarus was dead.

After they removed the stone, Jesus prayed, then spoke the words above.
Some have said that Jesus HAD to call Lazarus by name ... because
if He has said simply, "Come forth!", EVERY dead body in the entire
graveyard would have come forth. Now, a moment of truth. To make
things seem a little more real, imagine you are standing there and out of
that tomb walks a man who had been dead for 4 days, all wrapped up
like a mummy — and it is to YOU Jesus says, "Loose him and let him
go." Tell me, how fast are you going to run up to that figure and start
unwrapping? I bet they were ALL a little nervous ... even the sisters.

Jesus's reputation of healing was very well-known at this time, especially
among His friends. But what He displayed here by waiting until everyone
else thought it was too late, was nothing less than stunning. Had Jesus
arrived when Lazarus was "just a little sick," anyone could have suggested
that Lazarus got well all by himself and Jesus didn't have anything at all
to do with him getting well again, much less perform a healing miracle.
Jesus raising a man from his tomb who had been dead for 4 days sure
erased the possibility of that suggestion, didn't it? What Jesus did here
is great encouragement for us — the next time we think God's response
to us is too slow.

So the wall was completed on the twenty-fifth of the month Elul, in fifty-two days. When all our enemies heard of it, and all the nations surrounding us saw it, they lost their confidence; for they recognized that this work had been accomplished with the help of our God.
— *Nehemiah 6:15,16*

New Beginnings From An Old Foundation

If you have ever felt like your life was in ruins and beyond repair ... if it seems like everyone around you has looked at your life and circumstances as a lost cause — take heart, you are not the first person this has happened to. Over 400 years before Christ was even born, something happened that will encourage your heart. It is the story of Nehemiah and the rebuilding of the wall of Jerusalem.

Jerusalem had been destroyed by Nebuchadnezzar — burned to the ground. It had laid in ruins for 70 years. For many of us that is more years than we have been alive. Think about that. Then Nehemiah returned to that burned out pile of rubble that was Jerusalem — all that was left of the city of the once-proud, chosen people of God. He returned with a rag tag group of the Jewish people. His goal: rebuild the once-mighty wall that surrounded his city. It seemed like such an impossible task that all the regions surrounding Jerusalem ridiculed and mocked him. Some outright opposed him. In just 52 days the laughter stopped dead in its tracks.

Sometimes rebuilding our own lives from what has been turned into burned-out rubble might seem just as impossible as Nehemiah's wall. People around you might look at you and not even give you a chance of succeeding. It doesn't matter. Don't overlook by Whose hand the work is done. And what God did in Nehemiah's life, He can do in yours too. It doesn't mean it will be easy. Nehemiah had to be courageous and work very hard, but if you are willing to do your part, God is still in the business of new beginnings from old foundations ... still today.

This was in accordance with the eternal purpose which He carried out in Christ Jesus our Lord, in whom we have boldness and confident access through faith in Him.
— Ephesians 3:11,12

Nothing Lasts Forever

Randall Park Mall, North Randall, Ohio opened its doors in 1976 as the largest shopping mall in the world at the time — 2,000,000 square feet and 5,000 staff members. A scant 33 years later, closed and abandoned, the picture on the left is but a memory — replaced by the image on the right (until it was demolished).

The same thing happened to the Grecian Empire. The same thing happened to the Roman Empire. Monuments of human history to the truth that nothing man-made lasts forever.

In light of this, then why not give a chance to the one thing that never changes — and DOES last forever? The eternal purpose of the eternal and unchanging God. Just what is that purpose, which He accomplished in Christ Jesus our Lord? To love you — for an eternity. That is His purpose that has never changed, and never will. It will sustain you through — and carry you past — every worry and problem in your life.

If you are tired of shopping in life for everything that doesn't last, take a trip to God's Mall. It will never close its doors. It is always open, it is always full of love — and it is all free.

He has not dealt with us according to our sins, nor rewarded us
according to our iniquities. For as high as the heavens are above the
earth, so great is His lovingkindness toward those who fear Him.
As far as the east is from the west, so far has He removed our
transgressions from us.
— *Psalms 103:10-12*

A Light Sentence

In our system of justice, there is usually a range of punishments for someone
who is found guilty. Mitigating circumstances guide a judge in assigning
a sentence that can be the "minimum" all the way up to the "maximum,"
which can include a fine, imprisonment ... or both. Sometimes when we
see a person who has done something terribly wrong, but receives very
little punishment, we say they got "a light sentence." We could say the
very same thing about ourselves, couldn't we ... when it comes to standing
before the Lord God Almighty?

In fact, we didn't even get a light sentence. Our case got dismissed
altogether. Those of us who truly believe in the Lord Jesus Christ as
our Savior have a very, very long list of reasons to be extremely grateful
for God's grace in our individual lives. Of all the many items on the
list, I am not sure that ANY can rank any higher than what is contained
in these magnificent verses of scripture. Where would we be if God
dealt with us according to our sins instead of according to His grace?
If, instead of giving us His love, He gave us what we actually deserved?

But He doesn't. Instead of giving us what we deserve, He takes ALL our
sins away from us and throws them away from His presence "as far as
the east is from the west" — an expression which means a distance that
cannot be measured. The effect of the sacrifice of Jesus in our lives is at
the same time, both very precious and very powerful. Aren't you glad?

For as high as the heavens are above the earth, so great is His
lovingkindness toward those who fear Him.
As far as the east is from the west, so far has He removed our
transgressions from us.
— *Psalms 103:11,12*

How Far is Far For God?

This is sort of a companion devotional to "A Light Sentence" from Psalms
103:10-12. How far is far for God? Well, when it comes to removing
your sins from you, it is a distance that can't even be measured.

The voyager I and II spacecraft are arguably the most amazing stories
in all of space exploration. They were launched in 1977 with the short-
term purpose of exploring Jupiter and Saturn, which they completed,
and more — in 1989. Their continued performance, right up to today
has stunned everyone involved with the program. Built to last just 5
years, they will celebrate their 43 birthday this September (2020) — from
a distance of over 14 BILLION miles and still streaking away, at over
38,000 mph. They are the farthest manmade objects from earth and have
left our solar system and passed into interstellar space a number of years
ago.

That remarkable, almost incomprehensible distance doesn't even get out of
the driveway when it comes to how far God removes your sins from you.
With a mercy too great to be measured, God removes your sins a distance
too great to be measured. From eternity to the east to eternity to the
west. Go ahead, try to measure that. And remember it, the next time
the devil tries to beat your heart to death with your sins from the past.

And — if God removes your sins as far as the east is from the west, and
forgets them — you can too.

> "...I will forgive their iniquity, and their sin
> I will remember no more."
> — *Jeremiah 31:34d*

A Lapse of Memory

Ever have one of those? The truth is, with no medical excuse, I have been having them since I was a teenager. Some of my friends and family who have known me all those years might even be tempted to say that I am "absent-minded." Ok, ok … some of them have actually told me that. Fortunately for us, God doesn't have that problem. He never forgets anything. With one exception.

This is actually a follow-up to our time together with our two devotionals from Psalms 103. In that Psalm, when we ask forgiveness, God separates our sins from us "as far as the east is from the west," meaning a distance so vast that it is impossible to measure. Remembering this verse in Jeremiah along with that Psalm, paints a matchless beauty and finality to the way God deals with our sins.

The Lord God Almighty, infinite in His power, imposes a self-limitation on that infinite power in this one, single, solitary area: your sin. God remembers everything — except that. He forgets them, and never remembers them again. The next time the old devil tries to beat you to death with your past, remind yourself — it doesn't exist anymore. According to God's own promise it is gone … and forgotten. By God Himself.

But do not let this one fact escape your notice, beloved, that with the Lord one day is like a thousand years, and a thousand years like one day.
— *2nd Peter 3:8*

8-Day Alarm Clock

We are all familiar, some of us perhaps a little too familiar, with the expression, "wound up tighter than an 8-day alarm clock." It describes a person whose emotions and worries walk a tightrope every day, and they seem to eat stress like other people eat a chocolate bar.

If there was ever a group of people who had a reason to be wound up tighter than an 8-day alarm clock, it was the people to whom Peter wrote his two letters. They were confused, afraid, and deeply disheartened because they misunderstood the timing of the 2nd coming of Jesus. And it was happening in the middle of the merciless persecution of Christians by the emperor, Nero. It was to this group that Peter penned these beautiful and comforting words — and they reach across time to us today, too.

Maybe this little devotional is reaching someone today in the "8-day alarm clock" crowd. Your stress spring is wound tight over what seems like endless debt, or horrible work conditions, or kids making bad choices, or a marriage going bad — it can be a really long list. Real problems that really hurt ... and you pray, and God's answer seems to never come. It is for you, to whom these beautiful words reach out today.

Put away your 8-day alarm clock and live by God's timepiece. His timing is very rarely our timing. His clock doesn't operate on a 24-hour day. You don't have to live all wound up, because God takes care of all our worries. He just does it in His time. Peter said to never stop remembering that. It might not happen when you expect or want, but it doesn't mean that God doesn't hear you anymore, it doesn't mean that God doesn't care about you anymore, it doesn't mean that God doesn't love you anymore. Want proof? You need look no further than the cross of Jesus.

"Are not two sparrows sold for a cent?
And yet not one of them will fall to the ground apart from your
Father. But the very hairs of your head are all numbered. So do
not fear; you are most valuable than many sparrows."
— *Matthew 10:29-31*

I Never Forget a Hair

"I never forget a face." is a very common little sentence. God takes the meaning of that little sentence to an entirely new level when it comes to how much you mean to Him. Never forgetting a face is one thing, but ... never forgetting a single hair?

Have you ever felt worthless? I know I have. It often happens just about the time something occurs which shows you that your life — the life you thought mattered and had value to someone ... doesn't, actually. A friend turns their back on you, a spouse leaves you, if you are a parent it could be a child or children who reject you, it could be a boss that fires you. I have experienced the hurt of every one of those things, and you may have, too. Hard and hurting blows in life can leave us feeling worthless and unimportant sometimes.

When Jesus first spoke these words, His disciples would soon have their own hard, hurting blows coming their way. These were His words to them, and they are His words to us today. Jesus reminds us that the death of a virtually worthless bird will not escape God's attention. Never fall victim then, to the temptation to think that you are not of great value, especially to the One who matters most — God. You, whose every hair has a number. You, who are worth the life of God's only Son. That makes you valuable beyond measure ... and pretty important, too.

Therefore if you have been raised up with Christ, keep seeking the things above, where Christ is, seated at the right hand of God. Set your mind on the things above, not on the things that are on earth. For you have died and your life is hidden with Christ in God. When Christ, who is our life, is revealed, then you also will be revealed with Him in glory.
— *Colossians 3:1-4*

A New Family Album

Let's take a quick, little survey, ok? Ladies first, as always. Ok ladies ... how would you like it, if you saw your husband/boyfriend with a faraway look in his eyes, constantly looking at pictures of his old girlfriends? My guess is that you would not only be upset, but your mood would register somewhere between furious and livid — right? Ok, guys ... same thing. How would you like it, if you saw your wife/girlfriend with a faraway look in HER eyes, constantly looking at pictures of her old boyfriends? Your testosterone reaction would make your blood just about boil — right?

Why would we react that way? Isn't it because when we begin a new relationship, our interest, allegiance, not to mention our focus, should no longer be on the old relationship, but on the new one?

If you consider yourself a believer in Jesus and a child of God and yet, you seem to be missing hope, encouragement and joy in your life, I ask you to consider the message Paul wrote to the Colossians in these verses. Think of two "family albums." One old, one new. The old one is full of mental pictures of the life you used to have before Jesus: the wrong kinds of friends, the wrong kinds of places, the wrong kinds of attitudes, the wrong kind of lifestyle. The mental pictures in the new "family album" are different: the right kinds of friends, the right kinds of places, the right kinds of attitudes, the right kind of lifestyle. That is because since the Lord Jesus Christ became your Savior, you have been putting things in the new album that don't include "things on the earth."

Pay attention to the words "seek" and "set" here. They tell us how to start a new family album. You have a completely new life, a new family — and new experiences ahead. Your life in the family of God is not the same as your life before, and you should NEVER spend time in wistful thoughts of those days gone by and your past relationship with the world. Search passionately for the spiritual things of God — then firmly set your mind on them, not on things on the earth. Those old thoughts and memories are not worthy of a place in your new family album.

But the fruit of the Spirit is love, joy, peace, patience, kindness, goodness, faithfulness, gentleness, self-control; against such things there is no law.
— *Galatians 5:22,23*

The Holy Fruit Basket

The fruit basket of the Holy Spirit is very, very interesting. To understand just HOW interesting, one of the things we need to do is notice that the word is "fruit" (singular) and not "fruits" (plural). It may seem insignificant, but it is actually one of the things that makes this fruit so exceptional.

Think for a minute about all kinds of different, delicious fruits. Apples, oranges, peaches, plums ... on and on we could go, each having its own delicious flavor. Now, imagine you have a fruit in your hand — a single fruit — you take a bite and it taste like an apple, you turn the fruit and take another bite ... this time it tastes like an orange. Turn it one more time and it tastes like a peach. All from the same, single fruit. This is how the fruit of the Spirit shows itself in the life of a Christian. One person, many delicious tastes, depending on what life puts in his or her path.

And keep in mind, these fruits are not commands — for the Christian, they are descriptions. Descriptions of you. Character traits that show themselves because of "spiritual genetics" — because of the Holy Spirit who is living inside you.

The Lord bless you, and keep you; the Lord make His face shine on
you, and be gracious to you; the Lord lift up His countenance on
you, and give you peace.
— *Numbers 6:24-26*

Words of Gratitude

Sometimes events happen in our lives through friends or family around us —
acts of kindness or support — that are so significant it is difficult to find
words of gratitude sufficient to express how we really feel. This happened to
me a number of years ago. I live in Brazil, my home is Madisonville, Texas,
and after not being financially able to go home or see any of my family for
over three years, a group of my friends came together and prayed for us and
sacrificially donated the funds necessary for Claudia and I to return home for
a visit. What remains so inspiring and emotional for me to this day about it,
is that I had not seen or talked to some of those friends for over 40 years —
since we all graduated from high school. It was such a testimony to what real
friendship is all about, and it still brings tears to my eyes after all this time.

When all this happened, I dedicated these verses in Numbers to all of
them. Six actions of Jehova God for the lives of some very special people.
1. The Lord bless you — the goodness of God in your life.
2. The Lord keep you — the protection of God in your life.
3. The Lord make His face shine on you — the manifest favor and
   personality of God in your life.
4. The Lord be gracious to you — the mercy of God in your life.
5. The Lord lift up His countenance on you — the personal, providential
   work of God in your life.
6. The Lord give you peace — the victory of God over all trials,
   tribulations, worries and sorrows in your life.

(In Philippians 4:7, it is this peace that the apostle Paul says passes all
understanding.)

My friends I mentioned at the beginning are very special people — but,
so are you. How special are you? Special enough for Jesus to die for you,
so you deserve these words, too. And — If you want to thank a special
friend, or group of friends, and bless their hearts for something they have
done for you, you would be hard pressed to find a better way to do it than
these words of blessing written by Moses himself, over 3,000 years ago.

"I will ask the Father, and He will give you another Helper, that He
may abide with you forever;"
— *John 14:16*

I've Got Your Back

I so love this verse. It is a wonderful example of the expression "I've
got your back." This verse — all by itself — gives profound hope and
encouragement about our relationship with Jesus, with God, and with the
Holy Spirit. All three.

1. Because of your relationship with Jesus, Jesus prays on your behalf —
   "I will ask the Father ..."
2. Because of your relationship with Jesus, God acts personally in your
   life — "He will give you ..."
3. Because of your relationship with Jesus, and because of the gift of
   God, you have the Holy Spirit in your life. The "Helper" is the Holy
   Spirit. Verse 26 which follows, says it explicitly.
4. Once the Holy Spirit comes into your life, He never leaves. He is the
   "spiritual DNA evidence" that you have been born again, that you have
   become a new creature (2nd Cor. 5:17). We all know how powerful
   DNA evidence has become in solving crimes. It unmistakably
   identifies who a person is. The DNA of the Holy Spirit is marked by
   His gifts (1st Cor. 12:7-11) and His fruit (Gal.5:22-23).

You can quench the work of the Holy Spirit (1st Thess.5:19), you can
even grieve the Holy Spirit (Eph.4:30), but He will never leave. It is the
same promise of God in Hebrews 13:5.

Now, the subject of the Holy Spirit is much too big for a short devotional,
but from just this one verse you can rest assured that:

1. NO one in a white suit and patent leather shoes dancing around on
   a stage and waving his arms or coat around like crazy has the power to
   get the Holy Spirit anywhere NEAR you, much less give Him to you.
2. You have the Holy Spirit in your life because you have Jesus in your life.
   Period. It doesn't have ANYthing to do with speaking in tongues. Period.
3. The Holy Spirit doesn't "come and go" in your life. He NEVER
   leaves. Period.

How's that for some encouragement?

He only is my rock and my salvation, my stronghold; I shall not be
shaken.
— *Psalms 62:6*

Creating A Solid Foundation

Creating a solid foundation in the construction world is critical to building
anything. The same requirement is true in our Christian life, also. There
is one thing, however, that makes a spiritual foundation much, much
less complicated than a physical foundation. An indestructible spiritual
foundation has only one ingredient: God.

Sometimes our biggest mistake is just "including" God in the foundation
of our life. If you want a defense that never loses a fight, if you want
a faith that never fails, a foundation that never shakes, remember ... God
isn't PART of the foundation, He IS the foundation. Everything else is
merely shifting sand.

For you have not received a spirit of slavery leading to fear again,
but you have received a spirit of adoption as sons by which we cry
out, "Abba! Father!"
— *Romans 8:15*

Seein' Things At Night

This title is a hilarious old poem by Eugene Field, and one of my favorites about a little boy who sees all sorts of creepy things at night every time he has done something "bad" during the day.

Isn't that exactly how the ol' devil tries to work on us? No matter how hard we try we will never be perfect (nor does God expect that from us), we will always make mistakes, we will never deserve all that the Lord gives us with eternal life, and we will always stand in need of forgiveness for something. The devil tries to give us nightmares about that, tries to hide our hope with guilt, tries to make us forget that God loves us and forgives us — and tries to bury our joy with fear.

But the truth is that the Lord of all, and over all, keeps right on loving us — every minute of every day, and night. For all of us who have accepted the Lord Jesus Christ, the Son of God, as our Savior we have also become sons of God. It is a promise straight from our Bible, the word of God. That is not something that WILL happen — it has *already* happened. That is the promise and proclamation of this verse. No more bondage. No more fear. No more seeing things at night. Because the Lord of Light, the King of Kings and Lord of Lords is our Heavenly Father.

Just for fun, for anyone interested here is the entire poem, 'Seein' Things At Night', by Eugene Field (1850-1895):

I ain't afraid uv snakes or toads, or bugs or worms or mice,
An' things 'at girls are skeered uv I think are awful nice!
I'm pretty brave I guess; an' yet I hate to go to bed,
For, when I'm tucked up warm an snug an' when my prayers are said,
Mother tells me "Happy Dreams" an' takes away the light,
An' leaves me lyin' all alone an' seein' things at night!

Sometimes they're in the corner, sometimes they're by the door,
Sometimes they're all a-standin' in the middle uv the floor;

Sometimes they are a-sittin' down, sometimes they're walkin' round
So softly and so creepy-like they never make a sound!
Sometimes they are as black as ink, an' other times they're white—
But color ain't no difference when you see things at night!

Once, when I licked a feller 'at had just moved on our street,
An' father sent me up to bed without a bite to eat,
I woke up in the dark an saw things standin' in a row,
A-lookin' at me cross-eyed an' p'intin' at me—so!
Oh, my! I wuz so skeered 'at time I never slep' a mite—
It's almost alluz when I'm bad I see things at night!

Lucky thing I ain't a girl or I'd be skeered to death!
Bein' I'm a boy, I duck my head an' hold my breath.
An' I am, oh so sorry I'm a naughty boy, an' then
I promise to be better an' I say my prayers again!
Gran'ma tells me that's the only way to make it right
When a feller has been wicked an' sees things at night!

An' so when other naughty boys would coax me into sin,
I try to skwush the Tempter's voice 'at urges me within;
An' when they's pie for supper, or cakes 'at's big an' nice,
I want to—but I do not pass my plate f'r them things twice!
No, ruther let Starvation wipe me slowly out o' sight
Than I should keep a-livin' on an' seein' things at night!

"...and they said to Him, Then who can be saved?" Looking at
them, Jesus said,
"With people it is impossible, but not with God;
for all things are possible with God."
— *Mark 10:26,27*

Making the Impossible, Possible

When it comes to being saved, the concept of an "all-powerful" God
is pretty mind blowing, isn't it? In my 40+ years of trying to preach
and minister, any number of times I have had someone say to me things
similar to, "I am a lost cause." Or, "There is no way God could love me
after what I have done." If that is you today, my friend, that statement is
simply not true. In response to the question, "Who then can be saved?",
Jesus responded straight up that a manmade attempt no matter how
noble ... wasn't just unlikely to succeed, it was flat out impossible. But
God is NOT limited like man is. The promise of Jesus here is that with
God ALL things are possible.

Here is the truth — No matter how good you have been, without God in
your life you can't be saved.

Here is the truth — No matter how bad you have been, WITH God in
your life you can't NOT be saved.

That means that no matter who you are, no matter where you are, no
matter what you have done in the past, no matter how much you may
have ignored God ... if you will accept Him into your life through faith
in the Lord Jesus Christ, you not only MIGHT be saved — you WILL
be saved.

It is the promise of an all-powerful God, who loves you, and with whom ...
all things are possible.

The Lord is not slow about His promise, as some count slowness,
but is patient toward you, not wishing for any to perish but for all
to come to repentance.
— *2ⁿᵈ Peter 3:9*

God Always Delivers

"Neither snow nor rain nor heat nor gloom of night stays these couriers from the swift completion of their appointed rounds." This is the postal tribute chiseled in stone at the Smithsonian's Postal Museum. My friend, Mary, from my hometown of Madisonville, Texas delivered the mail for all of us for years just like that quote says.

God is in the delivery business too. Never a lost package. Never a delivery to the wrong address. Never late. When you put your faith in Jesus and repentance becomes a part of your life — God does His part, too. Always. He delivers the package of salvation right to the door of your heart. Immediately. Why should we think of salvation as a package? Well, because inside the "package" we have: eternal life in heaven, forgiveness of sin and removal of its burden, inheritance of all things with Jesus, abiding presence of the Holy Spirit, an Advocate (Jesus Himself) who prays to the Father on our behalf, and the power of God available — all the time.

The reason that I, personally, love this verse so much is two-fold. First: that little word "any" meant me too. I was included among those who God did not want to perish ... in spite of not deserving, ever, even one drop of His love. Two: that word "patient." It means "waiting" + "patience" + "grace." And God waited that way for me — for 28 years.

I was the one who was late. Not God.

Then, on the day I finally opened my heart to God, there He was ... right on time, with my package. And He will deliver the exact same "package" to anyone who asks for it. Always.

...and that you be renewed in the spirit of your mind, and put on the new self, which in the likeness of God has been created in righteousness and holiness of the truth.
— *Ephesians 4:23,24*

Before and After

Brazil, where I do my best to serve as a missionary, is famous for its beautiful butterflies. I have seen some almost as big as my hand. God is famous for His beautiful children. Not a cull in the bunch. If you know Jesus as your Savior, you are a child of God and that is you there on the right. If you are not — you can be.

The transformation God accomplishes in His children is stunning, to say the least. He takes the equivalent of what is on the left there, and when He is finished you have what is on the right. When you become God's child, the old mind disappears, the old heart disappears, the old self disappears — the caterpillar is gone. Forever. In its place is the new you ... in the likeness of God, created in righteousness and holiness. And unlike that beautiful Blue Morpho up there which will die in just 4 months, what God creates in you will never die. And in His eyes (which are the only ones that matter), no matter how many times you mess up, what God sees is the "you" there on the right. That is the power of His forgiveness in Christ.

There is one problem, however. The old devil. He never stops trying to hold up the picture of your old caterpillar self in your mind. He never stops trying to burden you with the guilt of the past. Don't let him get away with that. You are not the caterpillar ... anymore.

(By the way, for anyone who might be wondering, yes, that is the actual caterpillar for the Blue Morpho.)

Trust in the Lord with all your heart and do not lean on your own understanding. In all your ways acknowledge Him, and He will make your paths straight.
— *Proverbs 3: 5,6*

Accurate Directions

If you have ever gotten lost because of bad directions, you know from experience how frustrating it can be to know where you need to go, but not know how to get there. There is a path, a map, from point A to point B and you don't know what it is. Long years ago, I had a really funny key chain. On the fob it had a cartoon drawing of a guy in a convertible, hair blowing in the wind, hand over his head throwing a map into the air. The caption was, "Map??? I don't need no stinkin' map!!!" In life, we can also choose that attitude, but the smart thing to do is realize that in life we DO need a map ... and God is it.

For I consider that the sufferings of this present time are not worthy
to be compared with the glory that is to be revealed to us.
— *Romans 8:18*

What's It Worth?

That question gets asked a lot in a couple of places: the area of business,
and the area of personal suffering. We want to address the second area.
My bet is that just about everyone knows what it is like to suffer in one
way or another ... from physical suffering like a broken bone, all the way
to a ruptured bank balance or the pain of sickness. Perhaps you have
met suffering on the field of broken hopes or dreams. Suffering is real ...
but, so is hope. The good news is that the last word doesn't belong to
suffering.

The apostle Paul who wrote this verse knew a little about suffering, too.
Here is his list from 2nd Corinthians 11:24-27: frequent imprisonment,
flogged, exposed to death repeatedly, received 39 lashes 5 times, beaten
with rods 3 times, stoned, shipwrecked 3 times, a night and a day in the
open sea, constantly on the move, danger from rivers, bandits, his own
countrymen, Gentiles, danger in the city, in the country, at sea, danger
from false brothers, constant hard labor, often went without sleep, food,
water, clothing, suffered from exposure to the cold, and the daily pressure
of worry for all the churches.

And then he says that all of it, put together, isn't even worthy to be
compared with the honor that is coming for us. Nothing less than the
visible glory of the resurrected Lord Jesus Christ — revealed — in you
and me. That's pretty amazing, isn't it? Take heart, my friend. If you are
suffering today, there is a better day coming ... much better.

I don't know how to put a value on the worth of your suffering, but I do
know one thing. It isn't worthy to be compared with the glory that will
be revealed in you one day.

Trust in Him at all times, O people; pour out your heart before
Him; God is a refuge for us.
— Psalms 62:8

Heaven's Safe Deposit Box

One of the most secure places in the world to store something valuable to you is in a safe deposit box, which is stored inside the vault of a bank. In most instances it takes different keys operated at the same time, from both you and a bank employee, from inside the bank vault, to even open the box.

God is heaven's safe deposit box for all those who are His children, and you can open yours with a prayer. You can trust Him. Not some of the time. All the time. It is safe. You can pour your heart out to Him. Not part of it. All of it. It is safe. The encouragement of this Psalm of David is to trust in God ... not just when times are happy with no problems, but when life goes bad and you mess up as well. It encourages us to open up ALL our heart to God. Not just part of it ... pour out even the hidden corners where we are ashamed. Why? Because God isn't waiting for us with a whip and handcuffs when we mess up, that's why. First and foremost, God always wants to love us. You don't need to bottle up despair, or fear, or guilt. God is your refuge. According to Meriam-Webster, "refuge" is defined as follows:

1. shelter or protection from danger or distress.
2. a place that provides shelter or protection.
3. something to which one has recourse in times of difficulty.

If you will trust in God at all times, if you will pour out your heart to Him, you will find that God is exactly that in your life. A refuge. Where all is safe and secure — all the time.

"Do not fear, for I have redeemed you; I have called you by name;
you are Mine! When you pass through the waters, I will be with
you; and through the rivers, they will not overflow you. When you
walk through the fire, you will not be scorched, nor will the flame
burn you. For I am the Lord your God, the Holy One of Israel,
your Savior..."
— *Isaiah 43:1c-3c*

Signed, Sealed and Delivered

Yes! All three of these are in these beautiful verses from the book of
Isaiah. They are all there — in spades. Let's look.

"Sealed." You don't need to fear the future because if you belong to God,
you have a relationship with Him that places you firmly and eternally
in His love — He calls you by name and says pointedly, "you are mine."
The proof that you are His forever, is that He has already redeemed you
(bought back through the paying of a price, delivered). It is a settled fact.
No doubt. No fear.

"Delivered." This is what the whole middle of these verses are all about.
There is not a problem or a sadness deep enough to overwhelm you, there
is not a failure or a trial big enough to burn you down. For the one
who belongs to God, He is a constant Companion whose presence means
protection in the middle of all of life's storms. No doubt. No fear.

"Signed." For I am the Lord your God, the Holy One of Israel, your
Savior. It is the promise, the signature of Almighty God Himself for the
ones who are His. Written with the blood of Jesus — the same blood
that redeemed you. No doubt. No fear. No kidding.

...He cried out with a loud voice, "Lazarus, come forth." The man
who had died came forth, bound hand and foot with wrappings,
and his face was wrapped around with a cloth. Jesus said to them,
"Unbind him, and let him go."
— *John 11:43,44*

Back In Business

Well, if you are thinking that we have already used these verses one
time — you're right! Sometimes, however, when you are talking about
God's word, the same place is worth looking at more than once, or twice,
or even three times (or more). We are looking at these verses again, on
purpose, for a really beautiful reason.

In the sports world, we are all familiar with the expression, "one and done."
A team barely makes the playoffs and gets soundly whipped in the first
round. That's it. Out of the playoffs. One and done. God's word isn't like
that. The Bible is not a "one and done" book. When you read it, it is like
a diamond in the light. Hold it one way and its facets sparkle, turn it ever
so slightly and they sparkle a different way. Same diamond — different
sparkle. That is what the Bible is like every time you read it. Even if you
read it over and over. These verses show that in a beautiful way.

The first time we looked at Jesus raising Lazarus from the dead, we
focused on a great truth: we are often tempted to think — wrongly —
that God is not responding, or He is responding WAY too slowly. And
the whole time God is wanting to do something much greater than what
we asked.

Let's turn the diamond just a bit, shall we? It seemed like an impossible
situation.   Lazarus was dead ... and yet, Jesus told Lazarus, "Come
forth!" — and Lazarus came forth. And Lazarus was back in business.
There may be someone reading this who has known first-hand, the feeling
of an impossible situation with no way out, the feeling of having all the
hope crushed out of you, the feeling that you are of absolutely no use to
anyone. I have known all three of those, have you?

I know of no situation more impossible to change than being dead, more
hopeless than being dead, more useless than being dead, do you? That
means that if you are reading this, you are ahead of Lazarus in the game.

It also means that no matter what you have been through that caused the death of your hope or your joy in life — if you will give Jesus the chance, He can say "Come forth!" in your life too, and make you feel more alive, more hopeful, more useful than you ever thought possible. Back in business.

Let your speech always be with grace, as though seasoned with salt,
so that you will know how you should respond to each person.
— *Colossians 4:6*

Using The Right Recipe

What will happen if you are making a deeeelicious banana pudding and you decide to put about a cup of black pepper in it? What about putting beets in a pecan pie? Rib-eye steak grilled to perfection, topped with raw squid? All disasters, right? The wrong recipe can ruin any food, no matter how delicious it is.

The recipe for reaching a lost world for Christ is exactly the same, which is what this verse is all about. As Christians, we have the most delicious news in the world: the opportunity of eternal life through the sacrifice and forgiveness of Jesus. It gives us heaven to call home for eternity, and fills our hearts right now, with the kindness and loving characteristics of the Christian life.

The problem in reaching others for Jesus happens when we throw an ingredient into the recipe that doesn't belong there ... impatience instead of patience, anger instead of understanding, selfishness instead of kindness — and people are watching. Would YOU want a serving of banana pudding if you saw someone put a cup of black pepper in it?

These words of Paul to the Colossians are always the right recipe for letting the world see what being a Christian is like. Try it, and see what happens to your relationships, your witness for Jesus, and in truth, your day-to-day life. Deeeeelicious ...

Then the word of the Lord came to Jeremiah the second time, while
he was still confined in the court of the guard...
— *Jeremiah 33:1*

The Original Man of Steel

"Faster than a speeding bullet, more powerful than a locomotive, able to
leap tall buildings in a single bound ..." Many of us remember those
familiar words as the introduction to the show, "Superman," a.k.a., the
"man of steel."

There are, however, other ways to measure a "man of steel," and there are
many in the Bible. One such man was the prophet, Jeremiah. Nerves
of steel, resolve of steel, integrity of steel, faith of steel. He preached the
message of God faithfully for over 40 years with no visible response —
from anyone. He remained faithful even though he remained poor his
entire life. He was imprisoned, rejected by his neighbors, his friends ...
even his family. His entire life he stood alone, weeping over the judgment
he knew was coming on the country he loved. It was the weeping of
a broken heart. He cried so many tears he became known as "the weeping
prophet."

You may know the feeling of being rejected or ignored because of your
faith in God. Perhaps you have even been made fun of, or ridiculed.
Sometimes you may feel that you are all alone in your walk with God ...
just like Jeremiah. If so, you can take heart, and hope, and encouragement
from the life of this "man of steel." Did you notice in this short verse,
where Jeremiah was when the word of God came to him? Imprisoned
in the court of the guard. And — if you will let Him, God will speak to
you too, no matter where you are, or how sad you are, or how alone you
feel. Recorded in the book of Jeremiah, God spoke to — and through —
Jeremiah (as I count them), are you ready? ... 62 times.

What was the word of the Lord that came to Jeremiah that this verse
announces? Have a quick look at the very next verse — verse 3: "Call
to Me and I will answer you, and I will tell you great and mighty things,
which you do not know." That's the same God who wants to answer your
prayers, too.

> What then shall we say to these things?
> If God is for us, who is against us?
> — *Romans 8:31*

The Champion

Those of us who have been fans of the Dallas Cowboys for almost all our lives would bleed silver and blue if you cut us. In their "Golden Era" under the ownership of Clint Merchison, and the leadership of Tom Landry, Gil Brandt and Tex Schramm, the team came to define the essence of the word "champion." And they stayed that way until a new owner put the winning leadership "on the bench" by firing them.

Aside from winning 5 Super Bowls, here are just a few of their all-time NFL records:

** Most Conference Championship game appearances — 14
** Most consecutive winning seasons — 20 (18 of those in the playoffs)
** Fewest rushing yards allowed, 14-game season — 1,050.
** Most valuable sports franchise, not just in NFL history, but in the history of all United States sports. Value at this writing — $1.85 BILLION.

Sadly, until things change, today they are just another name in a long list of mediocre sports soap operas. That's what happens when you "bench" your winners.

Well, what in the world does all that have to do with what the Bible says here? The apostle Paul is responding to all we have in Christ, and a formidable list of trials and enemies. At the end of the list, he shouts triumphantly, " ... if God is for us, who can be against us?" It means no matter the opponent, no matter how fierce, no matter how strong, you are always a winner because God is in charge of your team. With God in the game, you never lose. Never.

In the game of your life, it is your choice, but — it is always, always, always a mistake to leave God on the bench. With God in control of your game you are always a champion ... always. You never ever lose.

> "Come to Me, all who are weary and heavy-laden,
> and I will give you rest."
> — *Matthew 11:28*

Rest In Peace

This is arguably the most famous phrase in the world when it is applied to someone who has just passed away. But the good news is, you don't have to die to experience it. The best time to experience "rest in peace" is while you are still alive. And the best place to find it? Jesus. Hands down. This comforting, beautiful promise of Jesus along with the next two verses exists only in the gospel of Matthew. Mark, Luke and John did not record it. Perhaps this tax collector-turned-disciple , who made his livelihood from people laboring and heavy-burdened found these words of Jesus particularly touching. And they are just as touching and comforting for us today, too.

The invitation Jesus gives here is not to read a book, or to follow a philosophy — it is to come to a person. Think about when you were little ... and how it felt to have your mom or dad, or the person in your life who took care of you wrap their arms around you, and hold you close when you were afraid or hurt. Would you have preferred for them to simply hand you a sheet of paper with first-aid procedures? That is the difference Jesus makes when He says, "Come to Me ..."

The invitation Jesus gives here is to everyone. That's what the word "all" means. And it means you too. He makes no distinctions or categories about your problems either. Whatever your "labors" are that keep you frantic, stressed out and exhausted ... whatever your "burdens" are (past or present) that keep joy and hope crushed out of you ... whatever they are — Jesus opens His arms and says, "Come to me ... and I will give you rest." Not might do it. Will do it.

It is a promise from Jesus to you — for right now in the present: rest in peace.

Draw near to God and He will draw near to you.
— *James 4:8a*

Making an Investment

Everyone knows that you have to "put some skin in the game" if you want to get something out of "the game." Even with something as simple as a savings account, if you don't put anything into it, you won't get anything out of it. These few, but powerful words from James here show us that a close relationship with God is like that. It isn't magic or automatic and oftentimes we can forget that. If we want to feel God near us, we have to do our part: draw near to God.

Make no mistake about it, God will not allow you to treat Him like a lap dog. The King of Kings and Lord of Lords will not be left in the corner and then respond to "here boy" when you are ready for some attention. You can't ignore God 99% of the time and then expect Him to "fetch" when you are ready to play. However, if you will take the time to draw near to God, He will most definitely draw near to you. And trust me, there is nothing sweeter than feeling God close to you.

How do you draw near to God?

1. Spend time talking with God in prayer.
    (that's real prayer, not just "a lick and a promise" at meal time)
2. Spend time listening to God through reading His Word.
3. Spend time being obedient to the way God expects ... and deserves, for you to live.

Do this, and trust me ... even in the hard times, you will feel God right over your shoulder.

"No weapon that is formed against you will prosper, and every tongue that accuses you in judgment you will condemn. This is the heritage of the servants of the Lord, and their vindication is from Me." declares the Lord.
— *Isaiah 54:17*

Staying True to the Lord

The twin towers before 9-11

9-11 is the day we remember one of the most tragic days in America's history. 2,977 people died and more than 6,000 were injured in coordinated terrorist attacks. If anyone ever asks you why it is so important — as an individual OR a nation — to honor Godly principles and remain a people of God, this verse is why.

"I will not leave you as orphans; I will come to you."
— *John 14:18*

Abandoned

PickensPhotos

My good friend, Danny Pickens, took these haunting pictures on a mission trip to Uganda. It is a little child who was left all alone to beg on the street. In the close-up it is easy to see his little hands in a begging position. Danny watched helplessly from the middle of a traffic jam as person after person walked by, completely ignoring the little child.

Someone may be reading this today — even as an adult — and yet, there are times you feel like this little child ... abandoned, in need, hands held out (and perhaps heart, too), desperate for some help from somewhere, hoping for at least a little attention from someone. Maybe even just a smile or friendly wave, which was all my friend was able to offer the little child in these pictures. And yet, just like this little child you are left all alone and the world just walks on by.

If you are that person, what Jesus would like for you to know today is that no matter how alone you may feel, no matter who else walks on by in your life, He will not. He loves you more than you can imagine and says to you today, "I will not leave you as an orphan; I will come to you." All you have to do is ask Him.

Let us hold fast the confession of our hope without wavering, for
He who promised is faithful;
— *Hebrews 10:23*

Timelines

Timelines are an indispensable part of life, even if we don't use the word. A farmer who wants to produce a crop follows one — it starts with the proper time to prepare the ground in order to have a harvest at the right time of the year. A builder uses a timeline when he signs a contract to have a building finished at the agreed time — from breaking ground, to framing, to roofing, to wiring, plumbing, painting ... all the way to the finished building. Each part has its place on a timeline. Examples are almost endless.

God has a timeline for your life, too. His timeline for you started before you were even a gleam in the eyes of your parents ... and before your parents were gleams in your grandparents eyes.

It all started before time began. That is when He started loving you:

"Just as He chose us in Him <u>before the foundation of the world,</u>
that we should be hold and blameless before Him in love ..."
— *Ephesians 1:4.*

It continued in your mother's womb:

"Your eyes have seen my unformed substance; and in Your book were
all written <u>the days that were ordained for me</u>, when as yet there
was not one of them."
— *Psalms 139:16.*

The thing that is so different and so marvelous about God's timeline for you though, is this: even though you can't see the end of it, God can.

In the meantime — between the "bookends" of God's timeline for you — is what this beautiful little verse is all about. Sometimes we don't understand why God lets some things happen, and sometimes we don't understand why He DOESN'T let some things happen. Sometimes He doesn't answer our prayers when, or the way, we think He should.

Sometimes it is only looking back that we understand why God did what He did. That is because God can see our timelines, even when we can't. There is one thing, however, that we DO know ...

"He who promised is faithful." He has promised to love you ... no matter what. And He does — even when the long night of loneliness makes you feel forgotten. He has promised to never leave you ... and He doesn't — even when the storms of your life may seem without end. He has promised you an eternal life in heaven, that all the demons in hell can't touch, because when Jesus saved you, He saved you forever, and your place in heaven is there, waiting for you ... at the end of your timeline.

Therefore, dear friend, no matter how long you need to do it, "hold fast the confession of your hope, without wavering." Your timeline is in good hands. Perfect hands. For He who promised is faithful.

The Lord is good, a stronghold in the day of trouble, and He knows
those who take refuge in Him.
— *Nahum 1:7*

A Cup Filled to the Brim with Hope and Encouragement

For avid coffee drinkers, there are few things in this world that excite our senses more than the aroma of a hot, fresh cup of fresh-ground coffee under our noses. When I was in the seminary, it is what helped wake me up every morning at 4:00 a.m. For others, chocolate does the same thing. What these and other things do for our physical senses, this little verse of scripture should do for our spiritual senses. It truly is a cup filled to the brim with hope and encouragement.

It starts even before the verse itself. In the very name of the book — Nahum. The name of this Old Testament prophet literally means "comforter." Even better than that, is what he prophesied: the destruction of Ninevah — the capitol city of the most vicious and powerful enemy Israel ever had: the Assyrian empire. It was thought that Ninevah was indestructible. It wasn't. And its violent destruction happened exactly the way Nahum said it would. Nahum's word can be trusted, just like all the rest of the word of God.

And what His word says right here in this one little verse gives us a precious cup of hope and encouragement filled to the brim. No matter what happens around us, <u>the Lord is good</u>. When bad things, or sad things, or confusing things happen, the Lord remains good. He is good not just some of the time, He is good ALL the time. No matter how powerful or indestructible our enemy may seem, the Lord is MORE powerful. He never gets weak, He never gets tired, He never gets scared. <u>He is a stronghold in the day of trouble.</u> All of them. All the time. And perhaps best of all — you are not just a nameless face in the crowd, <u>the Lord knows who you are</u>. And when you have the Lord Jesus Christ as your Savior, God loves you as His own child because you ARE His child. That is His promise to all who trust in Him. And no matter what happens in this life, that promise will remain with you all the way to eternity.

"Do not call to mind the former things, or ponder things of the past.
"Behold, I will do something new, now it will spring forth; will you not
be aware of it? I will even make a roadway in the wilderness, rivers in
the desert.
— *Isaiah 43:18,19*

Trailblazer

No, this isn't about Chevrolet's sport utility vehicle of the same name.
With all due respect to Chevy's version, this is about a much better
Trailblazer than that. Ever get stuck in one of life's ruts? Ever felt your
mind spinning in the mud of guilt from failures of the past? Ever felt
so lost you couldn't see the forest for the trees? Ever felt dried up and
burned out from living day after day with no hope? This verse is about
changing all that.

Welcome to Jehovah Trailblazer. For the person who will give God the
chance to blaze a new trail in their life, here is what will happen:

1. Freedom from all that has happened in your past. All the mistakes, all
   the guilt, all the remembering it.
2. God will give you a new start, a new life ... as fresh as artesian spring
   water.
3. Whatever is your wilderness, be it a besetting sadness, or illness, or
   failure, or problem on top of problem — God will blaze a roadway
   through what you cannot solve.
4. In the middle of the parched sand of hopelessness, God will cause
   rivers of joy to flow once again.

God can be this Trailblazer in your life too, making a new roadway. Just
give Him the opportunity to take the lead on your trail.

And answering him, Jesus said, "What do you want Me to do for you?" And the blind man said to Him, "Rabboni, I want to regain my sight!" And Jesus said to him, "Go; your faith has made you well." Immediately he regained his sight and began following Him on the road.
— *Mark 10:51,52*

Stating the Obvious

That could be said of the request of this man we call "Blind Bartimaeus," couldn't it? Seems obvious, doesn't it? If it were you who were blind, wouldn't the ability to see be the obvious thing you would ask for? Well, if the response IS obvious, why on earth do you suppose Jesus would even ask Bartimaeus, "What do you desire I should do for you?"

In answering that, there are a few things I believe we can safely assume: First, Jesus would not ask a stupid question. Second, Jesus already knew the answer. Third, Jesus would not ask what appears to be an obvious question of a blind man without a purpose. If all three of those things are true ... and they are, then there must be something beautiful here that is NOT obvious.

I, personally, believe that what is not so obvious here, but is truly beautiful is the resurrection of hope. It is really easy to overlook the fact that there was a time when Bartimaeus could see. Did you notice it in his answer to Jesus? " ... that I may REGAIN my sight." This blind man who assumed his place day after day alongside all the other beggars who lined the street, once was a man as normal as you and me. He had hopes and dreams and plans just like anyone else. Then something happened that robbed him of his sight. It changed his life forever, and hope disappeared. Then one day Jesus entered the equation of his life, and when He did, He restored Bartimaeus's sight, and his hope.

Bartimaeus lives today ... inside everyone who knows what it is like to lose all their hope in life. If that person is you today my friend, Jesus can do the same thing for you that He did for Bartimaeus. Sometimes when we lose all our hope, we forget that Jesus really can fix it. That is the reason for the question of the obvious, "What do you want me to do for you?" Jesus already knows ... He just wants to wake up your hope, and your faith, and remind you who it is that can heal everything in your life. Asking Him to do it is the first step back in the resurrection of your hope.

For our citizenship is in heaven, from which also we eagerly wait
for a Savior, the Lord Jesus Christ; who will transform the body
of our humble state into conformity with the body of His glory, by
the exertion of the power that He has even to subject all things to
Himself.
— *Philippians 3:20,21*

There's A New Day Coming

Matthew Stanford Robison was born severely disabled, blind and
paralyzed from the waist down — he wasn't even expected to live for
more than a few hours. He lived for just under 11 years, all of them in
a wheelchair. He never knew what it was like to stand up alone on his
feet. He never dressed himself. He never spoke more than a very few

words. When Matthew left this life, his father commissioned the making of this gravestone statue as a tribute to the healing, transforming power of the Lord Jesus Christ.

It is one of the most powerful and emotional images I have ever seen.

The freedom and transforming power that Matthew's statue represents is within the reach of anyone who will trust the Lord Jesus Christ as their Savior. Whatever your personal wheelchair might be, as a child of God you can rest assured that there is a new day coming for you. There will come a day when you leave it all behind.

Now to Him who is able to keep you from stumbling,
and to make you stand in the presence of His glory
blameless
with great joy,
to the only God our Savior,
through Jesus Christ our Lord,
be glory, majesty, dominion and authority, before all time and now
and forever. Amen.
— *Jude 24, 25*

Look What I Made For You, Dad

I believe one of the greatest joys and moments of pride in the world is displayed by children when they give something they have made out of love with their own hands to their mom or dad. Who of us has not seen that? Or done it, for that matter? This "coaster" was made by my youngest daughter 16 years ago when she was only 6 years old. She was so proud when she handed it to me. So was her dad. It is one of my most precious possessions.

These verses in Jude display that same kind of joy. I separated the phrases as they appear in the scripture reference on purpose, and if you read them slowly and carefully my bet is you will be captured by a strong desire to love and praise the Lord Jesus Christ. Spend a moment or two, not just reading, but thinking. In the glory of the presence of God — right now — you are faultless. Not "will be." Right now. Because of Jesus, God always sees you in eternity as the "finished product." That is the power of the salvation we have, and the power of the blood of Jesus Christ that paid for and washes away all our faults and sins. He lifts you up — the work of His own hands — and presents you faultless to God the Father. The joy here is actually three-fold: 1. — It gives Jesus great joy to present you faultless to the Father, 2. — It gives the Father great joy to receive you, and 3. — It gives you great joy to be there.

"Peace I leave with you; My peace I give to you; not as the world gives do I give to you. Let not your heart be troubled, nor let it be fearful."
— *John 14:27*

A Different Kind of Peace

Peace as defined by the world usually means "the absence of conflict," and world history is littered from past to present with one broken "peace accord" or "peace treaty" after another.

How much better, the peace of Jesus: "confident assurance in any circumstance." Nothing rattled Jesus — not even crucifixion — but ... the peace of Jesus is much more still:

** Whatever peace the world offers is fleeting and flawed.
The peace of Jesus is eternal and perfect, because He is.

** The peace of the world is usually costly, with conditions attached.
The peace of Jesus is a free gift with love attached.

** The peace of the world is enjoyed most often by the strongest.
The peace of Jesus is GIVEN by the strongest.

Jesus said: "All authority has been given to Me — in heaven AND on earth." The God of heaven and earth, the one with ALL the power and ALL the authority over everything, who has no need or cause to fear anything says, "MY peace I give to you."

If your heart is troubled or afraid, try the best "stress salve" in the world: the peace of Jesus.

Do not be deceived, God is not mocked; for whatever a man sows,
this he will also reap.
— *Galatians 6:7*

You Reap What You Sow

This is a very well-known verse in the Bible. My bet is, depending on how old you are, that you have heard it many times. I think however, that sometimes we short change this powerful verse. We pick up on its negative teaching, and often miss its golden key to hope and encouragement.

"Where is it?" you say. "I'm glad you asked.", I say. Now — to be sure, there is a stark warning to the negative here. It is a serious thing to "turn the nose up" at God. That's what "mocked" means here. You are free to "sow wild oats," but be advised ... wild oats can yield a very bitter harvest. You reap what you sow. We all know it. Ask any farmer the following question and note his response: "If I plant corn then change my mind and want peas instead, will peas come up?" The same is true in your life — it is the law of God. Plant anger, reap anger. Plant selfishness, reap selfishness. Plant deception, reap deception.

And the golden key to hope and encouragement? Spend some time sowing those two crops — hope and encouragement — and I will give you one guess what you will reap. Just read the next three verses here in chapter 6, and you will see.

He has told you, O man, what is good; and what does the Lord
require of you but to do justice, to love kindness, and to walk
humbly with your God?
— *Micah 6:8*

Course Requirements

Anyone who has ever gone to school knows what this means. Books you
have to buy, papers you have to write, areas of study you have to complete
in order to successfully obtain a high school or college degree. When
I was at the seminary, it seemed like I typed "In Partial Fulfillment for the
Requirements of the Course _'X'__" at least a thousand times for papers
I was required to write.

People in Micah's day worked themselves up into almost a frenzy of worry
about what God required. The two verses before this one show exactly
that: "With what shall I come before the Lord, and bow myself before
the High God? Shall I come before Him with burnt offerings, with
calves a year old? Will the Lord be pleased with thousands of rams or
ten thousand rivers of oil? Shall I give my firstborn for my transgression,
the fruit of my body for the sin of my soul?"

Sometimes folks today work themselves up into the same kind of frenzy
about what God requires. Whole denominations teach that you have
to speak in tongues to be saved. Wrong. Some name themselves "full
gospel" as though others are somehow only "partial gospel." Also wrong.
Some churches believe you need to jump up and down and wave your
arms in the air during the music to prove that you are "spiritual." Wrong
again. Some practice "laying on of hands" to heal the sick or confer
blessings (or ask for them) as if the power to do either exists in our
hands, instead of in the Lord Jesus Christ. Once again, this as well is not
a requirement of God. Simply because some gestures like that were used
in the New Testament, doesn't mean that the act itself either generated,
or aided, spiritual power. Jesus told us that all power and authority was
given to Him. That is where the power is. I choose to believe what
Jesus said about it. Laying our hands on anything for any reason is not
a requirement from God for Him to hear, treat as "more holy," or answer
our prayers. All those things may have some merit as rituals — but that
is all they are.

Now — to be sure, God absolutely deserves our very best when it comes to serving Him, but that same God also wants us to relax. The words of Micah 6:8 show us what is really important to the Lord. For Him, it isn't about ritual ... it is all about righteousness. Take heart and hope and encouragement today in knowing what the Lord really wants from you: to do justice, to love mercy, and to walk humbly with Him. Just these three things. God's very own list of requirements, for a lifetime of service that is pleasing to Him.

and let us consider how to stimulate one another to love and good deeds, not forsaking our own assembling together, as is the habit of some, but encouraging one another; and all the more as you see the day drawing near.
— *Hebrews 10:24,25*

Strength In Numbers

"Strength in numbers" is a familiar phrase, the truth of which just about everyone understands and accepts. In the Christian world, however, numbers can accomplish more than just physical strength. A lot more. Things like a more dedicated love, an increased passion to be kind and helpful, and mutual encouragement — and the very best place for that to happen is in a good church. Don't let ANYone tell you that going to church is not important ... because it is.

There is an old and well-worn story that to this day remains my favorite when it comes to painting a picture of the truth and importance of these two beautiful verses from the Bible. As it is told, there was an old pastor who set out one bitterly cold winter night to visit a person who was well-known for being just about as bitter as the winter weather. Anyone trying to encourage him to come to church had their heads instantly bitten off with, "I don't need the church, I am just fine by myself." The old pastor arrived and they sat down together in front of a nice fire in the fireplace. Before the pastor could even get started, the old man said, "Preacher, I know why you are here. Save your breath. I don't need the church. I am just fine by myself." The pastor didn't say a word, he just reached into the fire with a pair of tongs, removed one small, glowing ember and set it out by itself. As they sat by that nice, warm fire that continued to glow, they watched as the ember separated from the fire quickly went dark and cold. Then the old pastor stood up to leave, and with a kind smile all he said was, "Nice talking to you, brother."

If you are running a little low on hope and encouragement, one of the best places I know to rekindle them is around the warmth of a nice Christian fire.

"But I say to you that something greater than the temple is here."
— *Matthew 12:6*

In The Presence Of Jehovah

I don't think the Pharisees (the bean-counting, nitpicking Mosaic "lawyers" of Jesus's day) could have recognized the presence of Jehovah even if they had been with Moses at the burning bush. In this entire scene here from the gospel of Matthew (vs. 1-8), once again they were trying to pounce on Jesus for "breaking the law" on the Sabbath, by allowing His disciples to break off a few ears of corn to eat because they were hungry. Once again, Jesus made fools of them and their argument, and once again, they were oblivious to the fact that they were in the presence of Jehovah, even when the truth came from the lips of Jesus, Himself. By using the word "something" (according to the oldest manuscripts), and not "one," He was very likely referring not only to Himself, but Himself together with the Kingdom of God, and God's purpose in all of it.

This same sentence Jesus spoke over 2,000 years ago is as powerful, profound, and encouraging today as it was on the day He spoke it in that cornfield. Many of us love our church — our temple — and that is good, but all too often, come Sunday the focus is on the church, the "performance" of the worship leaders, and a service programmed almost to the minute to end at noon. When we are in church, what should always take our breath away is none of that. What should take our breath away is spending a few moments realizing, "something greater than the temple is here." If you come to truly worship, you are in the presence of Jehovah and the Kingdom of God.

Some who read this may have a different "temple" altogether. And like the early Jews and their temple, your life revolves around it. It may be the temple of career advancement, the temple of life as a party, or perhaps the temple of feeling important. Regardless, it is wise to understand that no temple lasts forever ... not even if King David, or Solomon builds it. Just ask Israel. Some who read this may have already had your temple destroyed, just like the early Jews. The good news is, the wonderful news is, "Something greater than the temple is here."

The presence of Jehovah and the Kingdom of God is forever — and He will never turn you away.

Because Your lovingkindness is better than life,
my lips will praise You.
— *Psalms 63:3*

Short and Sweet

Or, in the case of this beautiful-beyond-words verse in Psalm 63 — short and very, very, very sweet. Am I making too much out of a short sentence in the middle of a magnificent psalm of praise? I don't think so. God's lovingkindness is so wonderful and beautiful that we don't really have a word in our language that can truly capture its meaning.

This world is full of people who could be described as abundantly, profusely, maybe even obscenely successful in this life. It all stops when the lid closes on their casket. Life is short. But — God's lovingkindness is better than life. God's lovingkindness is eternal. Included in that lovingkindness is His mercy which is also eternal, and His forgiveness which is also eternal, and His love which is also eternal. All animals from whales to bacteria possess life, but only God's children possess His lovingkindness.

Perhaps best of all is realizing that the lovingkindness of God isn't seen in Him giving you a million dollars in a surprise that you don't expect. God's lovingkindness is realized best in seeing Him give you eternal life that you don't deserve.

> But in all these things we overwhelmingly conquer through Him
> who loved us.
> — *Romans 8:37*

Stainless Steel Love

This little phrase sits like a delicious slice of hope and encouragement right in the middle of an incredible "spiritual victory sandwich."

Just BEFORE this verse, Paul lists 8 stringent adversities: tribulation, distress, persecution, famine, nakedness, peril, sword, and ends with nothing less than martyrdom in verse 36. Then here, he says that not only do these things not stop us ... but, we are actually conquerors — and more — right in the middle of them. Paul's invented compound word here (and only here in the New Testament) for "more than conquerors" means to "vanquish beyond." Who is the agent of this astonishing victory? Jesus Christ who loves us!

Just how strong is this love? Well ... just AFTER this verse, Paul lists 10 MORE things: death, life, angels, principalities, powers, things present, things to come, height, depth, any other created thing — and says that NONE of them can separate us from the love for us that is in Jesus Christ.

... Stainless steel love ...

That ought to kick-start ANYone's day!

"I am the vine, you are the branches; he who abides in Me and I in him, he bears much fruit, for apart from Me you can do nothing."
— *John 15:5*

Well-Connected

Good things can happen when you are well-connected. At the end of a good connection with a professional sports team there can be some pretty snazzy seats to the games. At the end of a good connection with a supervisor, there can be a good job. At the end of a good connection with a banker there can be some fruitful financial advice.

When I was a teenager (a "few" years ago), my grandfather and I spent many hours on our farm clearing and building fence. MANY hours. One of those times as I was clearing some mesquite from the "bob war" I cut through a grapevine that was probably a little over an inch thick. Crystal clear water began to flow from the end. Not a drip — a flow. We worked on that section of fence for several hours. The flow never stopped. It never even slowed. There is a reason clusters and clusters of succulent grapes grow at the ends of grapevine branches — they are well-connected to an abundant source of water.

Jesus is like that vine. He is the source of not just crystal clear water ... He is the source of LIVING water, and it never stops or slows. And when He becomes your Savior, it flows into you, and through you like the branch of a vine. And because of that good connection there can be a lot of really good fruit at the end of your branch. Not here today and gone tomorrow fruit. Fruit that remains (John 15:16) — because you are well-connected to eternity's source of abundant life.

What is an example of that kind of fruit? The kind that remains? Well, imagine your arrival in heaven. You are turning in slow circles, beholding the incredible wonder of the beauty that heretofore was only words in the Bible. Your eyes fill with tears of unspeakable joy as you begin to realize the fullness of what salvation in Jesus and eternity in this beautiful place really means. As you stand there, eyes full of tears of joy, you feel a tap on your shoulder. There stands a person whose eyes are full of those same tears of joy, and that person says to you ...

"How can I ever say 'thank you?' — I am here, because of you."

THAT, is an example of fruit that remains.

... for I have learned to be content
in whatever circumstances I am.
— *Philippians 4:11b*

Carbon Steel Contentment

Even with new metals that have been developed in recent years, carbon steel remains one of the strongest alloy metals in the world. Tungsten has the highest tensile strength of any metal in the world, but it is brittle and shatters under impact. Who would want contentment that did that? Go with the carbon steel version, trust me.

This verse is about carbon steel contentment. It is very short, but oh so powerful. Many people think it is impractical and impossible to be content "no matter what" when they look at this verse. That is the wrong focus. First of all, it IS possible, but what you need to focus on are two beautiful points of hope and encouragement contained in this verse:

1. The peace of God is not connected with circumstances, and ...
2. Do NOT overlook the word "learned." You already know what "learned" means. So many people get discouraged because they think that when they become a Christian, they are automatically transformed instantly into an almost "perfect person" who is happy 24/7. The truth is, a lot of things in the Christian life take time to learn. This is one of them. Even the great apostle Paul had to learn it.

'Call to Me and I will answer you, and I will tell you great and
mighty things, which you do not know.'
— *Jeremiah 33:3*

What Did You Expect?

Have you ever been surprised by something and then have someone ask, "Well, what did you expect?" Most of us probably have. It might surprise you to learn that "call to Me" here isn't a polite invitation or suggestion from God. It is a strong admonition with the force of DO IT!! And, it is used again and again in the Old Testament when God's people are in real trouble.

Be honest now, there are times we don't call on God when we have a big problem because we don't REALLY think He's going to fix it, isn't that right? We trust in our own ability instead of God's. Or, we just give up. Am I plucking a few memory strings?

I'm going to tell off on myself to illustrate this — and show you a big difference between my wife, Claudia, and myself. A few years ago we were driving home on the freeway. We were beside an 18-wheeler and Claudia was driving. A woman trying to cross the freeway on a bicycle suddenly appeared right in front of us from the other side of the 18-wheeler. With nowhere to turn and no time to stop, we hit her broadside at about 50 mph. She smashed into the windshield and flew into a deep ditch in the median on our left. My instant and audible reaction was, "Oh my God, she's dead." My wife's reaction was completely different. She instantly began to pray that God would not let anything be wrong with that woman. This exact verse was what God brought immediately to her mind. When we got to the woman in the ditch, the bicycle was a mangled mess, but ... the woman was already sitting up, completely alert, with only a scratch on her right arm. True story.

Now, read this verse again and ask yourself, "What do I expect?"

Then I heard something like the voice of a great multitude and like the sound of many waters and like the sound of mighty peals of thunder, saying, "Hallelujah! For the Lord our God, the Almighty, reigns.
— *Revelation 19:6*

Heaven's Choir

I have heard music and majestic hymns from great choirs that have moved me to real tears, and I am sure you have too. I have to tell you though, I believe the best choir with the best musicians in the world will sound like a squeaky door hinge compared to heaven's choir.

Relax for a moment and strap on the sandals of the apostle John, the author of Revelation. Close your eyes and try to let yourself be transported into the vision he is experiencing — and trying to describe. The sound of the innumerable voices of heaven's choir shaking the walls and foundation of heaven itself with adoration and praise of the Lord God Almighty.

Be sure to note that God's kingdom isn't something waiting to happen. The King of Kings and Lord of Lords reigns — at this very moment. Now ... spend a minute or two remembering that the Lord God is also someone else, if you have trusted Jesus as your Savior. This mighty God who causes heaven to thunder with praise — you have the privilege of calling "Father." You are His child because Jesus is your Savior. That's a pretty sweet privilege, wouldn't you agree?

Then I said, "Behold, I come; in the scroll of the book it is written
of me. I delight to do Your will,
O my God; Your Law is within my heart."
— *Psalms 40:7,8*

The Servant Model

Prophetic words from these beautiful verses in this Psalm of David give us another "golden key" to hope and encouragement today — and of course, Jesus is the perfect example to whom the Psalm points.

Many times we approach the will and the law of God grudgingly, don't we? Jesus never did that. Sometimes in our human weakness we "obey" because we know we have to, or because we know it is the right thing to do — whether we like it or not. There is a better way ...

If you are a parent, think of the feeling you have had many times when you have held your children, or grandchildren in your arms. That is delight. If you have never had children, remember how it felt to be held that way when you were small. That is delight. Then, "Your law is within my heart" means "I cherish it in the center of my being." When that is where God's law resides, it is then that doing His will becomes a delight — because His will is your will, too.

So, as those who have been chosen of God, holy and beloved, put on a heart of compassion, kindness, humility, gentleness and patience; bearing with one another, and forgiving each other, whoever has a complaint against anyone; just as the Lord forgave you, so also should you. Beyond all these things put on love, which is the perfect bond of unity.

— *Colossians 3:12-14*

Dress-up

I don't know of anyone who didn't play this game as children. Girls put on their mother's dresses and shoes. Boys put on the clothes of cowboys and Indians, Batman, and Superman. My son went through a Batman phase, plus Ninja Turtles and Power Rangers phases, too. As kids we loved to "dress up" as someone we were not.

As Christians we are to "dress up," too. Only it isn't a game. It is an essential exercise for those who really want to follow Jesus. We are not only to "say" what we are, we are to match the "talk" with the "walk." That walk is the Christian's wardrobe. "Dress up" for real.

Let's start at the bottom of the list and work our way back up to the top. The first act of each day is to go to our wardrobe, pull out our Christian love, and put it on. After that: be prepared to forgive others in the same way the Lord forgave (and continues to forgive) you ... which is completely, without reservation, qualification or condition. And, as always, Jesus is our best example. If Jesus could leave His throne in heaven, come here for our sakes, and put on a human body, can we not at least start each day by putting on a little Christian love?

Tall order? Yes. Difficult? Most certainly. Impossible? No. These verses give us the "heart condition-list" that makes it possible. Two little words in front of the list makes it a verse of great hope for me: "put on." In those times (and they are legion) when I feel so less than what God wants me to be, it reminds me that a heart qualified to forgive is not acquired by magic. It is something I have to work at. It is something I have to ... put on. Most of the time it is a daily exercise.

... And daily exercise makes us stronger, right?

And you can do it, or God wouldn't give you the instruction. He has faith _in_ you, and love _for_ you. Don't forget — you are "holy and beloved" in His eyes.

How blessed is the man whose strength is in You, in whose heart are the highways to Zion! Passing through the valley of Baca they make it a spring; the early rain also covers it with blessings. They go from strength to strength, every one of them appears before God in Zion.
— *Psalms 84:5-7*

Proper Cultivation is Everything

You may be thinking "there is nothing about farming or preparing land in these verses." Oh, but there is — you just have to define what type of land you are talking about. When the land is your relationship with the Lord God, cultivation of that relationship opens a treasure chest of hope and encouragement for the one who does it right.

Two steps of that cultivation are given to you here and they can make a world of difference in your entire life.

First, let your supply of strength come from the One who is all-powerful, instead of trusting in your own strength. This provides you strength to trust in God's wisdom, strength to trust in God's ways, strength to trust in God's timing, strength to trust that God's love for you always surrounds you no matter what ... very handy in the valley of Baca.

Second, fill your heart with the goal of arriving in the presence of God in every highway of your life. In your family, God is the centerpiece. In your work, God is the centerpiece. In your social life, God is the centerpiece. In the plans for your future, God is the centerpiece.

The result? Blessings from God that can do this:
1. in the testing times of your life, turn your personal Baca (weeping) into springs water.
2. in your journey to arrive where God is, make you stronger and stronger with each step.

How to? Three very good places to start — going to Jesus, going to God's Word, and going to a good church.

"... the kingdom of heaven is like a merchant seeking fine pearls,
and upon finding one pearl of great value, he went and sold all that
he had and bought it."
— *Matthew 13:45-46*

Striking It Rich

Almost everyone I have ever known has had the dream, hope, wish ...
of striking it rich someday. The fact that millions of people play the
lottery every day bears testimony to that fact. The chances of winning are
abysmal, but the lure of striking it rich keeps people in the game.

Matthew, the tax collector disciple, is the only one of the four gospel
writers who records this parable of Jesus. He must have loved it because
he understood money and numbers and the value of things. And here
was the most fantastic strike it rich story he had ever heard.

What value would you put on citizenship in the kingdom of heaven, my
friend? The merchant in Jesus's parable found a pearl so precious, it was
worth trading all he had to possess it. In our journey of life today, Jesus
is the Pearl of Great Value. And although we don't have to pay anything
to have a relationship with Jesus, that relationship is still worth everything
we have — and more. Having Jesus means having the kingdom of heaven
too ... the joy of being a citizen of the kingdom now, and the joy of
knowing you already have an address there when eternity knocks on your
door.

It is an address with a mansion attached to it. An address with Jesus as
your neighbor. An address where you will never be sick, or old, or sad, or
in pain ... and the streets are paved with gold. That, my friend, is striking
it rich — and there is no lottery to it. For anyone who has trusted the
Lord Jesus Christ as their Savior, it is 100% guaranteed.

> ... I am He, I am the first, I am also the last.
> "Surely My hand founded the earth, and My right hand spread out
> the heavens; when I call to them, they stand together.
> — *Isaiah 48:12b,13*

Let Me Show You "Awesome"

Sometimes, I think "awesome" is the most over-used adjective in the English language. You hear it almost every day, used over and over, even about things that could barely be described as mildly interesting, much less "awesome." However, when the subject is God, it is always appropriate.

Sometimes, in our relationship with God, it can be good to put away the commentaries for a while, turn off the TV preachers, in fact turn off the TV period, forget about the latest, greatest study guide — then relax and just bathe ourselves in pure adoration of the truly awesome, Living God of the universe, who we also have the awesome privilege of calling "Father."

The Bible helps us do that with verses like these. No words can do justice to the power that can speak an infinite universe into existence, but verses like these help us form a picture in our minds. On earth, Jesus was a carpenter — a builder. He is still a builder as Master of the Universe. Look at the mighty grandeur from just the stretching out of His hand.

But the part that leaves me even more awestruck with wonder and adoration is that last phrase: "when I call to them, they stand up together." The earth and all of the universe snapping to attention, like children in front of a parent. That's a pretty awesome God that can do that.

Therefore, confess your sins to one another, and pray for one another
so that you may be healed. The effective prayer of a righteous man can
accomplish much.
— *James 5:16*

The Power of One

The whole context surrounding the first half of this one verse of scripture will
have theologians arguing until Jesus returns, but ... what is most important
about it for us today in our personal, day-to-day world, is to not lose sight of
the profound, simple and easy-to-understand truth it contains that can fill us
with hope and encouragement. That truth? The power of one.

Does it say, "the fervent, effective prayer of the church ministers?" ... "the
choir?" ... the Sunday School?" ... "the deacons?" ... "the church council?" ... "the
missions committee?" ... "a group of righteous people?" The answer is "no" —
to all the above. The answer is "a righteous person." Only one is needed.

Does God answer prayers of groups of people? Of course, He does. But that
doesn't diminish what He can — and loves to do — through just one person.
How about a very small sampling of this truth from God's word:

1. The prayer of Moses that saves the entire nation of Israel from
   destruction — Exodus 32:11-14.
2. The prayer of Joshua for the sun and moon to stand still — Joshua
   10:12-14.
3. The prayer of Elijah for fire to fall from heaven — 1st Kings 18:36-39.
4. The prayer of Elisha for his servant to see God's army and chariots of
   fire surrounding them — 2 Kings 6:17.
5. The prayer/proclamation of Peter to the lame man to rise and walk at
   the gate to Jerusalem — Acts 3:1-10.
6. The prayer of Jesus in the Garden of Gethsemane that opened the
   possibility of heaven for us all ... "not My will, but Thine be done." —
   Luke 22:42. And the next day, through the death of Jesus on the
   cross, the price for all our sin was paid.

Sometimes God does it instantly, sometimes in minutes, sometimes in
years — but, if you are willing to pray as passionately as you know how
and willing to live a Godly life as best you know how, this same God
can — and still loves — to use just one person to accomplish great things.

"This is My commandment, that you love one another, just as I have loved you. Greater love has no one than this, that one lay down his life for his friends."
— *John 15:12,13*

Love — More Than Just a Word

Popularly known as rodeo clowns, in the business they are known as "bullfighters." — because that is what they do. For those of us who grew up in the country and call rodeo our favorite sport, this is a powerful image. We have seen the value of a "rodeo clown" countless times — putting his very life on the line for his friends. I have never seen one even hesitate.

If we are going to call ourselves Christians, we should be so dedicated to our friends and Christian brothers and sisters, too. In fact, not "should," but "must." Even in the times when it isn't easy, because the alternative is to be disobedient to Jesus Himself. Did you notice His choice of words? Commandment. Not "suggestion." Not "advice." To love each other as He loved us. In fact, it is Jesus's very own plan to win the world (John 13:35). He also said, "If you love Me, keep my commandments" (John 14:15). Want to show Him that you really do love Him? Show Him a love willing to "charge the bull" for a friend. Willing to love … the way He showed us how to love.

Have I not commanded you? Be strong and courageous! Do not tremble
or be dismayed, for the Lord your God is with you wherever you go."
— *Joshua 1:9*

Side by Side

Have you ever caught the Bible in a lie? I haven't. And I have been studying
it for quite a few years now. Many skeptics have tried, many have told lies
ABOUT the Bible — but catching the Bible in a lie? It's just not gonna
happen. In fact, all physical evidence discovered to date, from the geological
to the archeological, unwaveringly supports with each new discovery, what the
Bible has maintained for thousands of years about people, places and events.

I can't resist just a couple of many examples we could pick from. Let's
take the first from geology. There is a treasure trove of fossils of ancient
sea life all around the world. Do you know where they are? High in the
mountains, a **long** way from the sea and all in a single, sedimentary rock
strata (which is important). Evolutionists have a really difficult time trying
to explain that. A worldwide flood as depicted in the Bible explains it with
ease. Example #2 — from archeology. For a long time the actual existence
of Sodom and Gomorrah (both destroyed by God with fire from heaven,
remember?) was vilified and scoffed at by many skeptics, they were treated
as little more than mere legend. That changed in 1973 when both of them
were discovered. And there are many, many other examples.

What's the point? Simply this: If what the Bible says is always true, then
when the Bible tells you that God is with you wherever you go, you can
count on that being true, too. Especially when it repeats it over and over
from cover to cover. The verse that says it here, is one of my favorites.
I never have to feel weak, I never have to feel discouraged, I never have to
feel afraid, I never have to feel demoralized. Why? Because God is with
me wherever I go. The same God whose power created the entire universe.
The same God who loved me enough to die for me. His is a presence
that is more sure than any physical company you could ever want. He is
with you in the valley, He is with you on the mountaintop — and He is
with you everywhere in between. All the time. With you. Side by side.

"Wherever" must mean, then, even up to — and into — the grave. And
because God is with you even there, if you have trusted Jesus as your Savior
you will come out of that grave just like Jesus did — victorious over even death.
That one truth alone makes everything in this verse shouting ground for joy.

For I am convinced that neither death, nor life, nor angels, nor principalities, nor things present, nor things to come, nor powers, nor height, nor depth, nor any other created thing, will be able to separate us from the love of God, which is in Christ Jesus our Lord.
— *Romans 8:38,39*

A Whole Lot of Nothing

This is one of the most beautiful, and majestic statements about God's love for you in the entire bible. Paul attempts to create a list which grows in its power and intensity with each item, to show that there is nothing you can even imagine, that can separate you from the love of God. Nothing.

If you are a believer in Christ, not even death can do it. No circumstance in your entire life can do it. The power of the good angels (the kind that can destroy 185,000 soldiers of the enemy ... an entire army in a single night) isn't enough to do it. The bad angels (like the ones that fell from heaven with the devil) can't do it. No event in this present time, no event in the future can do it. No evil power above or below the earth, not even satan himself has the power to do it. And just on the chance he might have left something out, Paul says "no other created thing," as if to say, "Nothing means nothing. Absolutely nothing."

That's quite a list of nothing. A whole lot of nothing.

Even if the entire rest of the world turns its back on you, God's love for you is permanent — and eternal.

You will not be afraid of the terror by night, or of the arrow
that flies by day; of the pestilence that stalks in darkness, or of
the destruction that lays waste at noon. A thousand may fall at
your side and ten thousand at your right hand, but it shall not
approach you.
— *Psalms 91:5-7*

The Bodyguard

In the movies, "The Bodyguard" would be the one with Kevin Costner
and Whitney Houston. Great movie about the dedication of a bodyguard
willing to take a bullet.

In life, that would be God. Having God as your Bodyguard is like being
with the biggest dog on the sidewalk. You will never have to be afraid of
anyone or anything ever again. Nothing that comes at you during the day,
nothing that comes at you during the night, nothing that comes at you
that you can't even see. No matter how many others may be affected, your
Heavenly Bodyguard has your back. God's Son is not called the Lion of
Judah for no reason.

And on that old rugged cross of Golgotha, a little over 2,000 years ago,
that Lion took a lot more than a bullet for you.

Some of the Pharisees in the crowd said to Him, "Teacher, rebuke Your
disciples." But Jesus answered, "I tell you, if these become silent, the
stones will cry out!"
— *Luke 19:39,40*

Dumber Than a Rock

Many of us grew up knowing this phrase, which describes an ignorance
so complete that it is compared to a rock. Well, believe it or not, it is my
opinion that this well-known phrase has a place right here in one of the
most renowned scenes in all the Bible. It is known as "The Triumphal
Entry." It was the last entry of Jesus into Jerusalem before His death on
the cross, and He was entering in the manner of a king of that time — on
a donkey ridden by no one else. A large crowd of followers and disciples
were praising Him, shouting with joy back and forth in front and behind
Him, recognizing Him as the long-awaited Messiah.

And some of the Pharisees (the politically correct, bean-counting nit-
pickers of the Jewish religious law) in the crowd couldn't stand it. So,
they ask Jesus to reprimand His followers for what they considered heresy.
His response was classic, and one of Jesus's most famous statements:
"I tell you, if these become silent, the stones will cry out." **Could that
really happen?** Well, let's see ... He created the heavens and the earth
(John 1:3), He made a bush burn and not be consumed (Exodus 3:2), He
made the sun stand still for an entire day (Joshua 10:13), He made the
head of an ax float like wood (2nd Kings 6:6), He made a donkey speak
(Numbers 22:28), He brought Lazarus back to life after he had been dead
for four days (John 11:43,44), He spoke a storm into silence (Mark 4:35-
40), performed countless other miracles (John 21:25), and as if all that
isn't enough, He rose from the dead after being crucified (Luke 24:1-6).
Now, if He could do all that — and He did — I'm putting my money on
Jesus being able to make the rocks cry out.

But why did Jesus say this, instead of something simple, like "Just leave
them alone."? I believe it was for a couple of reasons. One is because
nature itself bows before the presence of Almighty God. And the second?
Well, I can't prove it, but I believe it may have been Jesus's way of saying,
"Even these stones know what you should know — but don't." Or ...
"You are dumber than a rock."

So — the next time someone tries to make fun of your faith or tries to tell you Jesus isn't who He says He is, you are on pretty solid ground in thinking, "You are dumber than a rock." I wouldn't advise saying it, but you can sure think it.

Acquire wisdom! Acquire understanding! Do not forget nor turn
away from the words of my mouth. "Do not forsake her, and she
will guard you; love her, and she will watch over you. The beginning
of wisdom is: Acquire wisdom; and with all your acquiring, get
understanding. Prize her, and she will exalt you; she will honor you
if you embrace her. She will place on your head a garland of grace;
she will present you with a crown of beauty."
— *Proverbs 4:5-9*

The Perfect Partner

Have you heard of Irina Rodnina? Probably not ... unless you are an avid
student of ice skating history. She is the only pairs skater in history to
win 10 world championships — in a row (and no, that isn't a misprint).
From 1972-80 she also won 3 Olympic gold medals in a row. She also
won 11 European pairs skating championships. And she did it with
different partners. If you wanted to be a pairs skating champion, you
might consider her to be the perfect partner. In all walks of life, we
covet the "perfect partner," don't we? From matrimony, to fishing, to
partnerships like police work, where a person's life can be on the line.

In our own competitive event called "life," the Bible tells us of one of the
most beautiful and perfect partners ever: wisdom. Now, I know wisdom
doesn't sound "sexy" or "hip" ... but neither of those two will be of any
use to you at all when your life is approaching a dangerous cliff. Wisdom,
on the other hand can be the partner that saves your life. It is also a gift
of the Holy Spirit, but that doesn't make it automatic, nor does it mean
that everyone has it. You have to want it, and work passionately for it. Is
her partnership worth the effort? I believe these words from the book of
Proverbs speak very eloquently in response to that question. Read them
again slowly, and decide for yourself.

Where do you find this perfect partner called "wisdom?" That's an easy
one — God's word — between Genesis and Maps.

Now to Him who is able to do far more abundantly beyond all that
we ask or think, according to the power that works within us...
— *Ephesians 3:20*

Top Fuel Power

The incredible power generated by the engine of a Top Fuel dragster is
almost beyond comprehension for the normal person, even one who enjoys
racing. One Top Fuel dragster 500 cubic-inch Hemi engine generates
more horsepower than all the cars in the first 4 rows at the Daytona 500
combined. Burning 90% nitromethane it can accelerate to over 100 mph
in less than 1 second.

But enough talk about that piddlin' little bit of power. Let's talk about
some REAL power. How about God's power to create the entire,
infinite universe with its uncountable trillions and trillions of stars and
galaxies? Just from the creative power of His word — He SPOKE it
into existence. And He continues to sustain that same infinite universe
and hold it all together (Hebrews 1:3) — to this very hour — by that
same power. The same power that crushed mighty Egypt with plague
after plague, the same power that parted the Red Sea, the same power
that held the sun still for Joshua, the same power that let Elisha's servant
see himself and Elisha surrounded and protected by a heavenly army
with horses and chariots of fire filling the mountains all around them ...
and on and on we could go.

That same power is the power of which Paul speaks here. If you think
your problem or prayer is too much for God, think again. That same
power not only exceeds anything we can ask for, it exceeds anything we
can even think about. It is the Top Fuel power that only God has —
and — to the degree that you will submit to God, He will use that same
power to change your life.

Therefore, since we have so great a cloud of witnesses surrounding
us, let us also lay aside every encumbrance and the sin which so
easily entangles us, and let us run with endurance the race that is set
before us,
— *Hebrews 12:1*

Precedent

Precedent — n. — An act or instance that may be used as an example
in dealing with subsequent similar instances. (The American Heritage
Dictionary of the English Language)

This verse of immeasurable encouragement is actually the conclusion to
one of the greatest (if not the greatest) precedent statements in all the
Bible — Chapter 11 of the book of Hebrews.

Chapter 11 is so rich in its encouragement, that among Christian circles
it is famously known as "the roll call of faith." In exhilarating and rapid-
fire succession, the writer of Hebrews mentions, by name, the history-
changing faith of 17 people, plus the entire nation of Israel, plus all the
prophets, plus innumerable others martyred, tortured and imprisoned,

who he describes as "too good for this world." That entire chapter is the foundation of the "therefore" statement before us in this verse. A single verse of scripture, 12:1, that rings like every bell in every church steeple all over the world, all at the same time, saying "the plan of God and the Christian faith is worth our trust and our life."

It ignites our hope today with its incredible challenge. Witness after witness after witness bears testimony to the incredible plan and power of God, and what He wants to do with you ... and for you ... and through you. Raise high the banner of your faith. Refuse to let anything or anyone deter you. Refuse to let anything or anyone slow you down. Never pull out of the race. It is worthy of your best effort. You have a great cloud of witnesses as encouragement, and if you need a little more, read verse 2.

"Listen to Me, you who know righteousness, a people in whose heart
is My law; do not fear the reproach of man, nor be dismayed at
their revilings. "For the moth will eat them like a garment, and the
grub will eat them like wool. But My righteousness will be forever,
and My salvation to all generations."
— *Isaiah 51:7,8*

Setting Priorities

I have never met even one successful person who did not share the
following characteristics: 1. — a visionary goal, 2. — a clearly defined
strategy to achieve the goal, 3. — a prioritized agenda to implement the
strategy. Critical to success is getting those priorities straight.

God defines for us — very clearly — the priority of all priorities. The
choice between the temporal and the eternal. Everything else is a side-
issue. Nothing should turn your head, or your attention from that.
Those who are God's children have no need to worry or fear anything
that comes from man or this world. All of it is temporary and fleeting.
What God brings to the table is eternal.

Consider this: if you were to go shopping for an item of clothing —
a single item, would you spend every dime you have (including savings) to
buy it, even if you knew it would fade terribly and fall apart after just one
washing? My bet is that you would not. Those people and their lifestyle
who would belittle you for your Christian faith will be here today and
gone tomorrow, just like those cheap clothes. But — the priorities you
have set to follow the Lord will take you all the way to eternity.

...if you confess with your mouth Jesus as Lord, and believe in your
heart that God raised Him from the dead, you will be saved;
— *Romans 10:9*

Stop Trying to Make Something Hard
Out of Something Easy

If my grandfather told me that once when I was growing up, he must
have said it to me a thousand times. Especially when it came to math
problems. He could do more and faster math in his head than I could do
on a calculator. My brilliant sister has the same irritating gift.

Today, if I could offer counsel about salvation in Christ, it would be these
very same words my grandfather said to me all those years ago. I would
offer it both to those who are searching for the truth, and for churches
and entire denominations that consistently try to make something hard
out of something designed to be easy. Jesus did the hard part — so relax
already.

The steps to salvation in Christ are simple. They must be absolutely
sincere, but they are exceedingly simple. A theological library and a line of
philosophers of religion are not needed to explain Paul's words here. Put
simply, Paul here in his letter to the church at Rome, is just drawing —
for the culture of his day — an unmistakable line between a hot heart and
mere hot air when it comes to belief in Jesus. He is in NO way saying
that you have to (1.) — pray out loud to be saved, or (2.) — you have
to speak in tongues, or (3.) — any other of the seemingly endless list of
requirements that some religions today have tried to attach to salvation
in Jesus.

What Paul writes here is no more than the natural response of genuine
faith. Faith that believes in who Jesus is, and has put Him in the center
of its heart. Even though we are talking about salvation and eternal life
in heaven, you don't have to make something hard out of something easy.
Jesus designed it that way.

For He will give His angels charge concerning you,
to guard you in all your ways.
— *Psalms 91:11*

God's Faithful Protection

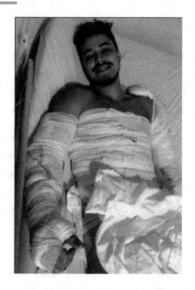

If you want to see what God's faithful protection looks like, just have a look at this picture.

Now, I know what you are thinking ... "this doesn't look much like God's protection to me." That's because sometimes God's protection doesn't necessarily fit our notions of it, and sometimes He doesn't save us from accidents. But if you think that this picture right here doesn't represent God's protection, it is only because you don't know the facts behind the picture. It doesn't always mean that we will never experience bumps and bruises as we travel life's road. As Christians our sins are forgiven, but that doesn't mean that they, or our own stupidity won't have consequences in this life. Meet my wonderful young nephew, Eduardo, the youngest son of Cláudia's sister, Heloisa. This picture was taken only hours after he had an accident on a motorcycle — going over 160 miles per hour. And no, that is not a typo. His front tire blew out, and you can imagine what happened after that. Injury report: three broken ribs, broken left arm, bruised lung, and a collection of scrapes and cuts (compliments of being launched into the air, then afterwards, rolling and sliding down the highway) which I imagine were very sore for quite some time. Here is the statement made by his attending surgeon, and I quote (as close to the Portuguese as I can get it): "You have been re-born, because it is impossible that you survived this accident."

Now, let me ask you something — if you had an accident, any kind of accident going 160 miles an hour, would you be happy to survive it with only the injuries my nephew sustained?... And, I would be willing to bet you something else. If you could ask him about it, I bet Eduardo would tell you that being able to smile for this picture had nothing at all to do with luck.

A poor widow came and put in two small copper coins, which amount
to a cent. Calling His disciples to Him, He said to them, "Truly I say
to you, this poor widow put in more than all the contributors to the
treasury; for they all put in out of their surplus, but she, out of her
poverty, put in all she owned, all she had to live on."
— *Mark 12:42-44*

The Value of a Penny

Jesus and His disciples were watching a bunch of rich people come into
the temple to give offerings in this passage. He didn't give a single one
of them any recognition. The one He gave recognition to was a widow
who, in the original language, was a pauper. Worse than poor, and with
very little opportunity or hope to ever change her situation. What she
contributed was about 1/64 of a day's wage ... but it was everything she
had. She held absolutely nothing back for herself.

Many of us today may not be able to make "big" contributions in church, as
others measure the word "big." Our voice in song may not be able to lead
the music ministry, our simple prayers may not lift people to the throne
of God as the prayers of others seem to do, our names may never appear
beside other names on a plaque in the church because of how much money
we gave to a project. When you do your best, and you are tempted to feel
disappointed because your best doesn't seem anywhere near the "best" of
others, remember the words of Jesus here dear friend, and remember —
Jesus doesn't measure sacrifice with size.

The neighbor women gave him a name, saying, "A son has been born to Naomi!" So they named him Obed. He is the father of Jesse, the father of David.
— *Ruth 4:17*

A Family Story

The book of Ruth is such a beautiful love story. It is a shame that it is largely neglected today. I say that because this love story is also a family story that God used in His eternal plans for you and me. It is a story involving two widows, Naomi and her devoted daughter-in-law (Ruth), a kind and caring man named Boaz who married Ruth, and their son.

It is beautiful as well because it reminds us that we don't have to be royalty for our family to be special to God and for Him to use us in His plan. Sometimes we might even be tempted to think that we are barely more than a small, insignificant cog in our family. Don't fall victim to that temptation, either.

How would you feel if your name was "Obed?" Would that make you feel important? Probably not, but this little verse in the Bible should give you encouragement that God can use you no matter what your name is or how common you might feel. Just who was Obed? — Well …

He was the father of Jesse,
… and Jesse was the father of David, the greatest king of Israel.
… It is the family tree of the Lord Jesus Christ.

Rejoice in the Lord always; again I will say, rejoice!
— *Philippians 4:4*

Indelible Joy

Do you know where these words were penned? They were penned from a jail cell in Rome. This is a picture of that jail cell, or more accurately, a dungeon. And yet, Paul uses the words "joy" and "rejoice" at least 14 times in this one, short letter. How could he do that considering all he had been through and where he was at the time? It is because there is a big, big difference in "joy" and "happy," and Paul understood the difference. "Happy" is a feeling based on a circumstance — but — "joy"

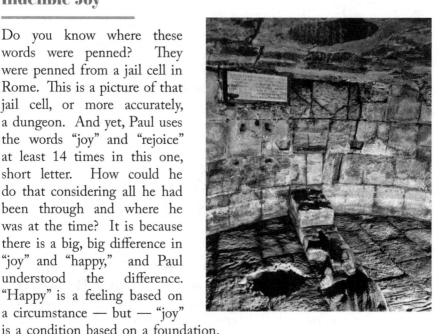

is a condition based on a foundation.

Bad circumstances can erase "happy," — but — they can't even put a scratch on real "joy."

Here is a partial list of bad circumstances: in prison like Paul, divorce, estranged children, lost job, lost home, lost savings, terminal illness, death of a child, death of a spouse, alone and no one cares, permanent injury that steals your future — and the list could go on and on. Any one of these bad circumstances can cause happiness to evaporate like a drop of water on a hot Texas sidewalk in the summer.

Here, is a VERY short, partial list of good things about the Lord:

1. Loves you enough to die for you.
2. Loves you enough that nothing can separate you from that love.
3. Chose to love you, even before the foundation of the world.
4. Gives you eternal life that nothing can take away.

5. Separates you from your sins as far as the east is from the west ... and forgets them.
6. Is never further than a whispered prayer away.
7. Is preparing a mansion in heaven for you.
8. Has a purpose for you, or He would take you to that mansion right now.
9. Has given you the abiding presence, peace and power of the Holy Spirit.
10. The entire contents of the 23rd Psalm.

— and the list could go on and on and on —

We may be sad sometimes, even deeply sad, when circumstances go bad in our lives. God knows how you feel, and cares. Don't forget, He knows what it is like to watch His own Son die. But, He also knew the end of the story — which lets Him write your name on the wall in eternity. That is the key for rejoicing in the Lord always ...

Joy is not determined by what your circumstances _**are**_ —
it is determined by who the Lord _**is**_.
He is the foundation of our joy.

fixing our eyes on Jesus, the author and perfecter of faith, who for
the joy set before Him endured the cross, despising the shame, and
has sat down at the right hand of the throne of God.
— *Hebrews 12:2*

Staying Focused

Staying focused is a very important part of life. Not only you staying
focused, but others around you as well. For example, a person not staying
focused while they are driving can affect my life as well as theirs. The first
phrase of this verse in the Bible shows us where the supreme focus of our
entire life should always be. In the middle of other important things like
our job, our family, our responsibilities, the focus that should never change
is the one we have on Jesus. "Fix your eyes on Him" is how God's word
puts it. His example, His instructions, His promises, His presence, His
power …and His love … all shine hope, and encouragement, and direction
into every corner of our lives, regardless of how dark the day may be.

Jesus is also "the author and perfecter of our faith," and our ultimate
example of how to stay focused. It was Jesus who created your path to
salvation, and it is Jesus who has completed and perfected the personal
story of redemption for each person who believes in Him. Heaven is your
home and nothing can change it, it is finished. It was not an easy thing
for Jesus to do — "He endured the cross, despising the shame," God's
word says. Make no mistake about it, the cross was not a joy for Jesus.
The thought of the horror of the cross caused Him to sweat blood in the
Garden of Gethsemane. It was not a joy. He ***endured*** it, and turned His
back on the shame of it for what was the real joy for Jesus — the one set
before Him — the joy of knowing it would bring you to heaven, with
Him, and that your own cross would forever be empty.

Jesus is the best example in all eternity of staying focused. His love for
you let nothing turn His head until your place in heaven was secure. Only
then did He sit down at the right hand of the throne of God. Nothing
else needs to be done. Ever. What He started, He finished. Jesus knew
how to stay focused … now it is your turn.

"... truly I say to you, if you have faith the size of a mustard seed,
you will say to this mountain,
'Move from here to there,' and it will move; and nothing will be
impossible to you."
— *Matthew 17:20*

The Right Tool For The Job

There are several variations, but, Archimedes is famous for the quote, "Give me a place to stand, a lever long enough and a fulcrum, and I can move the Earth." The principle is that with the right tool, there is no such thing as a weight too heavy to move. And the same is true with faith.

Many people think these words of Jesus to His disciples are about faith that is too small. It isn't. It is about "faith" that is virtually non-existent — and trying to move mountains with your own power. You don't need "big faith" to move mountains, you need a big God. It is the size of His power that moves the mountains in your life, not the size of your faith. Jesus taught that lesson here to His disciples by showing them that genuine faith need be no larger than the smallest seed of their world to move mountains and overcome any impossibility. Very small faith can access very great power when that faith is the real thing.

If we could have the license to paraphrase Archimedes just a bit, perhaps it would be: "Give me a place to pray, a genuine faith with which to pray — and nothing will be impossible for me."

Thank you for this wonderful truth, Lord Jesus!

And do not be conformed to this world, but be transformed by the renewing of your mind, so that you may prove what the will of God is, that which is good and acceptable and perfect.
— *Romans 12:2*

Mission Control

I remember visiting the Johnson Space Center just south of Houston, Texas a few years ago. What an amazing place. Part of it housed what is still known as the "Mission Control" room. It is where everything happened related to all of the spaceships and astronauts the United States put into space. From the first Mercury flight to the last shuttle flight. The first images of when man landed on the moon came from there. It is where the real drama of Apollo 13 happened. All the communications, all the decisions ... everything.

Our mind is like the mission control of who we are. God designed us that way. It is why the mind is mentioned in the Bible a lot more times than the heart — and it is why Paul wrote what he did here in his letter to the church at Rome. Many people believe we can live with one foot in the world and the other in the Kingdom and still be a Christian whose life is pleasing to God. You can't.

You don't have to become a nun or a monk, but you can't convince someone of a better way to take a bath by getting into the same mudhole with them. I heard it a million times after I became a Christian and stopped performing in nightclubs and dance halls: "I can go to nightclubs and be a witness for Christ there. People in nightclubs need Christ too." That statement is true, but my response to them has always been, "Yes, but DO you actually witness for Christ there?" The truth is, you don't and you won't. Related to that exact scenario is the beginning of this verse. It is a command, not a suggestion, and it is easy to understand.

How do you successfully live a life dedicated to God? Again, we have a command, not a suggestion, and it too, is easy to understand. "Renew" here doesn't mean to simply give your mind a "tune up." It means to make it new by a different way of thinking. "Transform" in the language of the New Testament is the word from which we get our word, "metamorphosis" — when something changes into something else that is completely different.

What is it we are to change? I love this part. Our MINDS. We have the expression "a change of heart" and we all know the Bible speaks about the heart, but it speaks more about the mind. A LOT more. Why? Because the truth is that our hearts don't feel a thing, and it never makes even one decision. All our decisions AND our emotions come from our minds. Our "mission control."

And now the best part of all — the purpose. In the spiritual trial against all the evil of this world — in God's courtroom — He wants you as the evidence ... your transformed and renewed mind — as proof of the good, and well-pleasing and perfect will of God.

Surely there is a future, and your hope will not be cut off.
— *Proverbs 23:18*

A Bridge Over Troubled Water

In 1969, Paul Simon wrote a song so powerful and beautiful that its popularity has endured for over 50 years (as of 2020) and counting. In 1971 it was awarded the Grammy Award for Recording of the Year and Song of the Year. To date it has been recorded over 300 times. Aretha Franklin brought it into the world of gospel music in 1971 and Simon said it was one of the most beautiful renditions ever, of his song, "A Bridge Over Troubled Water."

With God as your heavenly Father, you have a permanent bridge of hope over troubled water. That hope creates a bridge from right now, all the way to the day you see Jesus face to face. It is a permanent bridge that nothing can cut off — even if it is difficult to see at times. There may be days, weeks, months, or even years where problems and discouragements seem to try your faith and hope all the way to the bone. I've been there, have you?

Take heart. God doesn't think like us, act like us, or keep time like us. There will come a better day on the other side of the hard times. Neither God nor His Word ever fails. The bridge over troubled water will stand fast. No matter what.

"You did not choose Me but I chose you, and appointed you that you would go and bear fruit, and that your fruit would remain, so that whatever you ask of the Father in My name He may give to you."
— *John 15:16*

Who Found Who.

We've all heard it any number of times, haven't we? Someone is telling their story and says, "I found Jesus." Make no mistake about it, when anyone gets their life right with Christ, it is a beautiful story. But — if anyone thinks that they "found Jesus" one day, they need to read this verse again, and think again.

Long before you ever even start to look, Jesus had His finger on your name, and your future in His heart. Not only that, but He marked you out as His ambassador ... one that would do important and good things that really mattered, an ambassador that would have a lasting impact on others. That is the faith that Jesus has in you — specifically.

And not only that! Whatever you want or need **that is in the will and heart of Jesus ("in My Name)** — all you have to do is ask and it is yours. No executive boards, no committees, no chain of command. It doesn't mean that prayers are "wish lists" that are automatically granted the way we think they should be. Sometimes the will and heart of Jesus may take your prayers in directions you didn't expect. But rest assured — your request goes straight to the King of Kings and Lord of Lords, and when it is in the will and heart of Jesus ('in My Name"), you will have it.

Next time you are wondering if your life really matters, if your life counts for anything, let your heart take a deep, satisfying drink of the truth in this little verse — the truth of Who found who, and Who chose who.

And the city has no need of the sun or of the moon to shine on it,
for the glory of God has illumined it, and its lamp is the Lamb.
— *Revelation 21:23*

Light It Up

In our military culture, the expression "light it up" popularly means a command involving an immediate, violent military action against a target that can involve explosions, or massive fire balls from napalm or other incendiary ordnance. If we applied the term "light it up" to our religious world, it could no doubt refer to the effect of the shekinah glory that shines around the presence of God.

The glory of the Lord is a phenomenon incredible beyond all comprehension. When Moses came down from Mt. Sinai with the 10 Commandments, his face shone so brightly from being in the presence of the glory of the Lord, that the people were afraid and he had to wear a veil. When the disciples Peter, James and John saw that same shekinah glory around Jesus on the Mount of Transfiguration it made them want to build three temples; one each for Jesus, Elijah, and Moses ... and never leave the mountain.

Imagine an entire city never needing any light source because the glory of God "lights it up" all by itself. One day that Glory will be ours to behold with our own eyes — for all of eternity.

"The Lord your God is in your midst, a victorious warrior. He will exult over you with joy, He will be quiet in His love, He will rejoice over you with shouts of joy.
— *Zephaniah 3:17*

God's Happy Fit

We are familiar with assorted types of fits. Fits of anger. Fits of jealousy. In the midst of all the fits for all the negative reasons, why can't we have a fit of joy? A happy fit. God has one here, and be honest — how much time have you ever spent thinking of God behaving like this in your life? Let's change that today, shall we? When Israel repented and returned to its commitment to God, this verse was His reaction. He will do the same thing in your life when you return, in faith, to Him.

I would like to ask you to do something my Greek professor, Dr. Curtis Vaughan, challenged me to do in the seminary many years ago. It caused a whole new dimension of meaning and beauty of scripture to open before my very eyes ...

Read this verse — then read it again, slower. Then again, even slower. Do this, honestly, no cheating, until you have read it at least 10 times. This forces our minds and our hearts to slow down long enough for the Holy Spirit to actually have a chance to say something to us. I will help with just one phrase — "He will be quiet in His love." Some translations use "renew you" instead of "be quiet" because it seems to make better sense and it is only a tiny change in the form of the original word. I still prefer the unaltered, older translation. The word for "be quiet" here carries the same sense as in Genesis, when God's work of creation was completed, and all of it was very good ... and God "rested" in silent, satisfaction. It is still a "happy fit," just a different way to express it. God feels exactly the same way about His love for you.

Then Peter came and said to Him, "Lord, how often shall my
brother sin against me and I forgive him? Up to seven times?"
Jesus said to him, "I do not say to you, up to seven times, but up to
seventy times seven."
— *Matthew 18:21,22*

Raising the Bar

This is a borrowed phrase from the world of sports that we use in any number of ways today. Increase expectations, toughen the test, demand better performance — raise the bar. Jesus did exactly that with the subject of forgiveness.

It's easy to talk about. Doing it, however, is quite another proposition, isn't it? If we want to truly learn about that part (actually "doing" forgiveness), the place to go is the feet of the Master of forgiveness — Jesus — God's own expression of forgiveness in the flesh.

I love these verses here because they lay the lives of most of us open like a book, beside one of the great lessons of Jesus. We are SO much like Peter, are we not? The Rabbinic teaching of the day was that one was to forgive another three times. Peter thought he would impress Jesus by suggesting a whopping seven times, which was the symbolic number for perfection. As always, when we think we can impress Jesus with our lofty opinions of ourselves, He has a way of showing us just how far we still have to go. Like here. And my bet is that Peter and I are not the only ones to whom He has taught this lesson.

What Jesus does here is singularly beautiful. He answers unlimited revenge with unlimited forgiveness. He challenged Peter — and He challenges each of us — with a standard truly worthy of the gratitude we should all feel, because of the forgiveness God has shown to all of us.

One of the most beautiful quotes on forgiveness I have ever read speaks of both its beauty and its difficulty: "Forgiveness is the fragrance the violet sheds on the heel that has crushed it." (Mark Twain). Would that our own forgiveness could rise with such sweetness into the presence of the Lord.

in the hope of eternal life, which God, who cannot lie, promised
long ages ago,
— *Titus 1:2*

Promises, Promises

How many times have we heard that little two-word statement? How many times have we SAID it? Almost always it is spoken when something promised was not delivered, or when a person has little, or no hope that a promised action will actually be carried out.

Aren't you glad God isn't like that? God always means what He says, and He never goes back on His word. One of the Bible's strongest affirmations of this truth is right here in this short, little verse. Its truth is the foundation of our greatest hope and encouragement. There is a lot of "shifting sand" in this old world — success, possessions, relationships — but that which is most important and most precious is as solid as a rock. It is the promise of eternal life.

Your eternity with Christ isn't an afterthought with God. It isn't some last minute addition to His plan for you as a reward for something good you have done. If you have trusted Jesus as your Savior, your eternal life with God was set before time began — before "In the beginning, God created the heavens and the earth." It is an unshakeable, unchangeable promise. From the God who does not lie.

I will sing to the Lord as long as I live; I will sing praise to my
God while I have my being.
— *Psalms 104:33*

Music to my Ears

This is such an encouraging little verse for those of us who say they can't
sing — either physically OR in a spiritual sense. Hogwash. Yes, you can.
And God loves the melody because He loves you. In God's eyes you
couldn't hit a bad note if you tried because the melody of praise comes
from your heart. He would say of your praise, "It is music to My ears."

Don't overlook the fact of what is NOT said here, too. It does NOT say,
"as long as I get what I want," or "while I have everything going my way."
We think so often of prayer as asking for something, but the praise part
of prayer is very, very important too. Can I share a true story with you
that shows why?

Years ... and years ... ago, I was in the chapel service at my seminary
(Southwestern in Ft. Worth), listening to the sermon of a quite aged black
pastor. I have never forgotten what he said, even after all these years. He
was telling of an event in his own childhood when he was just a little
boy. It was time to start another school year and he was embarrassed
because he didn't have any shoes. In his house, shoes for the kids were
a luxury his single-parent mother simply couldn't afford. Again and again
he pleaded, and again and again his mother would say "no," each time
telling him to stop asking for things he knew he couldn't have.

SO — a few days before school he ran and jumped into his grandfather's
lap, hugged him and asked, "Pappy, can you buy me a new pair of shoes
for school?" And his grandfather responded, "Well, sure I will boy!" The
boy's mother was flabbergasted and irritated and said to her father, "How
can I teach him that he can't have something just because he jumps into
your lap and gives you a hug, if you always indulge him like that???" To
which the old grandfather replied, "Girl, I didn't tell him I'd buy him the
shoes just because he jumped up into my lap and hugged me. I told him
I'd buy him the shoes because of all the times he has jumped up into my
lap and hugged me — and didn't ...want ... nothin'!"

Bring the whole tithe into the storehouse, so that there may be food in
My house, and test Me now in this," says the Lord of hosts, "if I will
not open for you the windows of heaven and pour out for you a blessing
until it overflows. "
— *Malachi 3:10*

A Loophole in the Law

The law in God's word is very blunt and direct when it says, "You shall
NOT put the Lord your God to the test." (Deuteronomy 6:16). Jesus even
quotes this passage when satan tempted Him those 40 grueling days in the
wilderness.

Want to know the one area in the entire Bible where God grants an
exception to this law? Right here — in the area of giving back to the Lord.
In fact, He even INVITES you to test Him here — to see if you can out
give the Lord. It is a heartbreaking fact that not many take God up on His
offer. Less than 10% of the people who attend church provide 90% of the
financial support that sustains it.

In all my years of trying to do ministry however, I have had the honor
of meeting many, many true tithers and extremely generous and giving
Christians. Do you know how many of them — in all those years —
have told me that they found this verse to not be true? None. Not
a single one. Go on, put God to the test with your own giving. He
invites, and even challenges you to bring a tithe (or even more) to the
table — and see what happens.

My bet is that you will like what comes out of the windows of heaven.

"These things I have spoken to you, so that in Me you may have peace. In the world you have tribulation, but take courage; I have overcome the world."
— *John 16:33*

The Security Blanket

When Jesus spoke these words, he was only a few hours from the cross, and yet He gave these incredible words of hope to His disciples ... and to us. All that Jesus spoke for the last two chapters of John's gospel led up to this point.

Today there is no lack of TV "preachers" with perpetual Cheshire Cat grins, delivering cheap, inspirational one-liners sort of like — " 'happy' is out there for you, just reach up and grab it." I even heard one years ago say one time, "Stay tuned for a powerful message on how to put money in your pocketbook." You can't believe that sort of cheap gospel ... if you are going to believe Jesus. He teaches something much different, and much better.

Jesus said, "In the world you will have tribulation." Not "might have." Will have. I am betting that you already know that a new and exciting relationship isn't the answer to lasting peace and joy — is it? A better job isn't the answer to lasting peace and joy — is it? Is a move to a different place the answer to lasting peace and joy? ... No. Only Jesus is the answer for lasting peace and joy. Jesus said, "In Me you can have peace that the world will never give, and you can have confident courage in your trials in this world." Why? Because Jesus has overcome this world. He is our spiritual security blanket.

You need look no further than the empty tomb for proof.

I can do all things through Him who strengthens me.
— *Philippians 4:13*

The Key To Success

A whole lot of people have wasted a whole lot of money building libraries of "self-help" books. What is the key to success? The best way to help yourself? Here it is in a very short, single sentence in the Bible.

How much can we do through Christ? Something every now and then? A few things? No! ALL things. The problem many folks have is thinking that praying to Christ is some sort of "magic formula" where He comes running like some sort of Santa Claus in the sky and grants our every whim. That's wrong.

"Through Christ" means according to His will, according to His time, according to His way (all of which, some of which, or none of which may, or may NOT be, our own). To be able to know how to live that way, you need to (1) pray, and (2) invest the time necessary to read His book, the Holy Bible. You won't be sorry, as you watch this verse come alive in your life.

> This is the day which the Lord has made;
> let us rejoice and be glad in it.
> — *Psalms 118:24*

The Motivation of Our Joy

This verse is very well-known ... and very short, but its size is enormous when it comes to hope and encouragement. Not because of its "Pollyanna optimism" on the surface — but because of a profoundly deep and beautiful truth: our deepest joy as Christians comes not from the circumstances of our day — it comes from recognizing who created our day. I am writing this devotional about this verse today not so much for those who are already happy, as I am for those of us who have known days spent in the icy grip of sadness and despair. I know because I have been there.

A number of years ago I went through what was easily the worst time of my entire life when, as a Christian and as a missionary I watched helplessly as a divorce took my family. All my hopes and dreams disappeared before my eyes and I couldn't do anything to stop it. There were many days I curled up alone on my bed in a fetal position without the strength or the will to get up. God was so patient and loving toward me. Through His relentless love and the beauty of this verse and others, I began the return journey to a place of hope and joy. I will share with you how.

I cannot create a day, can you? If a day exists, it is because God created it. God does not create the problems in my day, but He most definitely creates the day. If I am a child of God — and I am — and if God really loves me ... and He does — then, if I am a part of this day God created, He must have a purpose for me in it (otherwise, He would simply take me home to heaven). And, if God has a purpose for me, it must be a good purpose because EVERYthing God does and makes is good. If God Himself has a purpose for me, then I CAN learn to rejoice and be glad in the day — even with a tear on my face and in my heart. I know ... because I have been there.

Behold, I stand at the door and knock; if anyone hears My voice and opens the door, I will come in to him and will dine with him, and he with Me.
— *Revelation 3:20*

Opportunity Knocks

See that old door? There was a time when it was the gateway to an important place for a lot of people. 100 years ago it was the front door to the First State Bank of Ben Wheeler, Texas. The stories it could tell. Opportunity knocked for many people who passed through it. It was the entrance to the place where many entrusted their life savings. Today it is abandoned, overgrown and forgotten in the woods.

There may be someone reading this today whose heart feels just like this old door: abandoned and forgotten, the day long past since it felt like an important place, longing

PickensPhotos

for a coat of paint, a couple of new hinges, a carpenter to fix it. That's what this verse in John's Revelation is all about. Jesus IS the Carpenter, and He never gives up on your heart, no matter its condition. He stands at it and knocks, wanting you to let Him come in and fix it. And He will. You just need to open the door.

Immediately Jesus stretched out His hand
and took hold of him, and said to him,
"You of little faith, why did you doubt?"
— *Matthew 14:31*

The Dream Catcher

A dream catcher is a beautiful example of Native American craftsmanship and tradition, originally hung over a sleeping person to catch bad dreams before they could enter the person's thoughts while sleeping. But, no matter how beautiful they may be, their ability to actually "catch" bad dreams is no more than folklore. There is, however, a very real dream catcher, and His name is Jesus.

This verse comes from the famous passage, recorded only in Matthew, of the disciples being caught in a storm in their boat and Peter wanting to step out of the boat and walk on top of the water with Jesus, who was coming to them ... walking on the water. You can read the entire fascinating event in verses 22-33. If someone were to actually try that today, some might be tempted to say something like, "Dream on, brother!" Well, don't let the people around you steal your hopes and dreams so easily with attitudes like that.

Just like Peter, there is nothing wrong with dreaming big even today — even WAY beyond what human logic says you can accomplish. For sure, storms of life will come and try to steal your dreams and cause you to doubt. Don't let it happen. Doubt has destroyed more dreams than failure ever has. And remember, when those storms do come, you have heaven's Dreamcatcher stretching out His hand to hold you up. Look to Jesus instead of the storm and doubt will never enter your dreams.

Seek the Lord while He may be found;
call upon Him while He is near.
— *Isaiah 55:6*

Getting Close to the Lord

What? You mean there are times when the Lord is not close at hand? That's right. But it's not really the Lord's fault, is it? Just being honest without calling any names ... we know whose fault it is, don't we? Without exception, when it seems difficult to find the Lord, or when He seems a long way off, it is because we don't give Him the chance to be close to us. And He always wants to be. Our days can get full and busy rather quickly, can't they? The reason it seems hard to find God sometimes is we cover Him up with all that "stuff" crowded into our day, and God will not accept second place in our lives ... or third or fourth ... and sometimes He gets relegated to a position even further down the list. Sound familiar? Sometimes we invite sin to be the guest in our hearts instead of God. And He will not intrude, even if you need Him.

It doesn't have to be that way. And we don't have to wait for a crisis when all of a sudden we remember to truly give God first place, and we find Him right beside us, faithful as always with His presence and love and power. James 4:8 tells us very succinctly how to get close to the Lord: "Draw near to God and He will draw near to you." And there are many places the Bible that tell us how to do exactly that (see the "P.S." at the end for a few examples). Basically, it involves two steps: 1. get rid of the wrong guest in your heart and invite God in, and 2. season your newly cleaned up heart with a healthy helping of humility.

I will be honest, it takes practice — sometimes a lot of it, because the devil doesn't like to let go of you without a fight. Also, everyone is different, but I can share with you what I like to do. What works for me is giving God the very best and the very first part of my day. That part when the day is fresh and new, before anything else is on the agenda. It is the time for me when God is always in first place. A time to read His word, a time to pray — a time with Him that doesn't get shared with anything, or anyone else. Set aside a time, every day, in your own life to do that and you won't have to find God. He will just show up, right there beside you.

"P.S."
Isaiah 55:7
Isaiah 59:2
Heb. 7:19
Heb.10:22
James 4:6-8
Ps.34:18

Let us not lose heart in doing good, for in due time we will reap if
we do not grow weary.
— *Galatians 6:9*

In Due Time

Have you ever eaten a tree-ripe peach? If you have, you know from
personal experience that it is one of the supreme pleasures of life. Think
with me for just a minute. If you planted a peach seed, would you expect
to have that tree-ripe peach from it the next day? Of course not. It
takes time to plant the seed, and even more time for the seed to become
a tree. The wait can seem excruciatingly long ... but then — in "due
season" it bears that succulent, juice-running-down-the-chin, delicious,
tree-ripe peach.

The Bible encourages us here, to not grow weary waiting for the peach.
God promises that it will come. And His promise is good enough, right?
Our part is to keep doing good — the things we should do as Christians,
without giving up — ever. You can't forget the condition of the promise:
"if we do not lose heart." Sometimes it is hard, I know, sometimes
REALLY hard, to keep doing what you know is right, especially if the
situation is difficult. But, if God's word is true — and it is — the wait is
more than worth the effort.

For a child of God due season will come — and it will be much better
than that tree-ripe peach.

"Now, Father, glorify Me together with Yourself, with the glory
which I had with You before the world was."
— *John 17:5*

A Little Refresher Course

From time to time, even those with the strongest of faiths among us can grow weary in that faith. It happened even to the great John the Baptist. We wonder about "unanswered" prayer, about why Jesus doesn't seem more real at times. Sometimes we may even be tempted to ask, as John the Baptist did — "Should we look for another?"

The Bible is full of little "refresher courses" for times like that. Verses that remind us of just who Jesus is. Verses that thrill us and restore our faith. Verses that remind us that the One in whom we have deposited our faith is not some sort of energy crystal, nor a contrived, carved idol, nor a dead fat man sitting with his legs crossed.

This verse is one of those verses. A conversation between God the Son and God the Father. Just a short snippet that lets us see behind the curtain of eternity — but enough to let us see that Jesus is ... and always has been, eternal. Glory equal to God's glory since before He ever said "Let there be light." Equal because Jesus IS God, and always has been. He really is the King of Kings and Lord of Lords, the Alpha and Omega, the Beginning and the End. Rest easy, my friend ... your faith is in the hands of the absolute Master of everything.

Put on the full armor of God, so that you will be able to stand firm
against the schemes of the devil. For our struggle is not against
flesh and blood, but against the rulers, against the powers, against
the world forces of this darkness, against the spiritual forces of
wickedness in the heavenly places. Therefore, take up the full armor
of God, so that you will be able to resist in the evil day, and having
done everything, to stand firm.
— *Ephesians 6:11-13*

Get Dressed, Soldier

There is a chilling scene in the first Jurassic Park movie that I will never
forget. A vicious dinosaur was moving along a perimeter fence, poking at
it with its nose. A person asked the expert who was with him, "What is
he doing?" The answer: "Looking for weaknesses."

That is exactly what the devil does in our lives every single day. He never
stops. In fact, it is most often the case that the harder you try to live
right and live for God, the harder the devil tries to find those chinks in
your armor — those "soft spots" in your perimeter fence.

Sometimes, you may feel like the devil has already crashed through your
weak spots and has left you wounded and bleeding on the battlefield of
your life. But — it doesn't have to be that way. God gives you a uniform
for the battle ... a suit of armor so strong and well-equipped that it can
protect you from anything the devil can throw at you. Want to know
what the pieces of God's armor are? Paul lists them in the next three
verses (14-17): 1.Belt of truth, 2. Breastplate of righteousness, 3. Gospel
of peace, 4. Shield of faith, 5. Helmet of salvation, 6. Sword of the
Spirit, which is the word of God.

The only way the devil can defeat you is if you let him. Take heart my
friend. Get up. Get dressed. Put on this armor. Don't let the devil take
the ground, soldier!!

> Your word I have treasured in my heart,
> that I may not sin against You.
> — *Psalms 119:11*

Biblical Insurance

A possession in our life might be thought of as a treasure when we have kept it and protected it through the years because it is extremely valuable and precious. Insurance is a plan we have paid into to help protect us in a time of need. When it pays for a health crisis or hospital stay that would have otherwise devasted us financially, it might even be thought of as a treasure. So what is Biblical insurance? Well, maybe this can explain it ...

A uniquely, beautifully gifted man named Angel Martinez was called as a boy, by God, to preach and be an evangelist. When he preached his first sermon at the age of 13, with the exception of his father, his entire family responded by giving their lives to Christ. When he went home to the Lord in 1995 at age 73 after a ministry that spanned some 60 years, he had personally led over 500,000 people to Christ.

In addition to his incredible gift to preach, Angel Martinez was also widely admired and respected for one other thing — he committed to memory the entire New Testament of the Bible, and could quote from anywhere in it without hesitation. When asked why he would devote such a monumental amount of time to accomplishing this amazing feat ...

Psalm 119:11 was his response.

Make sure that your character is free from the love of money, being content with what you have; for He Himself has said, "I will never desert you, nor will I ever forsake you."
— *Hebrews 13:5*

BFF

In the social media crazy world of today, "BFF" is a very well-known abbreviation. It means "Best Friends Forever." No matter what life throws at a person, the "BFF" is there. Always. Well, I hate to tell the social media world, but it is not the origin of the concept of "BFF." God Himself is the origin. He was the first BFF, is still the best BFF, and still extends His offer of love and friendship to anyone who will accept it.

This particular verse about the **H**BFF (Holy Best Friend Forever), is personally very special to me because it is the one the Holy Spirit used to finally slip through a small crack in my ol' stone-hard heart when I was a million miles from a relationship with Jesus. It was embedded in the middle of a sermon by Dr. Millard Bennett, the pastor of my home church in Madisonville, Texas. I can't remember the sermon, but I for sure have never forgotten this scripture. The truth is, I was in church to hide after being hurt really deeply, and on top of it all, I felt I had been abandoned by all the people I thought for years were my friends. I wasn't in church for Jesus at all. Then came this verse that nailed my entire life to the wall. I was consumed with the love of money, I wasn't content with ANYthing I had ... and then that last part that brings tears to my eyes to this very day and this very moment. It was as though God had created a moment between just Him and me, and it felt as though He was tapping me on the shoulder right there in the pew and saying, "You know that friend you have longed for who will stay even after the party stops, who will never disappear when you hurt and when you need someone to really care? I want to be that Friend ... and I have waited 28 years to tell you that." No one will ever be a better friend to you than the Lord God Almighty, and who — if He isn't already — would like very much to be your Heavenly Father.

He will not allow your foot to slip;
He who keeps you will not slumber.
— *Psalms 121:3*

Guard Duty

November 11th is a very special day each year on the calendar of the United States of America. We call it Veterans Day, and we set it aside to give honor and gratitude to all who have served so honorably in our armed forces. All around the world they have performed guard duty 24/7 that has kept America strong and free for a long time.

The 3rd U.S. Infantry Regiment, also known as "The Old Guard" is the oldest active-duty infantry unit in the Army, serving the US since 1784. Ever since July 2, 1937, soldiers from this regiment have been on guard duty at The Tomb of the Unknown Soldier. 24 hours a day, 7 days a week, the watch has never been broken — without regard to national calamity or events, or inclement weather, as is proven by this picture taken during a blistering rainstorm. Only a very few of the best of the best are chosen for the honor of this duty because it is a very demanding job.

That's what makes the guard duty mentioned in this Psalm so very important. You may be thinking, "Well, I don't know so much about this because my foot moves and stumbles a lot." You know why that happens? It is because you put yourself on guard duty, instead of the One who is actually qualified for the job. Guarding you, guarding me, guarding any of us in a world ruled by satan is a demanding job, too — and there is only one qualified to do it. Want fresh hope and encouragement and firm direction anew in your life? Let the Lion of Judah, who never sleeps, even when you do … secure your steps and guard your life.

Then the Lord God formed man of dust from the ground, and breathed into his nostrils the breath of life; and man became a living being.
— *Genesis 2:7*

A Matter of Faiths

When it comes to the subject of God and creation, there are actually two faiths involved. I could be wrong, but I don't think there were any photographers or journalists or scribes during the time creation happened and life began. So — let's look at these two faiths, shall we?

Faith #1: The group of us who believe in God and the Biblical account of creation and how life began. There is no "empirical evidence" so what we believe is based on faith.

Faith #2: The group that discounts our notion of an all-powerful God in favor of believing that everything came from nothing. Life evolved by chance from inorganic matter that, for no reason at all, appeared out of nowhere. Life evolved from this inorganic matter by sheer random accident, into the life forms that exist today. There is no "empirical evidence" for this theory either, so IT is actually "faith" as well.

Faith #2 is passionate about pointing to fossil records to prove their theory about evolution. But they have a problem: there is not a single example from the fossil records, of ANY species morphing by evolution into a different species. Not one. And there should be hundreds if not thousands and thousands of examples. And there is only a single strata of the earth where fossils are even found, they are not distributed evenly throughout the earth's crust over "millions and millions" of years, as one might expect. And — strangely, marine fossils and land animal fossils are all crushed together in this single strata — all over the world — almost as if there had been a single, cataclysmic, world-wide flood.

Hmmmmm …

Which is almost the greater faith? The faith that acknowledges a God with a power we could never hope to understand as the source of a creation that stretches to infinity, and is the source of life that is incredibly complex even on the microscopic level — or — the faith that scoffs at the suggestion that a robot could ever assemble itself out of nothing, yet refuses the notion that a human being — infinitely more complex than any robot — demonstrates any evidence of intelligent design whatsoever, and just evolved by accident.

I choose, unashamedly, faith #1 as the truth. But the greater truth still of God creating man, is not that a God this powerful created me — but that a God this powerful loves me. And He loves you too. And He sent Jesus Christ to prove it.

And my God will supply all your needs according to His riches in
glory in Christ Jesus.
— *Philippians 4:19*

A Quick Prayer Primer

"Guilty of a crisis-driven prayer life." It might be interesting to see how
many of our hands would have to go up on that one. The truth is, a deep
and satisfying prayer life comes only from a deep and intimate relationship
with God. It is only in this type of relationship that this verse will begin
to shed its magnificent fragrance into your life.

A short devotional cannot span the breadth of the subject of prayer —
indeed, book after book has been written on it, but we CAN extract one
of the pearls from its treasure chest: Philippians 4:19, which teaches
us that prayer is not a magic formula, but it IS a certain and beautiful
formula:

First — the word is not "might" supply, it is WILL supply.
Second — the word is not "some" of your need, it is ALL of your need.

Third — the word is not "supply according to your idea of answered prayer,"
it is supply according to His riches in glory.

Fourth — the word is not "supply according to the eloquence of your
prayer," but, supply through the power of the Lord Jesus Christ.

I, for one, am really grateful that God doesn't stop with my own limited
ideas about the way He answers prayer in my life — because His way is
always the best way.

But Jesus said, "Let the children alone, and do not hinder them from coming to Me; for the kingdom of heaven belongs to such as these."
— *Matthew 19:14*

A God-pleasing Faith

This is a beautiful statement of hope and encouragement from the lips of the Lord Jesus Himself. He is talking about a small group of children here, but the message is most definitely for adults. For those of us who can't pray the angels down with eloquent prayer, for those of us who are not spiritual giants, brilliant theologians, fire-breathing preachers or Biblical scholars ... and like as not never will be — good news — in fact, great news: We don't have to be.

In fact, God actually prefers something quite different. And a whole lot more simple. If you have a child-like faith, stop apologizing for it and praise God for it. He has given you the type of faith that is His favorite — open, honest, simple and trusting. Jesus used the best example on earth to illustrate it: a little child.

If a spiritual camera could take a picture of your faith and it looked like a little child, you may be a whole lot more pleasing to God than you think!

"For My thoughts are not your thoughts, nor are your ways My ways," declares the Lord. "For as the heavens are higher than the earth, so are My ways higher than your ways and My thoughts than your thoughts.
— *Isaiah 55:8,9*

Just Be Yourself

How many times have we heard that advice? How many times have we GIVEN that advice? Better still — how many times have we wished that we had actually TAKEN that advice? Do you suppose God ever thinks to Himself, "I wish they would just let Me be Myself!"

I know what you're thinking — no one can limit God. He can be Himself any time He wants. That's true, but that's not the way it works. And it is you who holds the key. God accepts a limited role in your life, not because that's what He wants — He accepts it because that is what YOU want, and God will not trample the free will underfoot that He, personally gave to you. In all honesty, we all do it. We tie God's hands when we force Him inside the fences we build in our prayers, the fences we build in our plans, the fences we build in our "bargains" with God (God if you'll just do this, then I will do thus and so …). If we are honest with ourselves, the way we approach God many times is like we want some sort of magic puppet, or a Saintly Santa Claus — instead of an Almighty God.

But, what if … just what if … we truly handed over our life to God and said, "Just be Yourself, Lord!" And instead of forcing Him to operate inside our own, small mental cube, we allowed God the freedom of exercising His limitless power, wisdom and ways in our personal life? The kind of wisdom and ways Isaiah writes about here. What do you suppose would happen if God could really be Himself in our lives? This, my friend is the spiritual altitude for which we should always reach — where faith fills its lungs with the air the angels breathe.

Now may the God of hope fill you with all joy and peace in believing, so that you will abound in hope by the power of the Holy Spirit.

— *Romans 15:13*

A Heapin' Helpin' of Hope

In the quest to discover hope and encouragement in God's word, Paul hits the "mother lode" right here. Stay with me for a minute here as we take an "amplified" look at the translation so we can get the full impact of the power and majesty, not to mention the beauty, of Paul's words here. Read it slowly. Here it is …

"Now may the God who is the author and source of all your hope, cram you so full of every bit of joy and peace possible because of your faith in Christ, that the Holy Spirit, through His power, puts in you a super-abundant overflow of hope."

God is the source of hope. He fills you with joy and peace because of your belief in Christ — and the Holy Spirit delivers all of it. In spades. That's what "abounding" means. It's a heapin' helpin' of hope.

"Wisdom is with aged men,
with long life is understanding.
— *Job 12:12*

A Word To The Wise

A word to the wise. Ok, here it is: Younger Christians (especially), lend an ear to some advice that I hope will serve you well in your life of learning about the Lord Jesus. Actually, I am hoping that these few words can be an encouragement to two groups: the young, and the "not so young."

Young folks ... you are tempted almost every day to make quick decisions based on thin information, isn't that so? Sometimes very thin. Rather than swallow a little pride and seek some real wisdom, sometimes you make the decision by yourself — and the decision ends up being wrong. The wrong person to date, the wrong people to go out with, the wrong place to go for a party, the wrong thing to drink, the wrong thing to do with your body, the wrong decision about a job offer.

Ask me how I know this is true ...

Young folks, let me encourage you to seek out some of those "grey-headed old fogeys" in your church, even if you are not currently in need of some quick wisdom. If you have never done that, you can't even begin to imagine the stories they can tell you ... stories that reside in their hearts, and beneath those crowns of silver hair. Real life stories of answered prayers and miracles that unfolded right before their eyes. The presence and strength and comfort of the Holy Spirit they have felt personally, when life seemed like one big storm with no end in sight. Feeling Jesus right there beside them when they went through fear so strong that it seemed it would shake them to pieces. The Bible is the most electric and exciting book that has ever been written. If you want to see it come alive in front of your eyes, spend some time with some of those bent over, older folks in your church.

Ask me how I know this will bless your heart ...

And now to the "not so young." Being a current part of this group I know how you feel, too. Life and usefulness seem to be passing you by. Church is not the same anymore, and seems more like a stage show now instead of worship. Full of guitars and loud, "modern" music repeating the same 5-word verse about 50 times — with all those beautiful and majestic old hymns all but forgotten. Sort of like you and me. May I be so bold as to offer an encouragement to you today that is really important? ...

Only you can help the wisdom and beauty of the Bible truly come alive for the younger people of the church. Why? Because you have lived it. Find a way to share it with those who need to see the wisdom and beauty and strength and truth in the Bible for themselves, from someone who has seen it first-hand. You have something to offer in church that no one else can provide.

> "... the cup which the Father has given Me,
> shall I not drink it?"
> — *John 18:11b*

When God's Answer to Prayer is "No."

God answers prayer. Yes, He does. Definitely. In one of the devotionals in this book we mentioned "well-worn" phrases in the church. Surely "God answers prayer" is another one. It is absolutely true, and one of the unshakeable pillars of our faith that gives us hope and encouragement. But ...

The mistake we make sometimes, in making this a churchy "well-worn" phrase is equating "God ***answers*** your prayer" with "God ***grants*** your prayer." They are not the same thing. No parent who really loves their child gives them everything they ask for — and neither does God. Just because He answers your prayer doesn't mean He grants your prayer. Sometimes the answer is "wait." And sometimes the answer is "no."

The deepest kind of hope in your life depends on how you respond when that happens, just like when it happened here to Jesus. This is the place in scripture where Jesus was about to be crucified and Peter was wanting to fight ... and Jesus had just been praying with such intensity and stress that He sweat great drops of blood from His face. The prayer? That God would remove the cup He was asked to drink. The cup of being crucified. God answered the prayer — and the answer was "no."

Jesus's response to God's "no" is the short sentence contained in this verse. Did He draw the sword of the King of Kings and Lord of Lords? No. Did He call down the Archangel Michael? No. Did He even allow Peter to fight? No. His response was, "Put the sword into the sheath; the cup which the Father has given Me — shall I not drink it?"

Accepting God's "no" as Jesus did here, with the faith that God has a bigger plan — bigger than you and I could ever imagine or understand — or deserve — is where the deepest kind of hope is found. We may not always understand God's plan, but we ***can*** always trust it. The size of that plan here in Jesus's life should give you great hope. The "cup" He drank on that cross paid the price for your sin and my sin, and gives us the future of eternal life in heaven. And that same future is there for anyone who will trust the Lord Jesus Christ as their Savior — all we have to do is ask Him for it.

He who overcomes will inherit these things, and I will be his God and he will be My son(v.7) and he carried me away in the Spirit to a great and high mountain, and showed me the holy city, Jerusalem, coming down out of heaven from God, having the glory of God. Her brilliance was like a very costly stone, as a stone of crystal-clear jasper (vs. 10,11). The material of the wall was jasper; and the city was pure gold, like clear glass. The foundation stones of the city wall were adorned with every kind of precious stone. The first foundation stone was jasper; the second, sapphire; the third, chalcedony; the fourth, emerald; the fifth, sardonyx; the sixth, sardius; the seventh, chrysolite; the eighth, beryl; the ninth, topaz; the tenth, chrysoprase; the eleventh, jacinth; the twelfth, amethyst. And the twelve gates were twelve pearls; each one of the gates was a single pearl. And the street of the city was pure gold, like transparent glass. I saw no temple in it, for the Lord God the Almighty and the Lamb are its temple. And the city has no need of the sun or of the moon to shine on it, for the glory of God has illumined it, and its lamp is the Lamb (vs18-23).

Home Sweet Home

YESSSSSSS!!!!! — Home, sweet home!! No comment necessary!!

Your word is a lamp to my feet and a light to my path.
— *Psalms 119:105*

God's Flashlight

When you grow up in the country, lots of times there are things that go "bump in the night" that you can't explain. That happened one night when I was just a young boy and my cousin and his dad (my uncle Floyd) were with us for the weekend. We had already gone to bed when ... the noise (a cat fight on the roof) happened. My city-cousin had never heard anything like that and cut loose with a blood-curdling scream. What followed still makes me laugh after all these years ...

In the pitch black darkness, I could hear my uncle (who didn't know where any of the light switches in the house were) crashing and banging into what seemed like every piece of furniture in our house — and offering some very "colorful commentary" during the process, while he tried his best to get to where we were as fast as he could — which finally, he did. It would have been much easier ... and much less painful, if he could have had a flashlight.

God's flashlight for us is His word, the Bible. Reading and studying it gives us a light switch for our whole life, so that we never — ever — have to worry about things that "go bump in the night," or have to stumble around in the dark.

"Father, forgive them;
for they do not know what they are doing."
— *Luke 23:34*

The High Cost Of Ignorance

Ignorance can become really expensive sometimes, can't it? There are even some famous quotes about it. A quote by the former president of Harvard University, Derek Bok, became known as "Bok's Law": If you think education is expensive, try ignorance." I also love what one of my professors at Southwestern Seminary, Dr. Bill Tolar, once said: "It is true that a little knowledge is dangerous ... but, so is a whole lot of ignorance." A good example would be trying to drive a car and not knowing how. That level of ignorance can get you killed. Quick.

The great majority of the people in Jesus's day were completely ignorant of who He was. It could have cost them a lot. But, the person who paid the cost of their ignorance was Jesus Himself. Such is His love. Jesus was misunderstood and rejected for most of His life. He was asked to leave town. The creator of the entire universe was reviled by the religious leaders of the day. In the hour of His greatest need His hand-picked disciples all turned tail and ran, never understood His teachings about sacrificing His life, and refused to believe in His resurrection until they saw Him face to face. And look at the setting of this verse — Jesus was beaten to a bloody pulp, almost to death, stripped naked in front of His own mother and nailed to a cross, laughed at, spit on, soldiers gambling for His clothes as He gasped for air and His body writhed in pain. And the crowd just stood there in morbid ignorance and watched, shouting, "Crucify Him!"

If anyone in the history of humanity had just cause to turn His back, and throw up His hands and say, "This is a lost cause! Every single one of you can just go straight to hell where you belong," it was Jesus. And He could have stood by and let every one of them go there. But He didn't. Jesus didn't turn His back. Instead, He said, "Father, forgive them for they do not know what they are doing." Jesus turned the high cost of ignorance into a day of salvation for all mankind.

Do you know what that means, my friend? It means He won't turn His back on you either. Ever. No matter what. For Jesus, no one is a lost cause. He died for you, too. The next time you are tempted to think that you are too far gone, that whatever you have done is too bad for Jesus to be able to forgive you, remember this scene at the cross, remember where He was ... and who He forgave, when He spoke the words of this verse. And He will forgive you too, if you will just ask.

The Lord's lovingkindnesses indeed never cease,
for His compassions never fail.
They are new every morning; great is Your faithfulness.
— *Lamentations 3:22,23*

Overgrown

PickensPhotos

Most all of us have seen old buildings like this, that nature is in the process of reclaiming. Left untended and alone it is surprising how fast it can happen. Have you ever let the same thing happen in your life? Piece by piece the things of the world can take us apart until we are only a shell of who we used to be, or until there is almost nothing left at all. If we allow it, the weeds of the world can consume us inch by inch, and before we know it, our lives have become over grown by the world. Sin can do that. Putting everything else in your life ahead of God can do that. Anyone besides me know how that feels?

The good news is that what is inevitably going to happen to this old shed doesn't have to happen to us. It might be too late for this old shed, but it is never too late for you. Why? Because God never gives up on you if you will just give Him the chance to love you. His lovingkindness never stops. His compassion never falters. His love for you is here to stay. And He can make you new again.

Where can I go from Your Spirit? Or where can I flee from Your
presence? If I ascend to heaven, You are there; If I make my bed
in Sheol, behold, You are there. If I take the wings of the dawn, if
I dwell in the remotest part of the sea, even there Your hand will
lead me, and Your right hand will lay hold of me. If I say, "Surely
the darkness will overwhelm me, and the light around me will be
night," even the darkness is not dark to You, and the night is as
bright as the day. Darkness and light are alike to You.
— *Psalms 139:7-12*

You Can Run But You Can't Hide

Ask Adam and Eve, they tried it. Didn't work. In fact, nothing works. It
doesn't matter what you use, it is still like trying to hide from God behind
a fig leaf (Adam and Eve's choice). You can try misdirection, by blaming
someone else for your own mistakes (Adam tried that, too: "the woman
that YOU gave me, God — she caused me to do it."). That didn't work
either. Using job stress as a cover for not giving the Lord the time He
deserves — another fig leaf. Hiding behind a bottle in the darkness of
a bar or nightclub — even smaller than a fig leaf. In fact, us trying to hide
from God paints about the same picture as when a raccoon covers its eyes
and thinks you can't see it.

The plain truth is, that you cannot hide from the presence of God. Ever.
But, there is a wonderful and beautiful upside to that. Try looking at it
through the eyes of David, king of Israel who wrote this Psalm. There is
also no place in life, no situation … no matter how alone you feel, or how
dark the future seems, where you will ever be all alone. God will forever
be there, even ahead of you, to lead you, protect you, love you, and to
shine His light into the darkest of nights.

"Whoever exalts himself shall be humbled; and whoever humbles
himself shall be exalted."
— *Matthew 23:12*

Upside Down Life Cake

Anyone who has ever baked a cake knows that, no matter what kind of cake you are baking, you have a list of ingredients, a process to combine those ingredients, some time in the oven, and then that delicious icing that goes on after you take the cake out of the oven. For a normal cake, even an upside down cake, that is how we do it, right?

With these wonderful words here, Jesus teaches us about a different kind of upside down cake. The cake of life. One way to real hope and encouragement in the here and now is getting this cake right, but a lot of us get it wrong. Even Christians. If we take a truly honest inventory of our "cake's" list of ingredients, we find "work time," we find "leisure time," we find "social time," maybe even a little "church time," we find "being a husband/wife/parent time," we find "trying to get ahead on the success ladder time" ... and then to make it a little more attractive, we cover it all with a coat of icing called "humility."

What Jesus teaches is — humility is the cake. Everything else is the icing.

Rejoice always; pray without ceasing; in everything give thanks; for
this is God's will for you in Christ Jesus.
— *1 Thess. 5:16-18*

Thanksgiving Day

(In 2021, that's today — November 25th)

Hint: It is more than just the fourth Thursday of November on the
calendar of the United States.

During class one day at Southwestern Baptist Theological Seminary, one of
my professors (I'm pretty sure it was Dr. Gray) said something about being
thankful that I never forgot. He said that if it were possible for everyone in
the entire world to put all their problems, worries and troubles in a sack —
and then everyone come together and dump all the sacks into one gigantic
pile — and then everyone leave with equal portions of problems, worries and
troubles in a new sack ... most people would be very happy to turn around
and leave with the sack they brought in the first place. That's really true, isn't
it? We all have more reasons to be thankful than we think, don't we?

As we think about that, and our own personal sacks, these verses right here
can help us get our priorities straight, even though they are three of the most
misinterpreted and misapplied verses in the Bible. They do **_not_** mean, and
have never meant, that we are supposed to rejoice or give thanks even for
sad or tragic things that happen. What they DO mean is: In the middle
of life's storms, we should never allow circumstances to throw a blanket of
doom and gloom over our joy, or our prayers, or our thanksgiving.

Why are we to never let that happen? Well, one big reason is this: it is
the will of God. But the harder question is "how," isn't it? How do we
do that? The answer is right there ... "in Christ Jesus." Because you have
Jesus in your life, you have a Friend who — loves you no matter what,
never leaves you, never forsakes you, forgives your mistakes, defends you
before God, bled for you, died for you, redeemed you, and has given you
a way to heaven and eternal life. You have all of that — present tense —
in Christ Jesus. And none of that goes away because of any circumstance
of life. That is why you can still rejoice in the middle of it all, pray in the
middle of it all, and give thanks in the middle of it all.

Take that sack to Jesus and let Him take care of it, my friend.

looking for the blessed hope and the appearing of the glory of our
great God and Savior, Christ Jesus,
— *Titus 2:13*

Grammar Can Be Exciting

Hang on to your hat. This is one of the greatest verses in all the Bible that proves who Jesus is. He is more than just a good man. He is more than just a good teacher. He is more than just a prophet. He is who the Bible says He is. He is God in the flesh ... and grammar proves it.

Some try to say that this verse does NOT say that Jesus is God, and the correct interpretation should be, in essence, like this: "looking for the blessed hope and the appearing of the glory of our great God, and the appearance of our Savior, Christ Jesus as well. The fatal flaw in that "interpretation" is that the grammar of the Greek language won't allow it. Stay with me here ...

"great God" in the Greek, is preceded by the definite article, "the." The word "Savior" has no article before it. Sound boring yet? It's not. Trust me. Literally it says, "the great God and Savior of us ..." When the grammatical structure is like this, it means that both nouns (God, Savior) refer to the same thing or person. This example should make it easy to understand: "All Country Music fans love the great singer and songwriter, George Jones." George Jones was both singer and songwriter.

The Lord Jesus Christ is both God and Savior. Anyone who tries to tell you differently doesn't know what they are talking about, grammatically *or* theologically.

He who gives attention to the word will find good,
and blessed is he who trusts in the Lord.
— *Proverbs 16:20*

The Encouragement Two-Step

Mention the words "Texas two-step" (a.k.a. "the Aggie Shuffle") to any of my Texas friends and two things will happen: our feet start twitching and we start looking for the nearest dance partner. Over the years, who knows how many boot soles have been worn out doing the Texas two-step. There is another two-step, however, that is even better. Much better. I call it the "encouragement two-step," and the steps to it are here in this little verse in Proverbs.

The first step is what you do with God's word. Notice, it is an action, not an idea. You can't learn the first step of the encouragement two -step if you leave your Bible unopened and neglected on the coffee table, fireplace mantle, or bookshelf. You have to pay attention to it and apply its truths wisely in your life. To do that, you have to read it — regularly. Not just when you have a crisis and need a miracle. God's word promises that the one who does this will find good. Tell me you are not encouraged when you find good things happening!

The second step in the encouragement two-step is trusting in the Lord. Again, an action, not an idea. Trusting in Him means even when you might not agree with something He does, or when you don't understand something He does. It means not leaving God in the corner of the closet until you have that crisis or need that miracle again. Trusting in the Lord is an everyday exercise. It builds your muscle called "faith." God's word promises that the one who does this will be happy and blessed. Tell me you don't feel encouraged when you are happy!

See how it works?! Shall we dance?

Jesus said to him,
"Because you have seen Me, have you believed?
Blessed are they who did not see, and yet believed."
— John 20:29

Bless You

The origin of the very common phrase, "bless you" is so old, and there are so many theories to how it began, that no one can really know for sure how it was first used. Today, we use it almost without thinking when someone sneezes.

Jesus uses it when someone believes in Him. Want some instant hope and encouragement? Here it is ...

If you are a believer in the Lord Jesus Christ, even with all your faults attached Jesus has a very high opinion of you. The opinions of all others pale in significance. Spend a few minutes thinking about this fact: The Creator and Lord of heaven and earth has personally, with His own lips, called you ... specifically ..."blessed." In the original language the word means "supremely blessed." It is the same word Jesus used nine times in what we call the Beatitudes in His Sermon on the Mount.

Here Jesus uses it again, especially for you. Notice, He did not say, "Blessed is your faith for believing." He said, "Blessed are YOU." Don't just read over that. Spend some time thinking about it.

You are of great value to the Lord Jesus.

I will give thanks to You, for I am fearfully and wonderfully made;
wonderful are Your works, and my soul knows it very well.
— *Psalms 139:14*

Different is Also Beautiful

PickensPhotos

To close our time together in the month of November, we are going to look at Psalms 139:14 — twice. I believe you will enjoy both looks. Here is look number one.

Take a good look at the old sycamore tree in this beautiful picture by my good friend and brother in the Lord, Danny Pickens. After reading Psalm 139:14, if you see just a dead, old tree you aren't looking close enough. I love what his wife, Paula, said: "If trees could talk, I wonder what stories each of those branches could tell." Look closely and you will see a tree that, even without leaves, stands out from all the rest behind it. You will see a tree, weather-worn, but still standing — alone in the field all by itself while all the others crowd in the anonymity of the grove behind it. In its difference, it is the most beautiful of them all.

No matter how different you feel or look, you are fearfully, wonderfully, beautifully, and marvelously fashioned by God's very own hand.

I will give thanks to You, for I am fearfully and wonderfully made;
wonderful are Your works, and my soul knows it very well.
— *Psalms 139:14*

Accidents of Evolution? Not.

Only a very few times have I used the same verse twice in this collection of devotionals. It is because sometimes a verse demands more than just one look. This is one of those times. Here is look number two.

Question: Does this verse say, "I praise You because I have fearfully and wonderfully evolved?" No. This mighty verse of scripture puts your creation squarely where it belongs ... in — and by — the hands of Almighty God. And so do the following verses. Created (not evolved) in His image. That makes you, personally and individually, astonishingly and wonderfully made. Sometimes through our own mistakes we can make a mess of His masterpiece, but make no mistake about it, you are an astonishing creation wrought by the hand of God Himself. Want just one, quick example that shows just how astonishing? ...

"If all the DNA in one of your cells were uncoiled, connected, and stretched out, it would be about 6 feet long. It would be so thin its details could not be seen, even under an electron microscope. If all this very densely coded information from one cell of one person were written in books, it would fill a library of about 4,000 books. If all the DNA in your body were placed end-to-end, it would stretch from here to the moon more than 165,000 times! In book form, that information would fill the Grand Canyon almost 30 times. If one set of DNA (one cell's worth) from every person who ever lived were placed in a pile, the final pile would weigh less than an aspirin! Understanding DNA is just one small reason for believing that you are "fearfully and wonderfully made."

Does that sound like an accident of evolution to you? Does that sound like something that grew up out of a schlogg of foam on top of a primordial mud puddle to you? Not to me either. Astonishingly and wonderfully made by the hand of God is the only explanation. Praiseworthy? Absolutely.

(Please join me in giving thanks to Dr. Walt Brown for his kind permission to use the italicized information above. It comes from his book, In The Beginning: Compelling Evidence for Creation and the Flood, which is completely free for all to read on his astounding website: www.creationscience.com)

"… and He will wipe away every tear from their eyes; and there will no longer be any death; there will no longer be any mourning, or crying, or pain; the first things have passed away."
— *Revelation 21:4*

God and His Handkerchief

For the person who is a Christian, life is always full of hope. Sometimes it may be hard to see, sometimes God asks us to wait for it and trust in Him in the meantime … but, it is always there. However, for a Christian it isn't just LIFE that is full of hope. Even death is full of hope. That's what this verse, with God and His handkerchief, is all about — when we arrive at heaven's gate. Pain of sickness, gone. Sadness of failure, gone. Sadness of broken relationships, gone. Despair of rejection, gone. Pain of a broken heart, gone. Sadness of death, gone. All gone … and gone forever.

When I was just a little boy, a cat bit me in my ear one night while I was trying to protect my dog's food. I was inconsolable, wouldn't stop crying and believed I was going to die of rabies. My grandmother got into bed with me, wrapped her arms around me, stroked my hair, and wiped all the tears from my eyes. All night long.

Whenever I read this verse, I always remember that night …

"Jerusalem, Jerusalem, who kills the prophets and stones those
who are sent to her! How often I wanted to gather your children
together, the way a hen gathers her chicks under her wings, and you
were unwilling ..."
— *Matthew 23:37*

Is This What You Call Encouragement?

I know you must be wondering where in the heck is the encouragement
in this? Trust me, it is here. Let's have a look. First, let's not try to
diminish the gravity of this scene. These words of Jesus contain crushing
sadness and in addition to this, His own crucifixion which He has
known about for eternity is now bearing down on Him like a locomotive.
Something else — try to keep in mind that this lament did not come
from just a man who life is about to end; these words, these thoughts,
came from the heart of the Lord God Almighty, Creator of heaven and
earth and who had watched the entire history of His chosen people of
Israel — people who had failed Him time and time again.

And through it all, He never stopped loving them. Ever. That's where
the encouragement appears in this verse of God's word. When He used
the words "How often I wanted to gather your children together, as a hen
gathers her chicks under her wings," He was using the same imagery
that comes from the beginning of Genesis — "and the Spirit of God
moved upon the face of the waters." And ... even though Jerusalem/Israel
rejected Him, He would not reject them. In a few days, He would still
carry that cross up Calvary and die on it. For them — and for you and
me. We fail God many times, just like Jerusalem. He still loves us, just
the same. He never says, "Your time is coming," or, "I will get even with
you." He just loves us, even though sometimes we break His heart. His
love for you never fails.

Now a challenge. We get hurt in this life too, don't we? By people.
Often times, by people who we love and who are supposed to love us.
Have we not all wept over our own Jerusalem at some point in our lives?
Of course, we will never be able to love as perfectly as Jesus, but we can
try our best. In the face of the hurt, we can love anyway. Because that's
what real love does.

"For you will go out with joy and be led forth with peace; the
mountains and the hills will break forth into shouts of joy before
you, and all the trees of the field will clap their hands.
— *Isaiah 55:12*

Return to Eden

This was the title of a television mini-series some years ago. It was full of murder plots and intrigue.

The real return to Eden is here — in Isaiah 55:12. It is one of the most joy-filled verses in all the Bible. In this poetic prophesy of Isaiah, he speaks of the day when the restoration and reuniting of the scattered nation of Israel will take place, but it doesn't end there. True prophecy has a present-day as well as a future significance.

Isaiah, in this beautiful prophecy, speaks of a coming day for us as well. Close your eyes for a moment. Do your best to "clean the mental blackboard" of all that is written, scratched and stained there so you can let your imagination soar free from stress. Imagine a day of "going out with joy and being lead out with peace," with your body finally perfected by God's very own hand, free from pain, free from sickness, free from death, free from all fear, free from all sadness, free from all worry — and free from sin. Imagine every single Christian in the world that way. The moral perfection of God that existed in the beginning has returned and it is so beautiful and exciting that nature itself rejoices.

In the Bible, creation is many times pictured as responding to the presence and activity of God, just like it is here in Isaiah's "return to Eden." Let your heart dwell in this place for a few minutes and you will have placed the tip of your tongue in the delicious taste of pure joy that our Heavenly Father intended for us from the very beginning.

"Are not five sparrows sold for two cents? Yet not one of them is forgotten before God. Indeed, the very hairs of your head are all numbered. Do not fear; you are more valuable than many sparrows."
— *Luke 12:6,7*

Forget-Me-Nots

I think the little Forget-Me-Not flower would be a wonderful nomination for "Best Biblical Flower." It is a really small wildflower that grows in big clusters, and I think they are beautiful. Biblical because we, just like them, can feel small and lost in a crowd sometimes, but — each displays its very own individual "sun" in its center, with "rays" coming off of it in all directions — exactly the way we should shine the light of Jesus, the Son, outward in all directions, from the center of our being. And then, there is that sweet name, "Forget-Me-Not" ...

Have you ever felt left out and forgotten? I know I have. I saw it many times as a pastor too, in nursing or retirement homes. As a free "sidebar" to the scripture today, may I offer an opinion? As Christians, we should find the time somehow to visit the fine folks in those places. It was one of my favorite places to go as a pastor. They are full of fine people with wonderful stories and beautiful hearts. Hearts that sometimes, sadly, have been forgotten by their own children.

God never does that to you. In our "work-a-day" world (or retirement world) we may slip into the feeling of being taken for granted by those around us, or just flat out forgotten sometimes … even by those who are supposed to love us. God never does that. He never forgets anyone. Including you and me. In fact, Jesus used the expression "the very hairs on your head are all numbered" to show the disciples that it is almost impossible to understand just how well God knows us.

And, if there is anything more wonderful to know than just how well God knows us — it's knowing just how much He loves us. Shine THAT out from your heart, Forget-Me-Not.

"His master said to him, 'Well done, good and faithful slave. You were faithful with a few things, I will put you in charge of many things; enter into the joy of your master.'"
— *Matthew 25:23*

Pay Day

The old story goes that once upon a time there were two farmers who had land next to each other. One of the farmers was a devoted Christian, the other was not. They both raised wheat. Every September at harvest time, the farmer who was not a Christian had about three times the size of harvest as the Christian farmer. Finally one year the lost farmer said to the Christian farmer, "You go to church every Sunday, you talk about the Lord all the time, and yet every September at harvest time my wheat yield is about three times as big as yours. How do you explain that?"

The Christian farmer replied, "The Lord does not always settle His accounts in September."

These words from Jesus in this little verse in Matthew describe the greatest pay day of them all. In the accounting system of the Lord, what is important isn't how much wheat you cut, isn't the size of your bank account, isn't the size of your house or car, isn't your position at work. What IS important is faithfully serving the Lord and taking care of what He has entrusted to your care. Sometimes it might be having to make do with an "old clunker" of a car, constantly patching a leaky roof in a small house, or working faithfully, showing up every day in a low-paying job.

But ... when the Lord settles your account, the pay day is more than worth it. All the success and riches this world has to offer is no match for hearing these words of Jesus when you see Him face to face: "Well done, good and faithful child; you have been faithful over a few things, I will make you ruler over many things. Enter into the joy of your Lord."

If it is disagreeable in your sight to serve the Lord, choose for
yourselves today whom you will serve: whether the gods which your
fathers served which were beyond the River, or the gods of the
Amorites in whose land you are living; but as for me and my house,
we will serve the Lord."
— *Joshua 24:15*

Putting Your Money Where Your Mouth Is

I doubt there will be anyone who reads this who doesn't know the meaning of the phrase "put your money where your mouth is." Talk is cheap. There comes a time when, if you want someone to believe you about something, they need more than just words from you. The same is true about our relationship with the Lord, and Joshua knew it.

... If you are going to say you believe in God ...
... If you are going to claim the blood of Christ for forgiveness of sin ...
... If you are going to say you are a disciple of Jesus ...

****There comes a time to stand up — or shut up.****

So — who's with me?

"And you shall love the Lord your God with all your heart, and with all your soul, and with all your mind, and with all your strength."
— *Mark 12:30*

Get To The Point

Have you ever been listening to someone and wished they would just "get to the point?" Some people seem to have a gift of being able to ramble all day and never get to the point. Jesus didn't have that problem. Jesus was a master at getting to the point. I don't think there has ever been anyone who could get to the point like Jesus could. No one. With one sentence, He could reduce the high and mighty (religious OR political) to intellectual dust, leaving them seething, mute and looking ridiculous. I love it. He did it here with one from the group called the Scribes — self-absorbed, and self-proclaimed experts in religious law — when he thought he would try to provoke controversy by asking Jesus which was the greatest commandment.

Jesus also gets to the heart of the matter in our own lives with this verse, doesn't He? If you are going through a rough time in your life, would you be willing to debate with Jesus about it? If He were to ask you, "Are you loving the Lord your God with all your heart, with all your soul, with all your mind and with all your strength?" could you say, "Yes."? I couldn't. I'd have to say, "I know I should try harder, because I fall short almost all the time."

And, my dear friend, therein lies the answer of hope to just about all our problems. Jesus ranked this as the number one most important commandment. Commandment — not suggestion. The distinction is important. When we obey it, things have a marvelous way of working themselves out.

Over the years when folks have complained about the impossibility of "keeping all those commandments," as I have mentioned several times throughout these devotionals ... I have always told them, "You don't have to worry about keeping all of them. Just keep the first one and all the rest will take care of themselves. Keeping the first one has the power to fix anything in your life. That's why Jesus got right to the point and ranked it first.

Your eyes have seen my unformed substance; and in Your book were
all written the days that were ordained for me, when as yet there
was not one of them.
— *Psalms 139:16*

I've Had My Eye On You

A teacher to an exceptional student, a coach to a gifted athlete, or perhaps an employer to a hard-working, promising employee — these are just a few examples of why this well-known phrase might be spoken to someone. God has had His eye on you, too ... for a very long time. If you are interested in knowing just how long, this little sentence from the Psalms tells you.

There has never been a single day in your life that God hasn't known who you are. There has never been a single day in your life that God didn't have a plan for you. There has never been a single day in your life that God didn't love you. So much so, that He wrote out a plan for every single day of your life. Sometimes our own stubbornness gets in the way, but God never gives up on His love for you. That's why He sent Jesus to die on the cross in your place.

If God's word means anything at all to a person, the question, "When does life begin?" is very, very easy to answer: before our mothers saw the first sunset with us in her womb.

Since before the end of your first day until this very hour, God has loved you.

"The King will answer and say to them, 'Truly I say to you, to the extent that you did it to one of these brothers of Mine, even the least of them, you did it to Me'."
— *Matthew 25:40*

Who Really Wants to Serve Jesus?

I'll give you a hint — it isn't the person who brags about never missing a tithe. It isn't the person who tries to sound like a Billy Graham sermon when they pray. It isn't the person who comes up to you in church and says something like, "Gaaaawd gave me a word for you today." It isn't the person who tries to impress everyone around them with how many Bible verses they have memorized. Jesus describes the person who really wants to serve Him in the verses just before the verse in this devotional (vs.35-39) ...

'For I was hungry, and you gave Me something to eat; I was thirsty, and you gave Me something to drink; I was a stranger, and you invited Me in; naked, and you clothed Me; I was sick, and you visited Me; I was in prison, and you came to me.' "Then the righteous will answer Him, 'Lord, when did we see You hungry, and feed You, or thirsty, and give You something to drink? And when did we see You a stranger, and invite You in, or naked, and clothe You? When did we see You sick, or in prison, and come to You?' Jesus's answer is the words in the verse of this devotional.

Really serving the King of Kings and Lord of Lords isn't our tithe — that is our duty. Nor is it our worship — that is our gratitude and praise. Performing real service TO Jesus is doing what He did: loving and serving the needy — and they are all around us with all manner of needs. And Jesus (not me) says that when we do it to them, we do it to Him. And in all my years of trying to do ministry, I have never met even one true servant of the Lord who said it wasn't worth it.

Are they right? Well, I'm glad you asked. One verse before the "servants list," in verse 34, Jesus reveals to His disciples, the fruit of this service: "Then the King will say to those on His right, 'Come, you who are blessed of My Father, inherit the kingdom prepared for you from the foundation of the world'." Eternal life, eternal joy. It is a promise to those who are His real servants. If that doesn't wind your "joy clock," your spring is broke!

Now the Lord said to Abram, "Go forth from your country, and
from your relatives and from your father's house, to the land which
I will show you; and I will make you a great nation, and I will bless
you, and make your name great; and so you shall be a blessing;
— *Genesis 12:1,2*

Comfort Zones

We all have them, don't we? Our personal comfort zones? Those places
outside which we don't like to venture. Big bank accounts, fancy cars,
luxurious homes, salaries that, compared to the rest of the world, let us
have our carefree choice of creature comforts, a lifestyle that is insulated
from the pain and needs of those around us. Even the church can be
a "comfort zone" that we don't like to leave to actually do those things, as
Christians, our Lord and Savior has commanded us to do.

It would have been very easy for Abram (Abraham) to stay in his comfort
zone when God told him to leave it. By today's standards he would have
been considered a middle-aged, very wealthy livestock owner. God was
telling him to leave it all — all his family, his country, all his land — and
go to a place that God didn't even name. All He said was, "I will show
you where." As a wealthy, middle-aged man he was asked to leave it
all and was told that he would be the founder of a great nation, and he
would be a blessing and would have a revered name. Could you have
believed that if it happened to you? Today I have difficulty getting people
to leave their "comfort zones" to be a part of mission trips that last for
just two weeks. Would you have left everything — for the rest of your
life — for an unknown land and a future that seemed almost impossible
to believe? Abraham did — and the rest of the Bible is a testimony to
the fruit that is possible through the faith of a single man willing to leave
his comfort zone and follow God's will in his life.

Now, I know what you are thinking — "I am no Abraham." Well, no
one else is either. But one of the things I love about the Bible is the
way it shows us time after time, how God uses people who are far from
perfect. Ordinary people for extraordinary purposes — people just like
Abraham. People just like you. You think it can't happen? Abraham lied
and compromised the personal integrity of his wife to save his own life,
he fell over laughing when God told him he would father a son at an old

age, he had concubines — he was far from perfect. Yet look what God did through him because he had the faith to follow God and step outside his comfort zone.

You are no different, my friend. You might not become the founder of a nation, or have your name immortalized, but God can — and will — and would like very much, to use you too. He has a wonderful plan for all of us if we are willing to not hide from it. Many, many, MANY times hope and encouragement and a new joy can be found just on the other side of your comfort zone — if you have the faith to step outside it.

At the ninth hour Jesus cried out with a loud voice, "ELOI, ELOI, LAMA SABACHTHANI?" which is translated, "MY GOD, MY GOD, WHY HAVE YOU FORSAKEN ME?"
— *Mark 15:34*

I Know How You Feel

There is incredible hope and encouragement in this verse, and it is powerful. Very powerful. Trust me.

To encourage me during the darkest hour of despair in my entire life, God took me to the darkest hour of despair of Jesus's life — and unveiled for me a truth that is so beautiful and powerful in its encouragement that I have never forgotten it. I have never heard it in any sermon or read it in any book. In fact, most commentaries avoid this verse entirely. But the beauty God showed me here brings tears to my eyes to this very day. I share it with you now —

When you reach the end of your rope, when you don't understand, when there is no explanation, when life affords no answers to anguish and despair and God seems silent — you don't have to feel guilty or that your faith is somehow small if you cry out to God, "Why?!!" Even Jesus cried out to God, "Why?!!" ... and He knows how you feel when you do it too. If you have never thought about that, let it sink in for a few minutes. Jesus was never separated from the love of God — but He WAS separated from the presence of God. For the first, and only, time in all eternity. It was the penalty for sin. Not Jesus's sin. Jesus never sinned. The sin for which Jesus suffered and died alone on the cross was not His. It was your sin and my sin that He died for.

Secondly, don't ever forget ... this was not the last thing Jesus said on the cross. The story was not over yet. The last thing Jesus said to us from the cross was "Finished!" It was a shout of victory meaning "Mission accomplished!" For the one who believes in Christ, life never ends in defeat. Never. Not even when we feel weak and without answers. There is a day past the despair. What Jesus experienced on the cross and what He accomplished for us there guarantees it.

How precious also are Your thoughts to me,
O God! How vast is the sum of them! If I should count them,
they would outnumber the sand.
When I awake, I am still with You.
— *Psalms 139:17,18*

What's On Your Mind

The first 18 verses of this psalm are one of the most beautiful eruptions of praise to God in the entire Bible. You can almost feel the pulse of David's heart as he loses himself in the wonder of God's abiding presence and care in his own life — having planned it from start to finish, even from the womb.

This praise was an exercise of such splendor for David that in numbering the great thoughts and care of God in his own life, he could think only of the number of grains of sand in the world as a comparison. And in David's world, there is a LOT of sand.

These words of David showed that his adoration of God's presence in his life was a constant pursuit. It was in his heart when he closed his eyes in sleep, accompanied him in his dreams, and was his first thought when he awoke. Years before the prophet Isaiah would pen the words, King David knew well this truth: "You will keep him in perfect peace, whose mind is fixed on You" (Isaiah 26:3). True for David. True for Isaiah. True for you.

But Jesus looked at them and said, "What then is this that is written: 'The stone which the builders rejected, this became the chief cornerstone.'?"
— *Luke 20:17*

Foundation, Foundation, Foundation

The expression "In real estate there are three things that matter: location, location, location." is familiar to just about everyone. In construction that would have to be amended to "foundation, foundation, foundation." Why? Because it doesn't matter how attractive the location is — if the foundation of the building isn't strong, all you will have in the end is a collapsed building on top of a pretty piece of dirt. Just like the apartment complex in this picture (NOT a photoshop, by the way), with a pretty view of the river.

When you are talking about where you will spend eternity, foundation, foundation, foundation is also of the utmost importance. Where are you going to build? On Mohammed who is dead? On Confucius who is dead? On Buddha who is dead? On any other dead false god or prophet? Or … are you going to choose the living, resurrected and reigning Lord Jesus Christ? The Alpha and the Omega, the Beginning and the End. The Kings of Kings and the Lord of Lords.

Who are you going to listen to? The "experts" who can't even tell you why life begins? -or- the One who created all life in the first place? Listening to the "experts" today as they try to minimalize the Person of Christ and build a world view without Him is like looking at the building in this picture and saying, "That's what I want." Want some real hope and encouragement today? Plant your life, your feet, your future and your faith firmly in the one and only Son of God, the eternal Head of the Corner. The One who is the sure foundation of all hope and eternity.

Then He said to Thomas, "Reach here with your finger, and see My
hands; and reach here your hand and put it into My side; and do
not be unbelieving, but believing." Thomas answered and said to
Him, "My Lord and my God!"
— *John 20:27,28*

Personal Encounters Make a Big Difference

Personal encounters are a lot different than a letter or even a conversation
on the phone, aren't they? If my Uncle Floyd were still alive, he would
certainly testify to that. When he was a young boy, he was deeply
infatuated with a young lady who lived not far from him. He wrestled
and wrestled with working up the courage to ride his bicycle over to her
house and ask her father if they could go out together for a "soda water"
at the drugstore. Finally he worked up the courage, rode his bicycle
over to her house, and knocked on the door. The young lady's father
answered the door and said, "Can I help you, young man?" My uncle
stood there speechless for a few seconds and then managed to weakly
reply, "Can I have a glass of water, please?" Personal encounters make
a difference.

A personal encounter with the risen Lord Jesus Christ makes a big
difference, too. If you could ask the disciple, Thomas, I believe he would
agree 100%. A scant week before this encounter with the resurrected
Lord Jesus Christ, when the other disciples had told him that Jesus
had risen from the dead, he refused to believe it. In fact, these words
that Jesus spoke here to Thomas were the very words Thomas used as
a demand in order for him to believe — to verify that Jesus was indeed
risen from the dead.

When Thomas's demand became a personal invitation from the risen
Lord, and he actually had the opportunity to do what he had demanded,
he simply fell to his knees and said, "My Lord and my God." He did
not say, "Oh my goodness, you really ARE alive!" ... or anything similar.
Instantly he knew the truth of what had truly happened on Easter Sunday,
and the truth — and fullness — of who Jesus really is.

There is something about an authentic, personal encounter with the risen
Lord Jesus Christ that completely erases doubt and disbelief. I have seen
it change men (and women) with hearts of stone who mocked Jesus only

the day before. After many years in ministry and a Master's degree in Theology from one of the finest seminaries in the world, my best and most scholarly response to the question "Why?" is — it just does.

Having an encounter with the risen Lord Jesus Christ and feeling His infinite love — for you — is a life-changing encounter. Or better yet, an eternity-changing encounter. And if you have never felt what Thomas felt, if you have never had a personal encounter with the Lord Jesus Christ ... it is only one, honest prayer away.

'He has redeemed my soul from going to the pit, and my life shall
see the light.' "Behold, God does all these oftentimes with men, to
bring back his soul from the pit, that he may be enlightened with
the light of life.
— *Job 33.28-30*

God and That Light of His

I struggle to find words that truly describe my feelings when I look at this
picture. Surreal and heartbreaking at the same time. A church abandoned
by its people — but, not abandoned by God. His light still wants to
shine through its leaning steeple, empty sanctuary and broken windows.

God's word tells us that believers in Christ are His church, each one with
a role to fill ... and yet, many times what we offer God looks so similar to
this old church — just an empty shell of what we should be. Or, maybe

you feel like this old church today. You feel empty, of no use anymore, headed deep into the pit Job writes about here — hopes and dreams long since gone, alone and abandoned. But — you are never abandoned by God.

If any of this is you, take heart my friend. God's light forever shines, and He wants to shine through you again too — no matter how badly your steeple may be leaning, or broken your windows are, or how empty you feel. His love for you is forever, and He will shine through you again just like this old church, if you will let Him.

"...and you will know the truth,
and the truth will make you free."
— *John 8:32*

Freedom that Lasts

This is normally not a verse that is used to bring a focus on Christmas ... but it should be. Israel's history, because of its disobedience and unfaithfulness to the very God who made it special, is one long story of being under the heavy foot of one conquering ruler after another, beginning with 400 years of bondage in Egypt — with a few years of relative peace (sometimes) between one conqueror and the next. The time of Jesus's birth was no exception. During this time it was the foot of Rome on the neck of Israel. They longed for a conquering Messiah to give them freedom at last.

What they didn't realize was that in Jesus, they had an even greater freedom. Jesus said, "I am the Way, the Truth and the Life ..." (John 14:6). Jesus did not say "I *have* the truth." He said, "I AM the truth." The truth Jesus speaks of in John 8:32 isn't just a teaching, it is a person. Him. Know THAT truth by asking the Lord Jesus Christ to become your Savior, and it will make you free indeed. It is a freedom that no one can ever take away. It is a freedom that will stay with you all the way to the gates of heaven itself. And it arrived a little over 2,000 years ago ... in a manger in Bethlehem.

> After coming into the house they saw the Child with Mary His
> mother; and they fell to the ground and worshiped Him. Then,
> opening their treasures, they presented to Him gifts of gold,
> frankincense, and myrrh.
> — *Matthew 2:11*

Presents for Christmas — It's in the Bible

Our present-day commercialization of Christmas has many faults. Many of these faults are justified, not the least of which is the way it takes the eyes of many away from the real focus of Christmas — the coming of the Lord Jesus Christ as the Lamb of God for the redemption of mankind.

I don't believe, however, that we should completely condemn the practice of gift-giving at Christmas — if it is done in the right way, and in the right spirit. Gifts were given at the very first Christmas by the Magi, or wise men. Very costly gifts of gold, frankincense and myrrh. Very costly indeed. We also know what God's gift to us was, on that very first Christmas. His only Son. And not just His only Son, but the sacrifice of the life of His only Son. Another very costly gift. Very costly indeed.

This year, as we gather with our loved ones and celebrate this most holy time of year ... and as we give gifts to each other, why not elevate the Christian approach to gifts at Christmas to its rightful place? We already know what Jesus has given to us for Christmas ... now the question for each of us is: (following the example of the Magi on that very first Christmas) — what is the cost of the gift that I will give to Jesus?

And she gave birth to her firstborn son; and she wrapped Him in
cloths, and laid Him in a manger, because there was no room for
them in the inn.
— *Luke 2:7*

Making Do With What You've Got

(I'd like to humbly ask your permission, just this once, to depart from the
familiar "no room in our hearts" lesson from this verse and see where it
can take us, ok?)

Most of us have lived that phrase "making do with what you've got" more
times than we would like to admit. We don't have what we would like, or
what we would prefer, so we have to make do with what we've got. The
clunker we drive to work, the tools that fall apart, the vacuum that spits
dirt, clothes that are frayed and a few years out of style ... sometimes it
gets old, doesn't it? When that happens (and for many of us, it happens
regularly at Christmas time), it might lift your spirits to look at Jesus —
the all-time Champion at making do with what you've got.

It started right here in this verse. Unable to have a room or a crib, Jesus
made do with a feed trough. It didn't diminish who He was, nor delay
the appearance of the King of Kings among us. Jesus made do, even
without a room, and the first Christmas arrived right on schedule.

Jesus didn't have the support of any of the religious leaders of His day ... so
He made do with a ragtag group of disciples made up of weak, common
men, fishermen, a tax collector — even a traitor. They ended up writing the
New Testament and launching Christianity permanently into the world.

On a hillside one time at the end of an exhausting day 5,000 people
showed up wanting Jesus to heal them and teach them ... 5,000 *hungry*
people. Jesus made do with what He had: a few pieces of bread and
a couple of fish. He fed 5,000 people with it and had 12 baskets full of
food left over.

Jesus wasn't given a long time on this earth — just about 33 years. He
wasn't given a long time in ministry either — just about 3 years. But
Jesus made do with what He had. No car, no private plane, no bicycle,
not even a camel for transportation, no white suit, or patent leather shoes,

homeless and penniless — and in just 3 years Jesus still managed to establish a faith that would change the world ... and is still changing it.

When Jesus was crucified, He didn't even own a tomb — He had to make do with a borrowed one. Did that dent the power or the hope of His resurrection? Not one bit. And the first Easter arrived right on schedule.

SO ... next time you are tempted to feel a little down from having to always "make do," take comfort in knowing that you are in good company — with Jesus — the all-time Champion at "making do." And while we are on the subject, if we are going to be honest, when it comes to each one of us, isn't it true that most of the time Jesus has to just "make do" with what we give Him? A tiny slice of our day instead of all of it, a piece of our heart instead of all of it, a piece of our life instead of all of it. And still He is preparing a place for us in Heaven. Think with me here: I wonder what Jesus could do with my life if I gave Him all of me and He didn't have to just "make do."

This will be a sign for you: you will find a baby wrapped in cloths
and lying in a manger."
— Luke 2:12

Christmas 365 Days A Year

Don't you just love the Christmas season? Not the commercialized
version, but the time of year we celebrate the real reason for Christmas.
Have you ever thought about how wonderful it would be if we could
celebrate it 365 days a year? Well ... we can.

The idea of there not being any room at the inn for Jesus, and the question
about not having room in our hearts is a familiar analogy to all of us who
have heard many lessons and sermons about Christmas. But — let's think
for just a minute about where there WAS room for Jesus: a manger, or
more exactly, a feed trough. It makes me feel really special thinking about
where Jesus laid His head His first day on earth. Not in the arms of
a king or queen in front of thousands of cheering people, not in some sort
of 5-star "baby hospital," not in a fancy golden crib. It was a common
feed trough.

It makes me feel special thinking about it because it reminds me that
I don't have to offer Jesus a life or a heart fit for a king. It's ok of we don't
have a heart that looks like a palace or a Presidential suite because life's
storms have laid waste to it. If all we have left is a manger, it is ok with
Jesus. All we have to do is offer what we have and Jesus will do the rest.

And that is a joy we can wake up with, 365 days a year.

And Mary said, "Behold, the bondslave of the Lord; may it be done
to me according to your word."
— *Luke 1:38*

Real Submission

If you haven't thought about it in a while, is there a better time to think
about submission to the Lord than Christmas? We see it all through the
Christmas story.

1. There was Joseph who accepted his wife's story that she was pregnant
   by the Holy Spirit and would give birth to the long-awaited Messiah.
   Could you have believed her?
2. There were the shepherds who left their sheep and their responsibility
   to guard them, in order to go and kneel by the baby Jesus.
3. There were the Magi who traveled a great distance to bring expensive
   gifts and worship the baby Jesus.

And then there is the submission of Mary in this verse. Have you ever
stopped for a minute and really put yourself in her shoes? Young teenager.
Virgin. Promised in marriage. The prospect of being pregnant out of
wedlock which would make her an outcast. She would be vilified by all
those who knew her. Who on earth would believe her story? And yet
with all of that crushing down on the conscience of a very young girl,
she uttered the words that would begin the entrance of the Savior of the
world:

"Behold, the bondslave of the Lord; may it be done to me according to
your word."

Imagine the difference it could make in the world today if all of us
who claim the Lord Jesus Christ as our Savior would make that same
commitment. What better time is there than Christmas to do it?

Now in those days a decree went out from Caesar Augustus, that a census be taken of all the inhabited earth. This was the first census taken while Quirinius was governor of Syria. And everyone was on his way to register for the census, each to his own city. Joseph also went up from Galilee, from the city of Nazareth, to Judea, to the city of David which is called Bethlehem, because he was of the house and family of David, in order to register along with Mary, who was engaged to him, and was with child. While they were there, the days were completed for her to give birth. And she gave birth to her firstborn son; and she wrapped Him in cloths, and laid Him in a manger, because there was no room for them in the inn. In the same region there were some shepherds staying out in the fields and keeping watch over their flock by night. And an angel of the Lord suddenly stood before them, and the glory of the Lord shone around them; and they were terribly frightened. But the angel said to them, "Do not be afraid; for behold, I bring you good news of great joy which will be for all the people; for today in the city of David there has been born for you a Savior, who is Christ the Lord. This will be a sign for you: you will find a baby wrapped in cloths and lying in a manger." And suddenly there appeared with the angel a multitude of the heavenly host praising God and saying, "Glory to God in the highest, and on earth peace among men with whom He is pleased."
— *Luke 2:1-14*

Again! ... Again!

If you are a parent, if you have ever read a favorite story for your children, how familiar are these words? "Again ... again, mommy!" "Again ... again, dad!" Sometimes you barely finish the words, 'happily ever after' and they are saying, "Again ... again!" In the hearts of children, some stories just never get old no matter how many times you read it to them.

Well, the story of the birth of our Lord and Savior Jesus Christ is one of those stories, isn't it? As God's children, who among us would say we get tired of the story of His birth? The birth of Christmas. The birth of eternal hope for all mankind. The story of Jesus coming to a manger, then to our hearts ... good news of great joy indeed.

Don't let it get lost in the food, and the presents, and the parties, and the football games. Make it a special time around the Christmas tree. Read it to your children, read it to each other, read it to your family and friends visiting for Christmas. "Again ... again!!!"

But the angel said to them, "Do not be afraid; for behold, I bring you good news of great joy which will be for all the people; for today in the city of David there has been born for you a Savior, who is Christ the Lord.
— *Luke 2:10-11*

Big Little Words

One of my favorite things to say about the Bible is how very big some of its smallest words are. Perhaps Christmastime is a good time to bring it up again, here in one of the most famous verses in the entire Bible. The announcement to mankind, of that which heaven had known for an eternity would happen.

The "big little" word in this verse may be especially important and helpful to someone who may feel a little "outside the circle" when it comes to Christmas. The one who perhaps hasn't felt a part of the eternal joy that erupts in the hearts of so many of us at the news of our Savior coming to earth. Because for some, perhaps He isn't your Savior. Yet.

Who knows why … Maybe you feel unworthy, or too bad, or beyond hope. No one else thinks much of you, so how in the world could the Savior of the world care about you? If that is you, the "big little" word in this verse is for you. It is the little three-letter word "all." The hope and the joy of heaven is for all the people. Including you. No one is left out. Feel unworthy? Doesn't matter. Feel too bad? Doesn't matter. Feel beyond hope? Doesn't matter. No one else cares about you? Doesn't matter. Jesus cares.

All the people means exactly that — all the people. Including you, my friend. Jesus loves you too.

A Gospel Harmony of the Christmas Story

(John1: 1-4,14) - (Matt.1:18-21,24-25) - (Luke 1:26-38, 2:1-18)

In the beginning was the Word, and the Word was with God, and the Word was God. He was in the beginning with God. All things came into being through Him, and apart from Him nothing came into being that has come into being. In Him was life, and the life was the Light of men. And the Word became flesh, and dwelt among us, and we saw His glory, glory as of the only begotten from the Father, full of grace and truth.
(John 1:1-4,14)

*****and it happened like this*****

Now in the sixth month the angel Gabriel was sent from God to a city in Galilee called Nazareth, to a virgin engaged to a man whose name was Joseph, of the descendants of David; and the virgin's name was Mary. And coming in, he said to her, "Greetings, favored one! The Lord is with you." But she was very perplexed at this statement, and kept pondering what kind of salutation this was. The angel said to her, "Do not be afraid, Mary; for you have found favor with God. And behold, you will conceive in your womb and bear a son, and you shall name Him Jesus. He will be great and will be called the Son of the Most High; and the Lord God will give Him the throne of His father David; and He will reign over the house of Jacob forever, and His kingdom will have no end." Mary said to the angel, "How can this be, since I am a virgin?" The angel answered and said to her, "The Holy Spirit will come upon you, and the power of the Most High will overshadow you; and for that reason the holy Child shall be called the Son of God. And behold, even your relative Elizabeth has also conceived a son in her old age; and she who was called barren is now in her sixth month. For nothing will be impossible with God." And Mary said, "Behold, the bondslave of the Lord, may it be done to me according to your word." And the angel departed from her. (Luke 1:26-38)

Now the birth of Jesus Christ was as follows: when His mother Mary had been betrothed to Joseph, before they came together she was found to be with child by the Holy Spirit. And Joseph her husband, being a righteous man and not wanting to disgrace her, planned to send her away secretly. But when he had considered this, behold, an angel of the Lord appeared to him in a dream, saying, "Joseph, son of David, do not be afraid to take Mary as your wife; for the Child who has been conceived in her is of the

427

Holy Spirit. She will bear a Son; and you shall call His name Jesus, for He will save His people from their sins." Now all this took place to fulfill what was spoken by the Lord through the prophet: "Behold, the virgin shall be with child and shall bear a Son, and they shall call His name Immanuel," which translated means, "God with us." And Joseph awoke from his sleep and did as the angel of the Lord commanded him, and took Mary as his wife, but kept her a virgin until she gave birth to a Son, and he called His name Jesus. (Matthew 1:18-25)

Now in those days a decree went out from Caesar Augustus, that a census be taken of all the inhabited earth. This was the first census taken while Quirinius was the governor of Syria. And everyone was on his way to register for the census, each to his own city. Joseph also went up from Galilee, from the city of Nazareth, to Judea, to the city of David which is called Bethlehem, because he was of the house and family of David, in order to register along with Mary, who was engaged to him, and was with child. While they were there, the days were completed for her to give birth. And she gave birth to her firstborn son (Luke 2:1-7a), and they called His name Jesus (Matt.1:25b);and she wrapped Him in cloths, and laid Him in a manger, because there was no room for them in the inn (Luke 2:7b).

In the same region there were some shepherds staying out in the fields and keeping watch over their flock by night. And an angel of the Lord suddenly stood before them, and the glory of the Lord shone around them; and they were terribly frightened. But the angel said to them, "Do not be afraid; for behold, I bring you good news of great joy which will be for all the people; for today in the city of David there has been born for you a Savior, who is Christ the Lord. This will be a sign for you: you will find a baby wrapped in cloths and lying in a manger." And suddenly there appeared with the angel a multitude of the heavenly host praising God and saying, "Glory to God in the highest, and on earth, peace among men with whom He is well-pleased." When the angels had gone away from them into heaven, the shepherds began saying to one another, "Let us go straight to Bethlehem then, and see this thing that has happened which the Lord has made known to us." So they came in a hurry and found their way to Mary and Joseph, and the baby as He lay in the manger. When they had seen this, they made known the statement which had been told them about this Child. And all who heard it wondered at the things which were told them by the shepherds. (Luke 2:8-18)

Wishing for all our wonderful and dear friends, a joyous and Christ-filled Christmas!

Kelly and Cláudia Adkins

For a child will be born to us, a son will be given to us; and the government will rest on His shoulders; and His name will be called Wonderful Counselor, Mighty God, Eternal Father, Prince of Peace.
— *Isaiah 9:6*

The Night Before Christmas

This devotional isn't about the well-known children's story of this same name. I will confess, this famous verse from Isaiah isn't exactly THE night before Christmas, either. In fact, considering that the book of Isaiah was written somewhere between 740 to 680 B.C. (guesstimation), this verse was about 255,000 + nights before Christmas.

But — if we could give our minds the freedom to wander for just a few minutes, what I would like to do is for us to try to imagine what the real night before Christmas must have been like. Everyone knows the beautiful announcement of the angels to the shepherds on the night Jesus was born. Have you ever wondered what it was like in heaven ... the night *before* Jesus was born? Can you imagine all the bottled-up excitement? With all the hosts of heaven knowing what was about to happen? Can you imagine the party in heaven? The rejoicing?

Now imagine something else — for all the heavenly hosts who live in eternity where there is no such thing as "time," the "night before Christmas" wasn't simply 24 hours, but since the beginning of time. That's how long the angels had known. Taking the liberty to "adjust" a couple of lines from the old children's story ...

Twas the night before Christmas, and all through God's house,
All the angels were rejoicing, all the angels did shout ...

And — I believe — for all that time, the song that the angels sang had to have been something like this verse right here. Here, where the prophet Isaiah gives all of us a little "peek behind the curtain" into the ground swell of the Christmas excitement that existed in heaven since the very beginning of time ... and before.

In the same region there were some shepherds staying out in the fields and keeping watch over their flock by night. And an angel of the Lord suddenly stood before them, and the glory of the Lord shone around them; and they were terribly frightened. But the angel said to them, "Do not be afraid; for behold, I bring you good news of great joy which will be for all the people; for today in the city of David there has been born for you a Savior, who is Christ the Lord. This will be a sign for you: you will find a baby wrapped in cloths and lying in a manger." And suddenly there appeared with the angel a multitude of the heavenly host praising God and saying: "Glory to God in the highest, and on earth, peace among men with whom He is pleased."

— Luke 2:8-14

It's A Boy!

Well ... the announcement brought a ***bit*** more news than that —

The first Christmas — the day that the joy known in heaven since the beginning of time, spilled out onto the earth. And hope began for all men. No comment necessary — the angel said it all ...

Wishing a blessed and Christ-filled Christmas for all our friends ...

Kelly Adkins

And Jesus came up and spoke to them, saying, "All authority has been
given to Me in heaven and on earth."
— *Matthew 28:18*

Power Source

If you tried to plug a toaster into a water faucet, how much power would
you get? You wouldn't get any power, would you? And you for sure
wouldn't get any toast. To get power to the toaster, you have to plug it
into where the power is.

It is the same with your life. There is only one place to get the power
you really need, and Jesus tells us where it is in this first verse of the
passage (vs. 18-20) we call the Great Commission. I absolutely love the
declaration with which Jesus begins: "ALL authority has been given to
Me in heaven and on earth." How much did He say? ... ALL of it!

The Greek work for authority here (exousia) is a word that means
"authority that comes inherent with power." (Sort of like when you say,
"Let there be light!" — and every star in the universe begins to shine.)
In fact, in many versions of the Bible the word is translated "power" here.
Sooooo ... tell me then — if Jesus has all the power and all the authority,

... how much — exactly — does the devil have?

"Then if anyone says to you, 'Behold, here is the Christ,' or 'There He is,' do not believe him. For false Christs and false prophets will arise and will show great signs and wonders, so as to mislead, if possible, even the elect. Behold, I have told you in advance. So if they say to you, 'Behold, He is in the wilderness,' do not go out, or, 'Behold, He is in the inner rooms,' do not believe them. For just as the lightning comes from the east and flashes even to the west, so will the coming of the Son of Man be.

— *Matthew 24:23-27*

Second Coming Swamis

If you want to do the research, you will find well over 200 predictions of the "end times" and the return of Christ. All of them wrong. One of the more recent ones even tried using the Mayan calendar. Wrong again. The famed Jean Dixon's prediction of somewhere between 2020-2037 (they are learning to not be so specific anymore) will also be wrong. Her first "end-of-the-world" prediction was February 4, 1962.

Pay attention. Are there signs? Yes. Progressive signs. BUT — regardless of what is happening around the world ... even the Middle East — here is what Jesus Himself says about it:

1. No one knows when it will happen except God (24:36).
2. No one will EVER know until it actually happens (24:36).
3. It will happen **very** quickly (24:27).
4. It will be UNexpected — as opposed to predictable (24:44).
And most importantly of all ...
5. BE READY — (24:44).

Where's the hope and encouragement? Well, I'm glad you asked. Here it is — the good news is that the Second Coming is really gonna happen. Who's coming? Buddah? Buddah's mama? Confucius? Confucius's mama? Muhammad? Muhammad's mama? NO!!! It will be the living, resurrected, reigning King of Kings and Lord of Lords ... the Lord Jesus Christ.

"Behold, I am coming quickly, and My reward is with Me, to render to every man according to what he has done. I am the Alpha and the Omega, the first and the last, the beginning and the end."
— *Revelation 22:12,13*

Cut to the Chase

A phrase from the early days of silent movies is a very good description of Jesus's style. In the early days before "talkies" began, silent movies very often ended with exciting chase scenes. Before the chase scene there was often quite a bit of useless, boring dialogue. "Cut to the chase" was a director's command to abbreviate the boring part and get to the exciting part that people were interested in. Today we use the phrase "cut to the chase" in almost exactly the same way — dispense with side issues and get to the point.

Jesus is the all-time champion when it comes to cutting to the chase. In the New Testament, in just a few words He could lay bare the disguised intents of the religious stuffed shirts of His day, and leave them chaffing with embarrassment. He does it again in these verses, addressing all the falderal that exists even to this day over the events of the second coming of Christ ...

It will be quick.
It will be rewarding for all believers.
Opinions to the contrary can argue with the authority of the Great "I AM."

Not one word about a date, or a millennial view, or what happens to our bodies. Because none of that is important at all. Interesting perhaps, but non-essential. Jesus cuts to the chase.

The advice of Jesus on the subject is — be ready. Period.

And He who sits on the throne said, "Behold,
I am making all things new." And He said,
"Write, for these words are faithful and true."
— *Revelation 21:5*

A New Year's Revelation

No, that isn't a misprint. In a few days most of us will take part in an annual ritual — the making of New Year's resolutions. This year there is going to be a new "me." I'm going to lose weight. I'm going to be a better mom, or dad. I'm going to work on my anger problem. Or any, of many, possibilities. Been there? Done that? Bought the t-shirt?

And ... there are more broken New Year's resolutions than there are broken cars in all the junkyards in the entire world. Been there too? I have a suggestion for all of us who have. Why not let the One with all the power to make ALL things new, make us new too? It is done through belief in the Lord Jesus Christ — the whole reason for the season of Christmas, and every other season, too.

If you would really like to make some changes in yourself this coming year — if you would really, truly like to see a "new you," — if you are tired of New Year's resolutions that are discarded almost as fast as Christmas wrapping paper ... why not go with the New Year's *revelation* instead? To paraphrase an old song, "Put your hand in the hand of the One who makes ALL things new." Including you. You can count on it because the words in this verse, unlike so many of our New Year's resolutions — are faithful and true.

> ... in a moment, in the twinkling of an eye, at the last trumpet; for
> the trumpet will sound, and the dead will be raised imperishable,
> and we will be changed.
> — *1ˢᵗ Corinthians 15:52*

Countdown to Blast Off

This is one of the rare times I have used the same verse twice in our year-long devotional journey together. Two reasons: One, there is more than just one encouragement in this verse, and two, it is perfect when we think about the countdown when a new year is about to arrive. As I write this, a brand new year is only two days away.

Astronaut John Grunsfeld describes the countdown and what it is like to blast off in the space shuttle. In his account, he says that the countdown begins, but they are all busy flipping switches and thinking about their training and the jobs they have to do. He said that it isn't until you get to the last 10 seconds in the countdown that you begin to think of what is about to happen. In a few seconds they are moving at 100 miles per hour. At the 6-minute mark, g-forces make them feel like they weigh 700 pounds. In a scant 8-and-a-half minutes following liftoff, they are outside the earth's atmosphere, the engines turn off ... and instantaneously they go from feeling like they weigh 700 pounds to being totally weightless. The transition is so sudden, he says that it almost makes you giddy. Sort of like in the twinkling of an eye, isn't it?

We don't know what the number is in God's holy countdown — but God does. What we DO know is that one day the number will reach "zero." This verse describes that day. What a blast off!! We go, in the twinkling of an eye, from being sinful, broken and corrupt ... to perfect and incorruptible. It is being the image of Christ time. As we all count down to the change and hope a new year brings, these beautiful words penned by the apostle Paul in God's word tell us of the most wonderful, incomprehensible countdown of all. Are you ready for when it reaches "zero?"

but I hope to see you shortly, and we will speak face to face. Peace
be to you. The friends greet you. Greet the friends by name.
— *3rd John 14,15*

When Christians Part

One of the most beautiful and comforting truths of the Christian faith
is that Christians never have to say "good-bye." For us, it is always just
'so long," because we know that whatever happens in this life, we will see
each other again someday in heaven.

The final words here of John to Gaius are wonderful words to finish our
devotional journey that we began a year ago on January 1. It has been
a wonderful blessing for me. My purpose was to create a journey of hope
and encouragement for you. I trust that it has been such a journey.

John expressed here a hope to see his friend Gaius soon. Because of the
hope and encouragement and future we have with the Lord Jesus Christ
as our Savior, I can say the same words of John to each person who has
shared this journey through God's word with me. From the perspective of
eternity's clock — which has no hands — I hope to see you shortly, and
we will speak face to face.

Until that day in heaven, may God bless you, and keep you, and may His
peace be always with you.

In His Love,
Kelly Adkins

A FINAL WORD

One of the most beautiful things that God has ever taught me over my many years of trying to do ministry is that He can display His beauty, His love, His hope, His encouragement — or His wisdom — from anywhere, or through anyone He chooses. Seeing this up close and personal any number of times has contributed greatly to keeping my heart tender and humble. It is also what makes every person on this little blue marble we call "Earth" profoundly special. Absolutely anyone can be a tool in the hand of the Master.

This truth was never brought home to me more powerfully than on my very first mission trip to Brazil as a first-year seminary student at Southwestern. Before the start of the mission, a lady in our host church in Brazil told her pastor she wanted to volunteer to help by being an interpreter for our team, if she could. She was not "super-fluent" in English, but she simply wanted to help in any way she could. Her name was Patricia. She was not a trained interpreter, a trained teacher, or a trained anything else. She was simply a loving person in the church who knew a little English, and who said, "Here I am, Lord, use me." And boy howdy, did He ever. Her own daughter became a Christian on the last night of the mission — and — in the car, on the way back to the hotel, we were all happy and celebrating, and in the middle of all the celebrating, Patricia said something that probably no one else even noticed. But I did. I never forgot it, and I never will. In the middle of Brazil, in the middle of all the noise of multiple conversations, God chose to use someone who had no Biblical training at all to give me a diamond ... one of the most profound things I have ever heard in all my years of ministry in a single sentence. She said this: "You know, all God ever wanted us to know is contained in John 3:16 ... He just gave us the rest of the Bible to try to understand it."

After 4 years in the best seminary in the world, being taught by some of the best professors in the world, those words from Patricia remain with me to this very day, as one of the most beautiful and profound statements I have ever heard about the love and the purpose of God. By the way, here is John 3:16:

> "For God so loved the world, that He gave His only begotten Son, that whoever believes in Him shall not perish, but have eternal life."

How To Ask the Lord Jesus Christ Into Your Life as Savior

It's as easy as 1-2-3.

The encouragement to ask the Lord Jesus Christ into your life as Savior appears in various places throughout these devotionals. If you have yet to do that, but would like to, it is not complicated or difficult. You can do it in less than one minute. That is no better illustrated than in Jesus's words to His own disciples in Matthew 18:3,4 — "Truly I say to you, unless you are converted and become like children, you will not enter the kingdom of heaven. Whoever then humbles himself as this child, he is the greatest in the kingdom of heaven."

Jesus does not require that we be theologians, or preachers, or teachers, or any other kind of religious "expert." His requirement is that we come to Him as little children, whose faith and trust is open and innocent, and He asks no more than what is contained in John 3:16 — "For God so loved the world, that He gave His only begotten Son, that whoever believes in Him shall not perish, but have eternal life." His promise is "Whoever will call on the name of the Lord will be saved." (Romans 10:13) You can do that with a simple prayer all by yourself that is as easy as 1-2-3:

(in your own words similar to these)

1. Lord Jesus, I believe in You, that you are the Son of God, and that you died on the cross for my sins.
2. I ask you now, Lord Jesus, to forgive me for all the sins in my life, and with Your help and strength, I promise to turn away from them and live for You.
3. Thank you, Lord Jesus, for coming into my life as Lord and Savior, for giving me eternal salvation right now, and heaven as my home when I die.

That's it. If you said that to Jesus — and meant it with all your heart — you are just as much a Christian and just as saved to eternal life in heaven as anyone else ... from prince to pauper ... who has ever believed in Jesus.

Believing in Jesus is a journey that begins with that simple prayer for salvation, and the promise of eternal life in heaven, the moment you put your faith and trust in Him. But — you will also discover that it is a journey which will take you a lifetime to complete. It will take you through both good times and bad, victories and trials that will test you and grow your faith each step of the way. You will feel the presence of Jesus both on the mountain top and in the valley. It will be a journey of learning, and blessing, and faith, and hope ... and fellowship with the King of Kings and Lord of Lords, who is also your Heavenly Father ... a journey that does not exist outside a personal relationship with Him, which begins when you invite Him into your life as your personal Savior. If you prayed that simple 1-2-3 prayer, I would like to be the first to welcome you to the family of God. Find a good, Bible-believing, evangelistic, mission-minded, service-oriented church where there will be a loving Christian community to encourage and help you grow in Christ. May He bless you deeply in your daily walk with Him.

ACKNOWLEDGEMENTS

This book, truthfully and literally, is the product of a lifetime of living and sharing life-lessons beyond value, learned from each one of the people I mention here. I know that not many people get excited about acknowledgements or want to take the time to read them, but I can promise, you will be blessed if you read these.

The problem with my acknowledgements and gratitude for those responsible for this book coming into existence, is knowing where to begin. Maybe the only way to truly do it is chronologically.

Dr. Millard Bennett

My first pastor who is now with the Lord. Dr. Bennett was the first man God used in the church to show me that Christian men were a long way from being wimps. One of his favorite free-time activities was hunting coons at night in the Navasota river bottom. The first time I shook his hand, I thought he was going to dislocate my knuckles.

Dr. Tom Robuck

My first pastor in Fort Worth when I moved there to go to the seminary. He also took me on my first mission trip to Brazil where God promptly stole my heart for missions and never gave it back. When I asked him for his advice on how best to pastor, He answered me with just 3 words. I thought he was just trying to be brief because he was busy. He wasn't. Turns out it was as profound as it was challenging. His answer: Love the people.

* * *

The following men were professors and leaders during my years at Southwestern Baptist Theological Seminary to whom I owe a Christian debt of gratitude that I could never hope to repay for all they taught me, both inside and outside the classroom. Their wisdom and Christian character appear on virtually every page of this book.

* * *

Dr. Russell Dilday

What I saw in Dr. Dilday, President of Southwestern Baptist Theological Seminary, was a depth and beauty of Christian grace and pastoral love that I have often tried to emulate, but seldom (if ever) achieved. And he maintained both during the very darkest days of the history of Southwestern. During my time there, I came to him one day after the hope had been crushed out of my heart. Instead of using his heavy and demanding agenda as an excuse to not have time for me, the President of the largest seminary in the world received me into his home, spoke to me and encouraged me with unbelievably kind, pastoral love. If the way Dr. Dilday ministered to me doesn't show in these devotionals, I have missed the mark.

Dr. Daniel Sanchez

My admiration and love for Dr. Sanchez did not come from the classroom, it came from personal interaction. Permanently stored in my heart are our conversations in the halls of the Theology building at Southwestern where he patiently listened to all my mission experiences, and unfailingly encouraged me in following God's call to missions in my life. And even now, after all these years (I graduated in 1986), he was still willing to help with this book and write words of support inside it.

Dr. Jesse Northcutt

My beloved preaching lab professor who literally wrote the definitive textbook on preaching, and who patiently taught me that instead of me being God's gift to preaching, preaching was God's gift to me.

Dr. Jack Gray

The person the Lord used to teach me that instead of me being God's gift to praying, praying was God's gift to me, and that kindness and humility are two of the most beautiful things on the earth.

Dr. Justice Anderson

The man responsible for establishing the World Missions Center at Southwestern, and for stoking the fire for missions that burns in my heart and soul even today. Inside class and out, he faithfully encouraged me again and again, in all my mission efforts during my time at Southwestern.

Dr. D. David Garland

Dr. Garland taught me about how close and personal God could truly be felt. Not from my Old Testament Survey class I had with him, but from the sheer humble and loving content of his prayers before each class. The scripture that promises "draw near to God and He will draw near to you" was personified in the prayers of Dr. Garland. There was no mistaking the presence of the Holy Spirit as our class began, from the sheer character of Dr. Garland's prayer.

Dr. Gerald Marsh

A professor who I had the honor of having on my ordination council and who brought pastoral ministries alive for me. What I learned from Dr. Marsh about how to give pastoral care is beyond price. It has served me well all these years, and definitely seasons the content of the devotionals in this book.

Dr. Charles Tidwell

Another professor who I had the honor of having on my ordination council. Dr. Tidwell taught me that if you want to be an effective teacher, good lesson plans don't happen by accident, and that the spiritual gift of administration was extremely valuable in leading a church. Most valuable of all, however, as was true of my other professors was what he showed me of his Christian heart. That is what I hope I have been able to reflect in this book. Dr. Tidwell even spent time with me in my home in England while he was conducting a class at Oxford — and — gave me the unspeakable privilege of speaking in one of his classes there. I always joked with him after that, "Now I can put 'taught at Oxford' on my resumé."

Dr. James Heflin

One more professor who is precious to my life, although I never had him for a class. He also spent time with me in my home in England during his sabbatical, taught in my church there, and after moving back home to Texas, he "sold" his car to me for almost nothing — just enough to make the paperwork legal — because I didn't have any transportation, or money. Dr. Heflin taught me a lesson about generosity to a brother in need that I have been able to pass on countless times through these many years.

Dr. Malcolm McDow and Dr. James Eaves

I mention these two professors together because they were the evangelistic "one, two" punch that poured gasoline on my soul-winning fire. I can't prove it, but I also believe they were directly responsible for me being given the Fred Swank Award for Evangelism when I was a graduating student.

Dr. William R. Estep

One almost has to say Dr. Estep's name with hushed breath because of the immense respect he commanded from all those who knew him. He was one of the greatest historians of Anabaptists, Baptists, and the Protestant Reformation who ever lived — and I had the privilege of having him for my Church History class. Dr. Estep gave me an undying appreciation for the important role historical knowledge plays in truly understanding the message contained in God's word.

Dr. J.N. Boo Heflin

Through my Hebrew and Old Testament classes with Dr. Heflin, my perception of just who God is grew about a thousand fold.

Dr. Jeter Basden

I dare not leave out the man who was singularly responsible for my admission to Southwestern in the first place. At the time (1984), a divorced person had a large, uphill climb to gain admission to a Baptist Seminary. Four times I drove from Madisonville to Forth Worth to meet personally with Dr. Basden, and he was kind beyond words to me each time. I will never forget how the last meeting ended. Dr. Basden said to me, "I see no reason why you cannot be accepted here. Welcome to Southwestern!"

Dr. Lawrence Klempnauer

I met the Vice President of Student Services on my very first day as a student at Southwestern — at orientation. During an inspiring welcoming address to us in the chapel, Dr. Klempnauer challenged all of us to do one thing: fight against the devil's efforts to cripple our seminary experience and our ministries by making the commitment to attend chapel service every day. A short time separated from everything else, dedicated just to the Lord. I took the challenge. Every day. First row, center section, center seat — even during semester finals. Because of Dr. Klempnauer's challenge I still carry with me today, the importance of a time — each day — separated just for the Lord.

Dr. Bill Tolar

I am grateful to Dr. Tolar on so many levels. His impassioned eloquence mixed with the love he wore on his sleeve as he preached in the chapel services at Southwestern, has flavored my own delivery of God's word all these years. Mercy, how this man could make a point. I can't resist just one example: "It is true that a little knowledge is dangerous ... but, so is a whole lot of ignorance." I remember his kindness when, as Dean of the School of Theology, he gave me special permission twice, to enter classes that had already been closed. The final mark he left on my heart was the supernatural, Christian strength he showed as Interim President, guiding Southwestern through her darkest hour.

Dr. Al Fasol

Dr. Fasol occupies a singularly special place in my heart, although he quite likely doesn't even remember me because I never had him for a class. The reason I didn't have him for a class is why he is so special. Here's how it happened:

I tried all my time at the seminary to have Dr. Northcutt for a preaching class, but he was so famous and popular I never got the chance. His classes were already closed every time it was my turn to submit my choices for classes. My last semester before graduation finally arrived, and you guessed it ... the same thing happened again. There would be no other opportunity. Even Jeanie Bell, secretary of Dr.Tolar who was the Dean of the School of Theology couldn't give me special permission. She said, "Even we can't grant special permission to add someone to Dr. Northcutt's class. Your only hope is trying to get permission from the head of the preaching department." Well, guess who was head of the preaching department — and — who the computer had automatically assigned as my professor for preaching lab? Dr. Fasol. The very person from whom I needed special permission to get into Dr. Northcutt's class. I was faced with the unnerving situation of asking to get out of his class so I could get into Dr. Northcutt's class. As I sat across from Dr. Fasol, nervously stuttering and stammering trying to explain and ask to get out of his class, his eyes simply began to sparkle a bit as he reached for the special permission slip and said, "I can't think of a better Christmas present to give to anyone, than a class with Jesse Northcutt." Guess what lesson still lives in my heart today because of Dr. Fasol ...

Dr. Curtis Vaughan

My beloved professor who became a dear friend. He was on my ordination council, and this world-renowned Greek scholar told all the others that he knew me so well he didn't need to ask me a single question. One of my most precious possessions is a book he gave me from his own library where he wrote in the front of the book: "Dear Kelly, you have been an inspiration and an encouragement to me this year." I had Dr. Vaughan for eight classes, including advanced Greek, even though he was known as one of the toughest professors at Southwestern. What he taught me about Christian grace, excellence in academics and how to truly study God's word, literally changed my life.

MindStir Media

A very special "thank you" to all the very kind, patient and talented folks at MindStir Media: J.J. Hebert, founder and owner and my personal mentor, Jen McNabney and Maggie Kelly my personal project managers, and all the talented design team assigned to my book. These fine, talented professionals took the raw material from a guy who knew absolutely zero about publishing and transformed it into a beautifully finished book.